An Independent Woman's Lake District Writings

Classics in Women's Studies Series

Jane Addams, Emily G. Balch, and Alice Hamilton, *Women at The Hague*

Susan B. Anthony, *The Trial of Susan B. Anthony*

Mary Roberts Coolidge, *Why Women Are So*

Matilda Joslyn Gage, *Woman, Church and State*

Charlotte Perkins Gilman, *The Man-Made World*

Harriet Martineau, *An Independent Woman's Lake District Writings*

Margaret Sanger, *The Pivot of Civilization*

Elizabeth Cady Stanton, *Eighty Years and More*

Mary E. Walker, MD, *Hit: Essays on Women's Rights*

Frances Wright, *Reason, Religion, and Morals*

An Independent Woman's Lake District Writings

Harriet Martineau

COMPILED, EDITED,
AND WITH AN INTRODUCTION BY
MICHAEL R. HILL

CLASSICS IN WOMEN'S STUDIES

an imprint of Prometheus Books
59 John Glenn Drive, Amherst, New York 14228-2197

Cover image of Harriet Martineau (1833), reproduced from
Harriet Martineau's Autobiography, edited by Maria Weston Chapman
(Boston: Osgood, 1877).

Published 2004 by Humanity Books, an imprint of Prometheus Books

Inquiries should be addressed to
Humanity Books
59 John Glenn Drive, Amherst, New York 14228–2197
VOICE: 716–691–0133, ext. 207; FAX: 716–564–2711

08 07 06 05 04   5 4 3 2 1

Martineau, Harriet, 1802–1876.
An independent woman's Lake District writings / Harriet Martineau ; compiled, edited, and introduced by Michael R. Hill.
p. cm. — (Classics in women's studies series)
Includes bibliographical references and index.
ISBN 1–59102–172–3 (pbk : alk. paper)
1. Lake District (England)—Social life and customs. 2. Lake District (England)—Social conditions. I. Hill, Michael R. II. Title. III. Series.

DA670.L1M34 2004
947.7'8081—dc22

2004006080

Printed in the United States of America on acid-free paper

Writer, sociologist, and public intellectual HARRIET MARTINEAU was born on June 12, 1802, in Norwich, Norfolk, England, into an upper-middle-class family. Her parents were Thomas and Elizabeth Rankin Martineau, devout Unitarians who passed their religious beliefs on to their eight children. Harriet's father was a textile manufacturer and businessman. Although attending two years of private, coeducational classes and a year in a boarding school for girls, Harriet was educated primarily at home by older siblings and hired tutors. Through disciplined self-study, Martineau mastered many subjects, including: the classics, languages, literature, history, philosophy, religion, mathematics, music, and poetry. At age twelve Harriet began to lose her hearing and by age sixteen required an ear trumpet, which she used for the rest of her life.

Coincident with the death of Thomas Martineau in 1826, the family business collapsed. Faced with financial exigency, and the unexpected death of her fiancé, Harriet supported herself thereafter as an independent single woman. She became the multifaceted author of essays, tracts, reviews, novels, guides and travelogues, biographies, how-to manuals, journal articles, newspaper leaders, histories, children's stories, didactic fiction, and sociologically informed nonfiction. Her first major success came during 1832–34 when she produced the *Illustrations of Political Economy*, a popular series of twenty-five didactic volumes that introduced rudimentary economic principles, largely via engaging fictional narratives, to appreciative lay readers. With success came fame, and she was lionized in London where she met the likes of George Eliot, Charles Dickens, Thomas Malthus, Charlotte Brontë, and Charles Darwin, among others.

Starting in 1834, Martineau toured the United States for two years, reporting her observations in *Society in America* (1837) and *Retrospect of Western Travel* (1838). In the United States, she met a host of well-known luminaries, including Ralph Waldo Emerson and William Ellery Channing, but she also visited with ordinary farmers, laborers, prisoners, housewives, shopkeepers, and the like. Her careful empirical studies benefited from her insightful understanding of the intricacies of sociological data collection, subsequently explicated in *How to Observe Morals and Manners* (1838), establishing her today as the world's first female sociologist. During her American travels, she became increasingly convinced of the justness of the abolitionist cause.

Martineau's strong abolitionist stance, her unflinching advocacy of women's rights, and her sharp criticism of American clerics, in *Society in America*, resulted in her growing reputation as an astute but controversial social analyst. She next wrote *Deerbrook* (1839), her most successful novel, and *The Hour and the Man* (1841), an experiment in historical fiction based on the slave revolt in Haiti. Her observations on *Eastern Life, Present and Past* (1841) were grounded in a trip to the Middle East, and in this work she revealed her embrace of atheism, again producing a storm of controversy. This evolving line of thought culminated in *Letters on the Laws of Man's Nature and Development* (1851), coauthored with Henry Atkinson, and her translation/abridgment of sociologist Auguste Comte's *Cours de philosophie positive* (1853). Her younger brother James, a prominent Unitarian minister and theologian, severely slammed her work with Atkinson in a published review—straining relations between the two siblings for many years.

Martineau's lifetime concern with health—her own was sometimes tenuous—resulted in her "Letter to the Deaf" (1834), *Life in the Sick-Room* (1844), *Letters on Mesmerism* (1845), *England and Her Soldiers* (1859), *Health, Husbandry, and Handicraft* (1861), and collaborations with Florence Nightingale on projects of mutual interest. Often acting behind the scenes, Martineau was an influential advisor to important officials in the British government. More publicly, and throughout her life, Harriet contributed to many periodicals, including: the *Atlantic Monthly*, *Edinburgh Review*, *Household Words*, the *Leader*, *Monthly Repository*, the *National Anti-Slavery Standard*, *Once-a-Week*, the *People's Journal*, *Sartain's Union Magazine of Literature and Art*, *Westminster Review*, and others. She also wrote more than fifteen hundred unsigned leaders for the London *Daily News*.

Following a prolonged illness, Martineau moved to the Lake District in 1845. Her health restored, she built a solid home at Ambleside, established a small farm, hiked the surrounding hills, became friends with the Wordsworths, and continued her writing and research. Not the least of her works from this period is the *Complete Guide to the English Lakes* (1855). Her magnificent *Autobiography* (1877) was posthumously published following her death on June 27, 1876, at the Knoll, Ambleside, Westmorland, England.

This book is dedicated to

LYNN MCDONALD,

intellectual pioneer, peripatetic scholar, collegial friend.

Contents

ILLUSTRATIONS

Preface

THIS BOOK BEGAN when the 2002 Bicentennial Working Seminar of the Harriet Martineau Sociological Society (HMSS) was a faint, as yet unrealized possibility on the academic horizon. The success of the 1997 HMSS seminar on Mackinac Island, combined with my favorable impression of Ambleside during a brief visit en route to Scotland in 1995, convinced me that our group ought to go to England—hopefully in concert with the publication of a special edition of Martineau's Lake District writings. I then set privately to work on what became the present volume. Vera Wheatley's published scholarship led directly to Martineau's delightful book of months, "A Year at Ambleside." Shortly thereafter, I identified additional candidates for this compilation and editing began in earnest. At the 2000 HMSS caucus in Washington, DC, Susan Hoecker-Drysdale's proposal that we visit Ambleside during the bicentennial year of Martineau's birth was seconded by all. Concrete plans for the seminar quickly unfolded (with a target date set in late May to take advantage of low-season transatlantic airfares). When the HMSS seminar subsequently convened in Ambleside 28–30 May 2002, editing was largely complete and seminar participants were presented with copies of seasonally relevant chapters from Martineau's "A Year at Ambleside" prior to their arrival in England. Thanks in large part to the perseverance, encouragement, and helpful suggestions of Ann O'Hear at Humanity Books, I now have the enjoyable privilege of presenting this robust anthology of Martineau's writings about the Lake District to a much larger audience.

My fellow participants in the 2002 HMSS seminar together explored the byways of Ambleside, walked in Martineau's footsteps, read scholarly papers, presented a public colloquium, broke bread together, and drank toasts to Harriet's memory and stellar accomplishments. These scholars comprise a special group of friends and colleagues: Jim Broschart, Kay Broschart, Mary Jo Deegan, Vicky Demos, John Drysdale, Susan Hoecker-Drysdale, Deb Logan, Lynn McDonald, Chris Penney, and Fred Peterson. Pat Lengermann, Jill Niebrugge-Brantley, and Caroline Roberts also presented papers in absentia via audio recordings. (Summaries of the seminar presentations are scheduled to appear in a special Martineau issue of *Sociological Origins*.) My thanks to all of you (and, as always, *especially* to my life-partner, Mary Jo) for having made Ambleside and the Lake District come alive for me in such a congenial and corporate way.

The HMSS seminar owed much of its success to several people in Ambleside who took pains to greet us with generosity and open hearts. To Fiona and Bryan Sparrow, convivial hosts who welcomed our seminar members to the The Haven and The Cottages on the Green, we send particular commendation. Thanks also to Barbara Crossley, author of *The Other Ambleside*, who so carefully outlined for us the history of the local social landscape since Martineau's time, and to Michelle Kelly who arranged our visit to the Armitt Library and Museum. Kath Teasdale provided the perfect venue for the seminar's finale: a public presentation on the Ambleside Campus of St. Martin's College. May the spirit of Harriet Martineau dwell with you always.

To the many readers who were unable to join us in Ambleside, allow me to suggest that there is no better introduction to the Lake District than Martineau's own words. This, of course, is the more important rationale for this book. Martineau's readable and lively descriptions demonstrate not only her narrative skills and story-telling prowess but also her proficiency in topographical and sociologically informed portraiture. Travelers to the English Lake District today—especially those wishing to visit this magnificent region as it was in earlier times—are well advised to make Harriet Martineau their expert companion.

It behooves me to thank those whose general cheerfulness and interpersonal encouragements always make my long days in Nebraska so much less grim, especially: Tom Carr, Miguel Carranza, Joleen Deats, Cinnamon Dokken, Connie Frey, Kathy Johnson, Kate Kane, Jennifer Lehmann, Teelyn Mauney, Dianna Parmley, Lori Ratzlaff, Barb and Tim Sandusky, Sally and Bob Stoddard, Morrie Tuttle, and Pat and Scott Wendt. Tony Blasi, Joe Feagin, Janusz Mucha, Raffaele Rauty, and Andrew Timming supplied digital inspiration from afar. During my semester as Visiting Scholar in the Department of Sociology at the University of Notre Dame, where I completed work on this book, material help and friendly smiles were provided by Brian Conway, Pat Kipker, Dan Myers, and Katie Schlotfeldt. Mike Keen and Scott Sernau welcomed me to Indiana University South Bend and Susan Weaver instigated my lectures on Martineau at Miami University of Ohio. Our home-away-from-home Michigan neighbors on Mizpah Park Road offered good words and camaraderie. My life-partner, Mary Jo Deegan, insures that life everywhere is not only joyful but also meaningful.

One technical point deserving notice concerns spelling, consistency, and faithfulness to Martineau's published manuscripts. I have retained British spellings and Martineau's now archaic punctuation where they appear in the originals, including *Sartain's Union Magazine*, and retained the Americanized spellings, as published, in the essay from the *Atlantic Monthly*. My introduction and my endnotes everywhere employ American spellings, with the exception of quotations and citations when British spellings are utilized in the referenced sources. In a very few instances, I broke some of Martineau's overlong passages into shorter paragraphs when I judged the result entirely felicitous to modern sensibilities.

Michael R. Hill
Notre Dame, Indiana

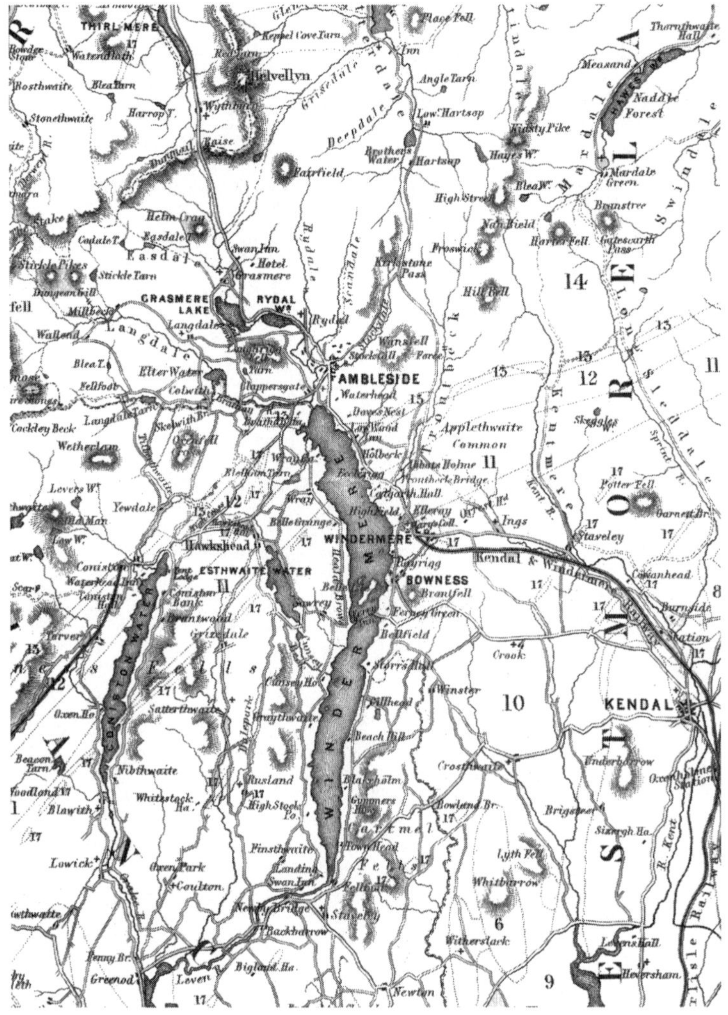

Fig. 1. Ambleside and Environs, circa 1855 (portion of a map from Martineau's *Complete Guide to the English Lakes*)

An Introduction to Harriet Martineau's Lake District Writings

by Michael R. Hill

THIS COMPILATION presents an engaging, insightful, and inspiring smorgasbord of essays (and one didactic tale) selected from Harriet Martineau's Lake District writings from the mid-1800s. As a source of inspiration, the English Lake District has been profitably mined by scores of writers, including Martineau. The selections included here are more or less available (usually less) in scholarly and rare book collections, but are not generally obtainable for a pleasant armchair read at home or, as Martineau would certainly encourage, to tote along in one's knapsack on a weekend ramble among the lakes and hills of Cumbria. The majority of the selections were penned prior to Martineau's full-length *Complete Guide to the English Lakes* (1855) and happily reflect her immediate first encounters with the topography and social life surrounding the English lakes. While the collection stands on its own, it by no means includes all of Martineau's works related to the Lake District. Avid readers will thus augment their "traveler's library" with copies of Martineau's 1855 *Guide*, her *Autobiography* (1877), and a relevant set of detailed Ordnance Survey maps. The *Guide* and the Osgood edition of the *Autobiography* (with its useful index) can still be had, at some expense, from rare book dealers.

As Martineau's texts remain the best introductions to her work and worlds, there remains little for an editor to do. As far as practicable, the selections are arranged so as to first introduce Martineau's more immediate surrounds in Ambleside, and then widen more generally to the Lake District as a whole (thereby playing somewhat footloose with chronology: for example, her essay on "The Lake District," written in 1848, is here placed *after* her 1850 series, "A Year at Ambleside"). Where terms or names are seemingly obscure, especially to American readers such as myself who are not steeped in the byways and byplay of English literary criticism, I have provided, where possible, brief annotations in the endnotes sufficient to ease one's recourse to the standard reference sources in local libraries. Martineau generally assumed, of course, that her readers were familiar with the cast of literary lights with whom she associated and occasionally frolicked. It remains only for this introduction to identify Martineau's skills as a descriptive writer, to sketch the outline of her happy first decade in Ambleside (during which most of the items were written), and to indicate something of the background and publishing history of each selection.

GEOGRAPHER AND SOCIOLOGIST

Harriet Martineau (1802–1876) became an experienced geographical and sociological observer and accomplished writer well before she took up residence in the Lake District. Her recognized place in the literary pantheon is the subject of an ever-growing number of readily available scholarly monographs, including notable recent additions by Deborah Logan (2002a) and Caroline Roberts (2002). Martineau's pioneering sociological acumen is now also well documented and widely accepted (Hill 1989; Hoecker-Drysdale 1992; Hill and Hoecker-Drysdale 2001; Deegan 2003), if not yet beyond perverse, recalcitrant disputation (e.g., Connell 1997; Hamilton 2003). Her fundamental observational principles and insights are fully and delightfully illustrated in the first methodological treatise in the social sciences: *How to Observe Morals and Manners* (1838a). No methodologist has yet improved on Martineau's core observational dictum: "The grand secret of wise inquiry into Morals and Manners is to begin with the study of THINGS, using the DISCOURSE OF PERSONS as a commentary upon them" (Martineau 1838a, 73). This said, her outstanding aptitude as a student of physical and human landscapes per se are somewhat less well recognized.

Martineau's topographical gifts are clearly and strongly revealed to readers of *Society in America* (1837), *Retrospect of Western Travel* (1838b), and, in a later work, *Eastern Life, Present and Past* (1848). Indeed, in that Martineau is now established as the first woman sociologist, we can also rec-

Fig. 2. Harriet Martineau, 1833 (from Martineau's *Autobiography*)

ognize her as an early woman geographer. In *How to Observe Morals and Manners,* she emphasized the importance of landscape description. To travelers, she advised, "those who do not draw should also note scenery." The reason being that "a very few descriptive touches will bring back a landscape, with all its human interest, after a lapse of years; while, perhaps there is no memory in the world which will present unaided the distinctive character of a succession of scenes" (Martineau 1838a, 235).

The landscape, she found, opens most fully to pedestrians: to travelers who *walk* from place to place. "The wisest and happiest traveller is the pedestrian," Martineau observed. "If gentlemen and ladies want to see pictures, let them post to Florence, and be satisfied with learning what they can from the windows by the way. But if they want to see either scenery or people, let all who have strength and courage go on foot" (Martineau 1838a, 63). When Martineau moved to the Lake District, she became an ardent walker, making long trips into the surrounding hills, virtually every morning and sometimes before dawn. This fundamentally independent mode of transport fit both her personality and her purpose. "The pedestrian traveller is wholly free from care," and, she continues:

> There is no such freeman on earth as he is for the time. His amount of toil is usually within his own choice,—in any civilised region. He can go on and stop when he likes; if a fit of indolence overtakes him, he can linger for a day or a week in any spot that pleases him. He is not whirled past a beautiful view almost before he has seen it. . . . He can reach almost every point his wishes wander to. The pleasure is indescribable of saying to one's self, "I will go there,"—"I will rest yonder,"—and forthwith accomplishing it. (Martineau 1838, 63)

A well-seasoned observer and an energetic walker, Martineau explored her world—and the extraordinary landscapes of the Lake District—with enthusiasm, integrity, and perspicuity.

Martineau first saw the Lake District in 1838 while en route to Scotland to complete on-site research for a series of topographical notes for Charles Knight's then forthcoming edition of Shakespeare's works:

> I therefore agreed to join a party of friends, to attend the meeting of the British Association at Newcastle first, and then proceed to the Lake District, which I had never seen, and into Scotland, visiting both Western and Northern Highlands. It is always pleasant, I find, to have some object in view, even in the direction of a journey of pleasure: and this was supplied to me by Mr. Knight's request that I would explore the topography of Shakspere's Scotch play now; and of the Italian plays when I went to the continent the next year. (Martineau 1877, 1:429)

The trip to Scotland provided Martineau with an indelible example of "the pleasure of a gradual approach to celebrated or beautiful places." She wrote:

> The first time that I felt this was on a pedestrian tour in Scotland, when I was at length to see mountains. The imagination of myself and my companion had fixed strongly on Dunkeld, as being a scene of great beauty, and our first resting-place among the mountains. The sensation had been growing all the morning . . . and we traversed it so freshly and merrily as to be quite unaware

> that we were getting towards the end of our seventeen miles. . . . We were deeply engaged in talk, when a winding of the road brought us in full view of the lovely scene which is known to all who have approached Dunkeld by the Perth road. We could scarcely believe that this was *it*, so soon. We turned to our map and guide-book, and found that we were standing on the site of Birnam wood; that Dunsinane hill was in sight. . . . (Martineau 1838a, 65–66)

Martineau's notes on the physical locations in Macbeth appear in volume 2 of *The Pictorial Edition of the Works of Shakspere*, edited by Charles Knight. It was a congenial project: "I do not know whether any of the air of the localities hangs about those notes of mine in Mr. Knight's Shakspere," she wrote, "but to me, the gathering up of knowledge and associations for them was almost as pleasant work as any I ever had to do" (Martineau 1877, 1:429).

The Macbeth project further sharpened Martineau's observational and descriptive skills, and, crucially, it introduced her, albeit as a serendipitous consequence, to the beauties of the Lake District wherein she would purposefully and independently choose to settle and build her home several years later.

LIVING IN THE LAKE DISTRICT

Martineau recovered, at the end of 1844, from a long, debilitating illness and confinement (Martineau 1844;

1877, 1:443–81). She confirmed her recovery with a change of scene, moving from Tynemouth to the Ambleside region, and quickly determined to make the Lake District her permanent home, living there from 1845 until her death in 1876. A new and independent era opened in her life. Of her first experiences in lakeland, she confided:

> I have been spending a delicious month on Windermere,—at Wansfell, (Mr. W. Greg's) & my friends in that neighbourhood made a plan for me which I could not resist, to take rooms at Waterhead (by Ambleside) for the whole summer & Autumn. I have done so, & shall be close by the Gregs and Davys, & within easy walks of the Arnolds, Wordsworths & Fletchers. Very many friends mean to visit us this summer. I wish you would. The delight of that month at Wansfell was unspeakable. (Martineau to Milnes, 22 February 1845, in Sanders 1990, 106–107)

And, after having built her home, The Knoll, she wrote to another friend:

> *When* you come here and see my perfect paradise of a home, and my dear neighbours, and have witnessed my daily life of honorable toil and gay enjoyment of both work and ease, I think you will feel a sort of surprise that there is on earth a lot of good so unmixed. The new experience of freedom from care,—of perfect ease of body and mind,—as new to me as Heaven itself could be—loses none of its wonder as yet. (Martineau to Wedgwood, 3 August 1846, in Arbuckle 1983, 90)

Martineau—hearing impaired, and without husband, college education, family fortune, or inherited position—had put it all together. Hers is a middle-class feminist success story of independence, hard work, self-discipline, and remarkable perseverance. The building of her home "went off without a difficulty" (Martineau 1877, 1:502). During the wonderfully full decade from 1845 to 1855, a period largely free from illness and pain, she exuberantly followed her inclinations, wrote what she liked, and visited as she pleased. Her day-to-day experiences repeatedly "confirmed my satisfaction with my independent plan of life" (Martineau 1877, 1:496).

When Martineau built The Knoll, the Lake District was already an established Mecca for friends and admirers of William Wordsworth and his circle, a brilliant set of Lake District "lights." To the growing list of lakeland callers, Martineau attracted her own illustrious visitors. For example, Ralph Waldo Emerson and Charlotte Brontë made notable, if brief, visits. Martineau met Emerson in 1836 during her travels in America—he "invited me to be his guest, in the midst of my unpopularity," she recalled. Emerson returned the favor, visiting England in 1847:

> Mr. Emerson did come. He spent a few days in February with me; and, unfavourable as the season was for seeing the district,—the fells and meadows being in their dunnest haycolour instead of green,—he saw in rides with a neighbour and myself some of the most striking features in the nearer scenery. I remember bringing him, one early morning, the first green spray

> of the wild currant, from a warm nook. . . . It was a great pleasure to me to have for my guest one of the most honoured of my American hosts, and to find him as full as ever of the sincerity and serenity which had inspired me with so cordial a reverence twelve years before. (Martineau 1877, 1:549)

It was for Martineau a memorable event, and she recalled it when writing to Emerson five years later, in 1852: "I have been over Loughrigg today, (you remember the mountain opposite my windows), & in returning found, & brought home, just such a sprig of wild currant as I got for you when you were here at the same time of year" (Martineau to Emerson, 25 February 1852, in Sanders 1990, 121).

From within England per se, Martineau was visited with great frequency by many luminaries of the current literary scene. Her Lake District writings are chock full of names and literary associations familiar to students of English literature. Details of many such visits are found throughout her *Autobiography* and her correspondence (Arbuckle 1983; Sanders 1990; Burchell 1995), but one visit that bears particular note is the pilgrimage made by Charlotte Brontë. When *Jane Eyre* appeared in 1847 under Brontë's pseudonym, Currer Bell, Martineau identified strongly with the novel and admired the work of the unidentified author:

> Can you tell me about "Jane Eyre,"—who wrote it? I am told I wrote the 1st vol: and I don't know how to disbelieve it myself,—though I am wholly ignorant of the

> authorship. I cannot help feeling that the writer must know not only my books but myself very well. My own family suppose me *in* the secret, till I deny it. With much improbability of incident, it is surely a very able book (outside of what I could have done of it:) and the way in which the heroine comes out without conceit or egotism is, to me, perfectly wonderful. (Martineau to Wedgwood, 18 February 1848, in Arbuckle 1983, 95–96)

Brontë, still disguised as Currer Bell, sent Martineau a copy of *Shirley* in 1849, accompanied by a note declaring that "C.B." sent the book "in acknowledgment of the pleasure and profit" she derived from reading Martineau's novel *Deerbrook* (1839). Between the appearance of *Shirley* and *Villette*, Brontë's final novel, Charlotte visited Harriet in December 1850. To George Lewes, who questioned whether Brontë correctly understood his views on Catholics, Martineau wrote: "Do you mean that she thinks you favour the Catholics? That is not like her. She is coming to me on Monday for a *cosy* winter visit; & we shall talk over all things whatever, I suppose;—& that among the rest; & I shall hear what she thinks" (Martineau to Lewes, 10 December 1850, in Sanders 1990, 120). Martineau later recalled, "our intercourse then confirmed my deep impression of her integrity, her noble conscientiousness about her vocation, and her consequent self-reliance in the moral conduct of her life. I saw at the same time tokens of a morbid condition of mind, in one or two directions . . ." (Martineau 1877, 2:24).

Brontë subsequently pressed Martineau to write a

review of *Villette*, but was deeply stung by Martineau's forthright critique and consequently rebuffed her invitation to make a repeat visit. As fate would have it, Brontë was the younger woman, but it was Martineau who wrote her obituary for the *Daily News* (reprinted in Martineau 1869, 44–50).

By January 1855, Martineau's old ailments returned; she wrote her *Autobiography*, and waited for death. The final curtain was far from down, however, and she produced a considerable body of work after this time. As Vera Wheatley (1957, 358) put it: "For the next ten or eleven years, her unremitting labour with her pen would have been remarkable enough in a perfectly healthy woman." Martineau's health never fully returned, however, and she increasingly curtailed her visitors, sharply limiting their number and eventually admitting only her closest friends and kin. Martineau died in 1876, no doubt in some sympathy with Mary Wordsworth who had once quipped, at age seventy, that the worst thing about living in the Lake District was that "it made one so unwilling to go" when death finally approached.

BACKGROUND AND PUBLISHING HISTORY

All of the selections in this compilation intersect at Ambleside, and dovetail with Martineau's larger *Autobiography* and *Complete Guide to the English Lakes*, thereby greatly enriching our appreciation of her talents as a topographer and social observer. Yet, with the exception of the two extracts from Martineau's *Autobiography*, the selections in this compilation were separately prepared and issued largely in disparate publications from 1848 to 1861, most during the oftentimes productive and generally pain-free period of Martineau's later life. The following inventory, arranged in chronological order, provides a brief commentary on the context and publishing history of each selection.

Frolics with the Hutchinsons

The essay reprinted here appeared originally with the prosaic title "The Hutchinsons in Grasmere." In her much later essay on "Lights of the English Lake District," however, Martineau referred to the earlier essay as "Frolics with the Hutchinsons," and I have here restored that more lively title. The article describes the visit of a singing troupe from the United States and details Martineau's central role in looking after the quartet and arranging the concert they gave at Ambleside. The account was prepared as the first of a three-article series on "Lake and Mountain Holidays" for the *People's Journal* (Martineau 1846a, b, c). The final two installments detail Lakeland rambles more or less recounted elsewhere in other writings, but Martineau's portrait of the Hutchinson quartet is a fairly singular account. William Howitt and his wife, Mary Howitt, were copartners with John Saunders in the production and editing of the *People's Journal*, a magazine oriented to popular education for members of the working classes, and Martineau contributed several articles during the first years of publication. She was not on particularly friendly terms with the Howitts—indeed, she readily kept her distance:

> An . . . unintelligible claim to my friendship has been advanced in print by the Howitts. I can only say that I do not remember having seen Mrs. Howitt more than twice in my life, and that I should not know her by sight: and that I have seen Mr. Howitt about four or five times:—three or four times in London, and once at Tynemouth, when he came with a cousin of mine to cool himself after a walk on the sands, and beg for a cup of tea. This he and Mrs. Howitt have represented in print as visiting me in my illness. Such service as they asked of me in London, (to obtain a favourable review of a book of Mr. Howitt's in which he had grossly abused me) I endeavoured to render; but I really was barely acquainted with them; and I was glad the intercourse had gone no further when I witnessed their conduct to their partner in the People's Journal, and in some other affairs. I so greatly admire some of their writings, in which their fine love of nature and their close knowledge of children are unmingled with passion and personal discontent, that I am thankful to enjoy the good their genius provides without disturbance from their unreasonable and turbulent tempers. (Martineau 1877, 1:313)

In addition to several meditations on largely political matters (most published under the series title "Survey from the Mountain" during 1846), her treatise on *Household*

Education (1849) was partially serialized first in the *People's Journal*, also during 1846–1847. In commencing her "Survey" articles, she noted:

> Sitting here in my quiet home, in the quietest of valleys, or crossing the mountains which close it in, I watch the ways and fortunes of the world; and with so much interest, that I sometimes long to seek for sympathy by saying what I think and feel of the world's ways and fortunes. Will you permit me to send you monthly some of the comments I cannot help making as I read of human life and its affairs? (Martineau 1846d, 303)

This was work she enjoyed: "I do like writing for that Journal,—the host of readers are so earnest!" (Martineau to Fanny Wedgwood, 3 August 1846, quoted in Arbuckle 1983, 91).

The Lake District

Close reading of this essay reveals numerous precedents, illustrations, and turns of phrase that subsequently appear not only in "A Year at Ambleside" (1850) but also in Martineau's *Complete Guide to the English Lakes* (1855). Her easy recycling of phrases, examples, and even whole passages explains part of her astonishing efficiency as a writer. Nonetheless, each telling of a favorite example provides Martineau with opportunities for shifts in nuance and perspective. When she occasionally repeated selected accounts nearly verbatim, the new *context* in which an old story is retold tends generally to deepen the weight and significance of the example. By 1855, Martineau was acquainted more intimately with the lakeland region, and the encyclopedic character of her *Guide* makes it a landmark in tourist writing equally as interesting as William Wordsworth's earlier *Guide to the Lakes* (1835). Travel guides aside, "The Lake District" is a fresh, compact geographic description revealing a comprehensive grasp of Martineau's new environs, without burdening the reader with the prosaic detail required in a full-blown travel guide per se.

In 1846, having recovered her health, Martineau set herself the ambitious task of learning thoroughly the physiography surrounding her newly adopted home:

> I set myself to learn the Lake District, which was still a *terra incognita*, veiled in bright mists before my mind's eye: and by the close of a year from the purchase of my field, I knew every lake (I think) but two, and almost every mountain pass. (Martineau 1877, 513)

Her lakeland travels garnered almost immediate utility in her writing. Work on the essay, published by Charles Knight as "The Lake District," began in August 1848. Martineau (1877, 2:4) recounts that at that time "I was writing 'Household Education,' and I had promised him [Charles Knight] an account of the Lake District, for the work he was publishing called 'The Land we live in.'"

The Land We Live In comprises fifty-seven individually prepared chapters on various institutions, cities, and regions of the British Isles. Knight expressed the coordinating theme, in comparing the perspective of historical writers to those of his own age, thus:

> But *we* have also to look upon many things, some of which are scarcely picturesque, some wholly modern, but which have the elements of grandeur in their vastness and their moral influences. The course and offices of government, legislation, and the administration of justice; the halls of science, art, and letters; the seats of education; the emporiums of commerce and manufactures; the havens of maritime power; the material improvements of our day viewed in connexion with the moral; the manners and social characteristics of the people. All these features, and many more which it is better here to suggest than enumerate, make up the wonderful whole of "The Land we live in." Be it our aim to seize upon the most permanent and most universal of these features; in the desire to amuse as well as to inform,—to advance all safe and benevolent progress,—to nourish a just patriotism.

The separate chapters were initially published as numbers of Knight's *Weekly Volume* series, and issued subsequently as a handsomely bound four-volume set. The general aim was to provide authoritative, inexpensive, interesting, and attractive materials for the instruction and betterment of working-class readers (much along the lines as the *Penny Magazine* issued by the Society for the Diffusion of Useful Information, a reform-oriented organization in which

Knight played a significant role and that also courted the publication of Martineau's earlier didactic tales). It bears notice that Martineau (1877, 1:428) claims credit for having been instrumental in thinking up the "Weekly Volume" scheme in the first place, with the idea being somewhat later implemented by Knight. Each installment was profusely illustrated with drawings and usually included a well-executed plate, adding substantial visual interest to the accompanying text. The illustrations that accompany Martineau's essay are classic examples of the picturesque style then in vogue (Peterson forthcoming). In launching *The Land We Live In*, Knight was likely encouraged by the success of a similar project, a six-volume series of essays on *London*, published in 1841, which did for the prime city what he now envisioned for the British Isles as a whole. The first edition of the bound volumes of *The Land We Live In* was not dated, but Rivlin (1947, 102) suggests that the work appeared incrementally, from 1847 to 1850. Inasmuch as Martineau's contribution appeared in volume 2, and was not commissioned until 1848, a publication date of late1848 or early 1849 is a plausible conjecture.

Our Farm of Two Acres

Many aspects of Martineau's life may be seen metaphorically as experiments. As a writer, she experimented with new forms of imaginative writing, including didactic fiction to teach the principles of economics. But she also conducted real-world experiments and "Our Farm of

Two Acres" and "The Cost of Cottages" are two prime examples. Once having thought through a pragmatic problem, and having outlined a plan of action to accomplish stated ends, she was virtually compelled by some inner force to bring her ideas into pragmatic realization. Her life became an experiment, a *demonstration* of how to live independently, thoughtfully, rationally, and in social harmony—if not in intellectual agreement—with one's neighbors. "Our Farm of Two Acres" demonstrates, with grace, brevity, and somewhat more convivial social insight than Henry David Thoreau's *Walden* (1854), how a single woman might simultaneously increase her personal independence and social usefulness.

The pastoral, comforting imagery of "farms" and "cows" danced temptingly in Harriet's head at an early age. She reports that, as a youngster of five romanticizing about death, she contemplated various schemes of escape from a situation in which she perceived that "nobody else cared for me," and in one such plan she clearly equated farming, rural life, and cows as a suitable haven:

> I used to lean out of the window, and look up and down the street, and wonder how far I could go without being caught. I had no doubt at all that if I once got into a farm-house, and wore a woollen petticoat, and milked the cows, I should be safe, and that nobody would inquire about me any more. (Martineau 1877, 1:14)

But, years later, after Martineau undertook her complicated experiment in small-scale agriculture, inquiries and onlookers were frequent. "In 1848 (I think it was) I had begun an experiment of very small farming, which I never intended to become an affair of public interest" (Martineau 1877, 2:33):

> At first, we were abundantly ridiculed, and severely condemned for our methods; and my good servant's spirits were sometimes sorely tried: but I told him that if we persevered good-humouredly, people would come round to our views. And so they did. First, I was declared deluded and extravagant: next, I was cruel to my live stock; then I pet them so that they would die of luxury; and finally, one after another of our neighbours admitted the fine plight of my cows; and a few adopted our methods. At the end of a year's experience, I wrote a letter, by request, to an Assistant Poor-law Commissioner, who was earnest in his endeavours to get workhouses supplied with milk and vegetables, by the labour of the inmates on the land. To my amazement, I found my letter in the "Times," one day while I was at Bolton. How it got there, I know not. Other papers quoted portions of it which, separated from the rest, gave rise to wrong impressions; so that I found it necessary to write a second letter, giving the result of a second year's tillage; and to issue the two as a small pamphlet. I need say nothing here about our method of farming, as the whole story is told in that pamphlet. I may simply add that we go on with it, very comfortably; and that my good farm-servant is a prosperous man. Strangers come every summer to see the place as a curiosity; and I am assured that the invariable remark is that not a foot of

> ground is lost, and not a sign of neglect appears in any corner. (Martineau 1877, 2:34–35)

The farm operation increased Martineau's independence in direct and practical ways, significantly reducing her household's previous dependence on local shops and suppliers for fresh meat and produce. And, it was fun! "I am enjoying, as my third interest, my little farming. O! it is so pleasant,—our fine cream and butter, and hams and bacon, and fowls and eggs,—and vast prospects of vegetables and fruit to come" (Martineau to Wedgwood, 2 January 1849, in Arbuckle 1983, 102–104). The magazine version of "Our Farm of Two Acres" appeared in *Once a Week* during July 1859, and was reprinted in Martineau's *Health, Husbandry, and Handicraft* in 1861. A later pamphlet edition, according to Rivlin (1947, 110), was published in the United States in 1865.

A Year at Ambleside

Martineau's remarkable book of months appeared serially over the course of 1850 in *Sartain's Union Magazine of Literature and Art,* published in Philadelphia by John Sartain and edited by John S. Hart and Mrs. Caroline M. Kirkland. Kirkland was a noted abolitionist, pacifist, and writer. "In its earliest days under K[irkland]'s leadership the *Union* was considered one of the best family magazines of its kind" (A. Roberts 1980, 472). Poetry, essays, and fine art prints surrounded Martineau's monthly "Ambleside papers."

Americans today will particularly recognize the name of Edgar Allan Poe, whose posthumously published essay on "The Poetic Principle" appeared in the October 1850 issue. Close readers of "The Lake District" will note Martineau's revisiting of several themes and examples, but the exposition in "A Year at Ambleside" is essentially temporal (month by month), whereas the organization of "The Lake District" is fundamentally spatial (quadrant by quadrant). The factual bases of several vignettes recounted in both essays are subsequently fictionalized for use in "The Highest House in Wathendale," the one example of didactic fiction included in the present compilation.

Having, by 1850, completed the construction of her house and established her financial situation, Martineau began contributing to various causes and projects, and such she did with the proceeds from writing her "Ambleside papers," as the following letter to Ellis Gray Loring (a Boston lawyer whom Martineau met during her US travels) reveals:

> It is very long since I wrote to you: & now I have a favour to ask of you. Messrs Sartain of Philadelphia owe me money for contributions to their Magazine. I write by this same post to request them to pay to you £20 of the balance in my favour. What I have to ask of you is to be so kind as to receive this sum, & to pay half of it to Mr. Garrison for the benefit of "the Liberator," & the other half to "the Anti-Slavery Standard."—I hope it will turn out all right. I have no reason what ever to doubt it. I wrote 12 papers at their & Mrs. Kirkland's

> request; & they duly paid me for the first three. Seven more are now printed, I suppose; & their value being £35, I suppose there is no doubt of your getting the £20. (Martineau to Loring, 23 October 1850, in Burchell 1995, 80)

Thus, by writing about the physiography and society of Ambleside, Martineau actively linked the Lake District to her vigorous support of abolition in the United States. The latter topic, it should be noted, has been recently explored in substantial depth by Deborah A. Logan (2002b).

The Highest House in Wathendale

This story appeared in *Household Words*, a well-known journal edited by Charles Dickens, in July 1851. Martineau's contributions to this journal were unsigned, but Anne Lohrli (1973, 360) provides authentication of Martineau's authorship. Martineau contributed to *Household Words* during its first year of publication, 1850, and thereafter submitted articles on a regular basis. "Mr. Dickens sent me an invitation to write for 'Household Words,'" Martineau (1877, 2:25) recalled "That kind of work does not, in my own opinion, suit me well; and I have refused to write for Magazines by the score; but the wide circulation of 'Household Words' made it a peculiar case; and I agreed to try my hand." Her last contribution appeared in 1855—by which time Dickens's virulent anti-Catholic stance had become to her personally intolerable.

"The Highest House in Wathendale" is the only

example of Martineau's fiction included in this compilation, but its place is well deserved. It illustrates vividly how Martineau drew directly on personal experiences to construct didactic tales. Her surveys of the mountain country, encounters with peddlers, visits to auctions, and concerns for the general health and well-being of her community all find utility and purpose here. Her social-psychological analysis of the pros and cons of "pledges" made at revivals and meetings of teetotalers is especially perceptive.

Two Autobiographical Reflections

Martineau began serious, concerted work on her *Autobiography* in 1855 when, faced with a recurrence of earlier symptoms of illness, she presumed that she would soon die. Her presumption was, in this instance, quite wrong. Two short excerpts are included here, as preface ("On Society and Independence") and conclusion ("The World and the Terrace: Two Views from the Knoll"). Both "essays" capture her sense of independence and privacy combined simultaneously with an extraordinary regard for the affairs of the wider world. Readers interested in further details of Martineau's life generally, and in Ambleside in particular, are well advised to pay special attention to the *Autobiography*—it is replete with references to the Lake District. Without the spur of quick demise, she might never have completed her memoir—she added nothing to it during the last twenty years of her life. The *Autobiography* was published posthumously, in accord with Martineau's instructions, in 1877.

The Cost of Cottages

Two essays included here are striking in providing windows on Martineau's life in Ambleside some five years after the completion of her *Autobiography*. The first, "The Cost of Cottages," is a sort of "progress report" on an experimental project begun in 1848 when she conceived the idea of putting small-scale farming to a practical test. As part of her "farm," she built a stone cottage for a Norfolk couple who in return conducted many of the day-to-day chores. She soon thereafter widened the project, to include good, healthful cottages for working-class families. And, there was more at stake than just good housing: this was also an investment scheme in which Martineau took a direct, personal, and profitable hand (see Martineau to Wedgwood, 21 November 1855, in Arbuckle 1983, 135). Published initially in *Once a Week*, in January 1860, Martineau reprinted the essay the following year in her *Health, Husbandry, and Handicraft.*

Lights of the English Lake District

The second post-*Autobiography* essay addresses the disparate array of writers and personalities identified traditionally as "the lake poets." Martineau published "Lights of the English Lake District" in the *Atlantic Monthly* in 1861. At nearly sixty years of age and increasingly ill, Martineau looked out from the terrace at the Knoll, presumably, and still saw the wider world in her mind's eye—as earlier noted in her *Autobiography*: "the magnificent coast of Massachusetts in autumn, or the flowery swamps of Louisiana, or the forests of Georgia in spring, or the Illinois prairie in summer. . . ." At the least, she put pen to paper with her American friends clearly in mind. Looking back on the past fifteen years of her life in the Lake District, she recalled—for her American readers—anecdotes and characteristics of the major literary figures she either knew firsthand or remembered through her studies: Elizabeth Smith; the Wordsworths; Robert Southey; Samuel Taylor Coleridge and his son, Hartley; Thomas De Quincey; Mrs. Hemans; and the Arnolds, among others.

AN INVITATION

It is high time to put aside introductions and turn instead to Martineau's texts. Read now her simultaneously appreciative, critical, and prescriptive commentaries and visit the Lake District as her vicarious guest. Look outward from your respective terrace, wherever it may be—in Massachusetts, Louisiana, Georgia, or Illinois—to gaze on gentle Loughrigg, the rushing Rotha, the high crest of Scawfell Pikes, the winding road up Kirkstone Pass. With maps in hand, retrace her routes, hear the waterfalls, smell the blossoms, observe her neighbors. Rise with Martineau at dawn, walk the streets of mountain villages, feed the cows, collect the eggs. Make life a true and meaningful experiment—observe, take notes, try new schemes, build new worlds.

REFERENCES

Arbuckle, Elisabeth Sanders, ed. 1983. *Harriet Martineau's Letters to Fanny Wedgwood*. Stanford, CA: Stanford University Press.

Burchell, R. A., ed. 1995. *Harriet Martineau and America: Selected Letters from the Reinhard S. Speck Collection*. Berkeley: Friends of the Bancroft Library.

Connell, R. W. 1997. "Why Is Classical Theory Classical?" *American Journal of Sociology* 102 (May): 1511–57.

Deegan, Mary Jo. 2003. "Textbooks, the History of Sociology, and the Sociological Stock of Knowledge." *Sociological Theory* 21 (September): 298–305.

Hamilton, Richard F. 2003. "American Sociology Rewrites Its History." *Sociological Theory* 21 (September): 281–97.

Hill, Michael R. 1989. "Empiricism and Reason in Harriet Martineau's Sociology." In *How to Observe Morals and Manners*, by H. Martineau, sesquicentennial edition with introduction, appendix, and analytical index by M. R. Hill, xv–lx. New Brunswick, NJ: Transaction.

———. 1991. "Harriet Martineau." In *Women in Sociology: A Bio-Bibliographical Sourcebook*, edited by M. J. Deegan, 289–97. New York: Greenwood.

Hill, Michael R., and Susan Hoecker-Drysdale, eds. 2001. *Harriet Martineau: Theoretical and Methodological Perspectives*. New York: Routledge.

Hoecker-Drysdale, Susan. 1992. *Harriet Martineau: First Woman Sociologist*. Oxford: Birg.

Knight, Charles, ed. n.d. *The Pictorial Edition of the Works of Shakspere*. New York: P. F. Collier.

———, ed. 1841. *London*. London: Charles Knight.

———. [1847–1850]. *The Land We Live In: A Pictorial and Lit-*

erary Sketch-Book of the British Empire. London: Charles Knight.

Logan, Deborah Anna. 2002a. *The Hour and the Woman: Harriet Martineau's "Somewhat Remarkable" Life*. DeKalb: Northern Illinois University Press.

———, ed. 2002b. *Writings on Slavery and the American Civil War*, by Harriet Martineau. DeKalb: Northern Illinois University Press.

Lohrli, Anne. 1973. *Household Words: A Weekly Journal 1850–1859 Conducted by Charles Dickens*. Toronto: University of Toronto Press.

Martineau, Harriet. 1837. *Society in America*. London: Saunders and Otley.

———. 1838a. *How to Observe Morals and Manners*. Sesquicentennial edition with introduction, appendix, and analytical index by M. R. Hill. New Brunswick, NJ: Transaction, 1989.

———. 1838b. *Retrospect of Western Travel*. London: Saunders and Otley.

———. 1839. *Deerbrook*. London: E. Moxon.

———. 1844. *Life in the Sickroom*. London: E. Moxon.

———. 1846a. "Lake and Mountain Holidays: No. 1. The Hutchinsons in Grasnere." *People's Journal* 2 (4 July): 1–3.

———. 1846b. "Lake and Mountain Holidays: No. 2." *People's Journal* 2 (8 August): 72–74.

———. 1846c. "Lake and Mountain Holidays: No. 3." *People's Journal* 2 (12 September): 149–50.

———. 1846d. "Survey from the Mountain." *People's Journal* 1 (30 May): 303–305; (20 June): 351–53; 2 (11 July): 19–21; (25 July): 49–52; (1 August): 58; (29 August): 120–22; (26 September): 172–75; (31 October): 247–49.

———. 1846–1847. "Household Education." *People's Journal* 2

(18 July): 36–38; (1 August): 65–67; (5 September): 128–130; (10 October): 205–207; (14 November): 274–76; (19 December): 345–47; 3 (9 January): 23–25; (6 February): 90–92.

———. 1848. *Eastern Life, Present and Past.* London: E. Moxon.

———. 1849. *Household Education.* London: E. Moxon.

———. 1850. "A Year at Ambleside." *Sartain's Union Magazine of Literature and Art* 6 (January–June): 38–41, 139–42, 291–98, 355–58, 381–84; 7 (July–December): 28–32, 88–91, 150–53, 227–30, 268–71, 344–47.

———. 1851. "The Highest House in Wathendale." *Household Words* 3 (19 July): 389–96.

———. 1859. "Our Farm of Two Acres." *Once a Week* 1 (9 July): 37–40; (16 July): 44–47; (30 July): 96–100.

———. 1860. "The Cost of Cottages." *Once a Week* 2 (14 January): 61–65.

———. 1861a. *Health, Husbandry, and Handicraft.* London: Bradbury.

———. 1861b. "Lights of the English Lake District." *Atlantic Monthly* 7 (May): 541–58.

———. 1865. *Our Farm of Two Acres.* New York: Bunce and Huntington.

———. 1869. *Biographical Sketches.* New York: Leypoldt & Holt.

———. 1877. *Harriet Martineau's Autobiography*, edited by Maria Weston Chapman. Boston: Osgood.

Peterson, Fred. Forthcoming. "On the Picturesque." *Sociological Origins* 3 (2).

Poe, Edgar A. 1850. "The Poetic Principle." *Sartain's Union Magazine of Literature and Art* 7 (October): 231–39.

Rivlin, Joseph B. 1947. *Harriet Martineau: A Bibliography of Her Separately Printed Books.* New York: New York Public Library.

Roberts, Audry. 1980. "Caroline Matilda Stansbury Kirkland." In *American Women Writers*, vol. 2, edited by Lina Mainiero, 471–73. New York: Frederick Ungar.

Roberts, Caroline. 2002. *The Woman and the Hour: Harriet Martineau and Victorian Ideologies*. Toronto: University of Toronto Press.

Sanders, Valerie, ed. 1990. *Harriet Martineau: Selected Letters*. Oxford: Oxford University Press.

Thoreau, Henry David. 1854. *Walden: or, Life in the Woods*. Boston: Ticknor and Fields.

Wordsworth, William. 1835. *Guide to the Lakes*. 5th edition. London: Longman. Reprinted with an introduction by Ernest de Sélincourt. Oxford University Press, 1970.

An Independent Woman's Lake District Writings

Fig. 3. The Knoll, Ambleside, 1846 (from Martineau's *Autobiography*)

Chapter One

On Society and Independence[1]

As to this matter,—of society. There is a perpetual change going on in such neighbourhoods in the Lake District as that of Ambleside. Retired merchants and professional men fall in love with the region, buy or build a house, are in a transport with what they have done, and, after a time, go away. In five or six years, six houses of friends or acquaintance of mine became inhabited by strangers. Sorry as I was, on each occasion, to lose good friends or pleasant acquaintances, I did not call on their successors,—nor on any other new-comers: nor did I choose, from the beginning, to visit generally in Ambleside. When I made up my mind to live there,[2] I declined the dinner and evening engagements offered to me, and visited at only three or four houses; and very sparingly at those. It did not suit me to give parties, otherwise than in the plainest and most familiar way; and I had some idea of the mischiefs and dangers of such society as is found promiscuously cast into a small neighbourhood like this. I had not time to waste in meeting the same people,—not chosen as in London, but such as chanced to be thrown together in a very small country town,—night after night: I was aware how nearly impossible it is to keep out of the gossip and the quarrels which prevail in such places; and there was no adequate reason for encountering them. I foresaw that among a High-church squirearchy, and Low-church evangelicals, and the moderate-church few, who were timid in proportion to their small numbers, I might be tolerated, and even courted at first, on account of my reputation, but must sooner or later give deadly offence by some outbreak of heresy or reforming tendency, stronger than they could bear. I therefore confined my visiting to three or four houses, merely exchanging calls with others: and it is well I did. Of those three or four, scarcely one could endure my avowal of my opinions in 1851.[3] Even with them, I had before ceased, or did then cease, to exchange hospitalities. As they had sought me, and even urgently pressed themselves upon me, (one family in particular, whose mere name I had never heard when I arrived) they were especially in need of my compassion at the plight they found themselves in,—with goodness of heart enough to remember that our acquaintance was all of their seeking, but with too much narrowness and timidity to keep up intercourse through such opprobrium as my opinions brought on me among their High-church neighbours. They had the shame (which I believe them to be capable of feeling) of being aware, and knowing that *I* was aware, that they sought me, as they were wont to seek and flatter all celebrities, for my fame, and to gratify their own love of excitement; and that their weakness stood confessed before the trial of my plain avowal of honest opinions. It made no difference that, after a time, when the gossip had blown over, and my neighbours saw that I did not want them, and did not depend on their opinions in any way, they came round, and began to be attentive and kind:—their conduct at a moment of crisis proved to me that I had judged rightly in declining Ambleside visiting from the beginning; and their mutual quarrelling, fierce and wide and deep, certainly confirmed my satisfaction with my independent plan of life. My interests lay among old friends at a distance; and I had as much social intercourse as I at all desired when they came into the district. I was amused and instructed by the words of an ingenuous young friend, who, taking leave of me one winter afternoon at her own gate, said: "Ah! now,—you are going home to a comfortable quiet evening by your own fire! Really, I think it is quite hypocritical in us!—We dress and go out, and seem to be so pleased, when we are longing all the time to be at home! We meet the same people, who have only the same talk; and we get *so* tired!" It was not long before that family withdrew from the Ambleside visiting which I had always declined. A very few faithful friends, whose regard did not depend on the popular nature of my opinions, remained true and dear to me; and thus I found that book,—the "Atkinson Letters,"—do me the same good and welcome service in my own valley that it did in the wide world;—it dissolved all false relations, and confirmed all true ones. Finally, now that that business has long been settled, and that all my other affairs are drawing near their close,[4] I may make my declaration that I have always had as much society as I wished for, and sometimes a great deal more.

CHAPTER TWO

A YEAR AT AMBLESIDE[5]

JANUARY

AFTER A LONG illness, during which I never saw a tree in leaf for upwards of five years, and passed my life between my bed and my sofa, I recovered—to my own surprise, and that of every one who knew me.[6] In September, I crept out of doors, and lay on a bit of grass a few yards square. In October, I walked down to the sea-shore, and by degrees extended my rambles to a fine beach three miles from home. By this time there was no doubt of my being well; but it was evidently desirable to change the scene, and break off all associations of sickness with my daily habits, and I eagerly accepted the invitation of friends who lived on the banks of Windermere, to spend a month with them. That month determined my place of residence for, probably, the rest of my life.

I had seen the Lake district in a cursory way, some years

Fig. 4. Lake Windermere, circa 1855 (from Martineau's *Complete Guide to the English Lakes*)

before, merely passing through it on my way to Scotland. Its beauty had struck me with a kind of amazement. As I looked down into some of the vales, or around upon a wall of mountains, I was almost incredulous of what I saw. If I had been told that after a long and dreary season of hopeless illness, I should come and sit down for life in this region, I should have looked upon the prospect as one of the most marvellous of the shifting scenes of life.

Its beauty is not the only, nor to some people, the chief interest and charm of the Lake district. The mountains, by their conservative influence, have here hedged in a piece of old English life, such as is to be found nowhere else within the island. They have always hedged in a piece of the life that had passed away from the rest of the country. When the Romans were elsewhere building walls around the towns, and stretching out roads from point to point of the island, the Druids were still collecting their assemblage of wild Britons under the forest shades of this region. The remains of coppices of oak, ash, birch, and hollies, show how high up the mountain sides the ancient forest extended, and under those trees stood of old the long-bearded, shaven-headed, white-robed Druidical priests, sending up a flame of sacrifice, which scared the red deer, and the wolf, and the wild bull in their coverts, and brought the eagles from their highest perch by the scent of a prey. But even here change must come, though later than elsewhere, and the Romans drew near, at last, to invade the region, and pave a road through it. It must have been a curious sight to the skin-clad Britons who were posted as sentinels, when the Roman standards appeared among the trees, and helmets and spears glittered in the pathways of the woods. The Romans took possession of Windermere, and made a camp at its head. If the circles of stones planted by the Druids are visible here and there in the district, no less distinct are the marks of Roman occupation. In a field at the head of Windermere, the outlines of their camp are obvious enough to the eye; and on a mountain ridge, still called High Street, are the fragments of pavement, which show that even here, above the highest tree-tops from which the British sentinels could look forth, the Roman soldiers made a road for their standards and their troops. What a sight it must have been from below! How the native mother must have shrunk back with her children into the caves of the rock, or the covert of the wood,—less afraid of the wild beasts than of these majestic invaders, against whom her husband was gone out with his scythe or his club! How she and her companions must have listened to the shock of falling trees, and the cleaving of the rocks, which gave notice that the enemy were making themselves a broad highway through the heart of the district. I always think of those cowering Britons now, when I go by the old Roman road, which descends upon Grasmere. The scene is open enough now, but I can conjure up the forests which clothed the mountain slopes down to the very brink of the Grasmere lake, in the days when the wild boar came down to drink, and the squirrel could (as the country people tell) go from Wythburn to Keswick—ten miles on a straight line,—on the tree-tops, without touching the ground.

Fig. 5. Grasmere, circa 1855 (from Martineau's *Complete Guide to the English Lakes*)

After all, the Romans passed away before the Britons. The natives remained in considerable numbers in the fastnesses, when the glittering soldiers were no more seen on the paved ways, and the trumpets no longer echoed from one mountain peak to another. But the Saxons and Danes came in to take possession of the fertile spots as the Romans left them. They never obtained possession of the district, however. For six hundred years, the Saxons held some of the fine alluvial lands about the lakes, and lived in settlements where there were natural facilities for defence; but they needed all these facilities, for the Britons had learned from the Romans how to arm themselves better, and to fight; and for those six hundred years they held their ravines, and forests, and even their villages and hamlets, so that the Saxons could never feel secure. After those six centuries, more and more Saxons crowded to these West Moorlands, now called Westmoreland; but they came not to conquer territory, but to seek shelter from the Normans, who were upon their heels. The Saxon men of substance, who were driven out from their estates in the south by the Norman invaders,—robbed, oppressed, outraged in every way,—came up among the Fells to nourish vengeance, and form themselves into bands of outlaws, for the torment of as many Norman usurpers as they could reach. The Britons had long ceased to appear elsewhere; and from this time we hear no more of them among the Fells, and, as before, the Saxons were to be heard of as holding the Fells, long after their race had mingled with the Norman everywhere to the south. The Normans came as near as they could, but they never so far penetrated the West Moorlands as to build castles in the midst, and settle down there as inhabitants. They obtained grants of land, but they never practically took possession of them. They built monasteries and castles in the level country which stretches out around the cluster of mountains; but they only sent out their herdsmen with their flocks to encroach gradually up the mountain slopes, and over the nearer vales; or drew the inhabitants towards them by the temptations and privileges of the abbeys and the castles. First, these Normans built Furness Abbey, on a plain to the south of the mountain group; and then between the mountains and the sea, Calder Abbey, to the west. Afterwards, they restored the religious house of St. Bees, on the coast, and then a great Norman noble founded Lanercost Priory, to the northeast. Thus they invested this noble fortress of nature,—this mountain cluster,—but they never took it. Their race at last mingled with the Saxon, and dwelt here as everywhere else, but it was by gradual penetration, and not by force or stratagem. The feudal retainers, sent to do service in tillage and herding, became more and more free and independent of their lords, and as they became more free, they found easier access to the heart of the region, till, in course of time, they were in fact owners of portions of land, under a mere nominal subservience to the great men at a distance. This state of things is kept in mind by old customs at this day. I pay ninepence a year to Lord Lonsdale for my field, and am nominally his tenant, while my land is, to all practical purposes, freehold. The tenure is called

Customary Freehold, and the nominal lord has no power when I have once acknowledged his old feudal claim by being "made a tenant," and paying my ninepence a year.

The holders of the crofts on the mountain sides, and in the vales (the inclosures built of stones, for the protection of the flocks from wild beasts, and for promoting the growth of the coppice on which they browsed), these tenants gradually becoming owners, were the original of the Dalesmen of our time. Since the union of Scotland with England, and the consequent extinction of border warfare, these dalesmen have become some of the quietest people in the world. No more summoned to war, nothing calls them out of their retreats, except an occasional market, or a sale of household furniture in some neighbouring valley. They go on practicing their old-fashioned methods of tillage and herding, living in their primitive abodes, and keeping up customs, and even a manner of speech, which are elsewhere almost obsolete. It will not be so for long. Their agriculture cannot hold its ground against modern improvements. Their homespun linen and cloth do not answer now in comparison with Manchester cottons and Yorkshire woollens. Their sons part off to the manufacturing districts, to get a better maintenance than they can find at home; and the daughters must go out to service. Still, the old croft will not support those who remain: the land is mortgaged more deeply. The interest cannot be raised; and, under this pressure, the temptation to the sinking dalesman to drown his cares in drink, becomes too strong for many a one who has no resources of education to fall back upon. Then comes the end,—the land and furniture are sold, the family disperse, and a stranger comes in who can make the land answer under modern methods of tillage.[7] Some of these strangers have a sufficient love of what is consecrated by time, to retain as much as they can of the ancient character of the region, in the aspect of their dwellings, and the arrangement of their estates, but all cannot be expected to do this; and the antique air of the region must melt away. I have myself built a house of the gray stone of the district, in the style of three centuries ago; but I see flaring white houses, square and modern, springing up in many a valley; and I feel that from this time forward our West Moorlands will not lag behind the world—two or three centuries in the rear of adjoining counties,—so charmingly as they have done from the dawn of British history till now.

As in many other mountain districts, the highest of our peaks are in the middle. Scawfell is the highest, and Bowfell next, and they are nearly in the centre of the cluster. From this centre, not only do the ridges decline in height, but the valleys decrease in depth; so that on the outskirts, we have only gently sloping, green hills, and shallow vales, whence, in clear weather, we look up to the lofty central crags. In approaching from the south, through Lancashire, Windermere is the first of the lakes that is encountered. Gentle hills surround its southern end; and these rise and swell through the whole ten miles of its length, till, about its head, the diverging valleys are closed in by the heights of Fairfield, and the remarkable summits called the Langdale

Pikes. Bowfell appears beyond them; and from some points on the lake, Scawfell itself is seen peeping over a nearer ridge. It was night when I arrived at the house of my host; and all that I knew of the road, for some miles, was that it was bordered by tufted walls, and overhung with trees which on the left hand separated it from the lake. In the morning, what a scene it was! The road was hidden, and the lawn before the windows seemed to slope down to the fringe of trees, and the graceful little wooded promontory which jutted out into the lake. The gray waters spread out here about a mile in breath. To the south they were lost among a group of wooded islands, while the head of the lake rounded off among green meadows, with here and there a rocky projection crested with black pines, which were reflected in the waters below. A hamlet of white houses appeared in and out among the trees, at the foot of the rugged mountain, called Loughrigg, which separates the two diverging valleys at the head of Windermere. From my host's porch we looked up the quiet valley of the Brathay, where a beautiful little church, built by a mercer from Bond Street, crowns a wooded rock, and overlooks the rattling river Brathay, to the glorious cluster of summits and ridges which the winter morning sun clothes with orange, crimson, and purple lines below where the snow cuts out a sharp outline against the sky. When I came to live here, I soon learned that if I wished for a calm, meditative walk after my morning's work, I had better go up this valley of the Brathay, where I was sure never to meet anybody. I could look out from its high churchyard upon its unsurpassed view, and then go down and skirt Loughrigg, and lean upon a gate, or rest upon a heathery perch of rock, without much probability of seeing a face for three hours together. Whereas, if I was tired of thinking, and socially inclined, I had better take my way up the other valley—that of the Rotha, where the little town of Ambleside nestles under the shelter of the swelling Wansfell, and which is scattered over with dwellings throughout its circuit. In going round this valley, a walk of about five miles from my friend's house, it was pretty certain that we should meet the majority of our acquaintances, on any fine winter afternoon.

On going forth, the first thing that strikes the stranger's eye is probably the great abundance of evergreens. To me, the wintry aspect of the country is almost annihilated in the neighbourhood of dwellings, by the clustering and shining of the evergreens. The hollies in the hedges are tall and tree-like; and near the breakfast-room windows of their houses, the inhabitants plant a holly, to be an aviary in winter, when birds come flitting about for the sake of the berries. Then, the approaches are hedged in with laurels; the laurestina is in full flower on the lawns; the houses and walls are half covered with ivy; and wherever, along the road, a garden wall stretches away, it runs over with evergreens, which shake off the snow as the breeze passes over them. Well, we go down the road to the toll-bar, where the good woman lives who likes her calling so well that she has no wish to leave her gate to see the world. She saw the world one afternoon for four hours, when her employer sent her to Bowness for a frolic; and she got so tired and dull that she was glad to see her toll-house again, and declared she would never more go pleasuring. I was in the boat with her that day—a packet-boat steered by Professor Wilson,[8] who had his friend Dr. Blair with him. The contrast of the three faces was curious,—the forlorn dulness of the woman, who looks the picture of content when taking toll,—the abstraction of the philological Dr. Blair, and the keen, observing, and enjoying countenance of Christopher North! Just through the toll-bar, lies Waterhead, a cluster of houses on the northern margin of the lake, the prettiest of which is the low cottage under the massy sycamores, with its grass-plat spreading into the waters—the cottage where I lived while my house was building. Passing behind this cottage, the road winds somewhat inland, leaving space for a meadow between it and the lake, till it passes the Roman Camp before mentioned. Then on the right we see, across a field and almost hidden among evergreens, the cottage of poor Hartley Coleridge's tutor, the singular old clergyman who died at upwards of eighty, without a will, as if summoned untimely! Then we pass the beautiful house and most flowery garden of a Quaker friend of mine,—a place which seems in all weathers to look as cheerful as its benevolent master. In my early walk, before it is light in the winter morning, I choose this direction in February, because in a copse of my Quaker friend's which overhangs the road, there is always a more glorious tumult of singing-birds than in any other spot I know. To hear these birds on the one hand, and the gush of the rapid Rotha on the other, when the day is breaking over the waters, is enough to enliven the whole succeeding winter day. The Rotha is here spanned by a bridge, which we must cross if we mean to go round the valley. We leave the highway now, and pass through a gate which makes the winding road half private for the whole time that we are skirting Loughrigg. Under wooded steeps and through copses we go, looking over the flat valley to the green swelling mountains on the other side, whose woods run down the ravines, and hang on the slopes, and peep out where the vales hide between. When I first came, there was a green knoll swelling up out of the meadows, under the opposite hills, with a chapel roof rising behind it, and a row of lowly gray stone cottages near. When I first marked that knoll, I little thought that on it I should build my house, and that it would afford that terrace view which would be the daily delight of my life. But there now stands my graystone old English house, with climbing plants already half covering it, and a terrace wall below, inviting my fruit trees to spread themselves over it.

Our road now skirts the Rotha, a stream too clear to fish in, except after heavy rains. There is no beguiling the trout in water as translucent as the air. We do not now cross the little Millar Bridge, by which I am wont to go almost daily to Fox How; but we walk on to Fox How, through whose birch copse we have to pass. Every one knows that Fox How is the abode so beloved by Dr. Arnold—the house he built, and the garden he laid out to be the retreat of his old age. The trees that he planted spread and flourish, his house is almost covered with roses and climbing plants, his younger children are growing up there, and his friends assemble in his home; but he has long been gone. Perhaps there is not one of us that ever passes through that birch copse without vivid thoughts of him. As for me, I usually take my way through the garden, even if I have not time for more than a word at the window, or even for that. We now see the recess of Fairfield, its whole *cul-de-sac*, finely, unless mists are filling the basin, and curling about the ridges; and Rydal Forest stretches boldly up to the snow line. Lady Le Fleming's large, staring, yellow mansion is a blemish in the glorious view; but a little way back, we saw near it what puts all great mansions out of our heads,—Wordsworth's cottage, a little way up the lower slope of Nab Scar—the blunt end of the Fairfield horseshoe. Of that cottage we must see more hereafter; it does not lie in our road now. After passing four or five dwellings, more or less prettily set down in their gardens, we come to Pelter Bridge, where we cross the Rotha again, and join the mail road. The river still sweeps beside us, among stones and under bending trees, joined here and there by a beck (brook) which has been making waterfalls in the ravines above. When we part company with it, we pass by more and more dwellings, one of the most striking of which, from its exquisite position on a hill-side, is the large gray house built by the brother of Sir Humphry Davy. That gate is near my own. After passing both, and skirting the wall of Mr. Harrison's grounds, we come to the little town of Ambleside. We had better pause at the foot of the hill leading up to the church; for we have more to say of Ambleside than we have room for here.

FEBRUARY

THE HILL on which the church stands is steep; and it would be out of our way to ascend it, in making the circuit of the valley. So I will merely say, in a few words, what lies in that eastern part of our little town. As we go up the ascent, there are houses on each side,—built on limestone, with gushing water within hearing, and on a slope so steep as to make a natural drainage;—yet are these houses, for the most part, undrained, ill supplied with water, close and unwholesome. Dung-heaps and other collections of dirt are before our eyes and under our noses, wherever we turn; and one consequence is,—and a very natural one,—that the men of the place, finding little comfort in an unsavoury home, (which besides is usually over-crowded,) resort to the public houses,—which seem to me to be full whenever I pass them. This is one token of the old-fashioned character of the place. The morals of health have not been preached, or taught, or thought of here; and other morals have a poor chance while such is the state of things. From the time when I became a resident, I saw that something must be done about this. The bad state of health and of morals in the place was evidently a gratuitous evil. The site of the town seemed made for health,—with its slopes, and its abundance of water, and its open position, fronting the valley. The two great evils of there not being houses enough, and of the existing houses being, in a large proportion, unwholesome, seemed to me presently remediable; and we may perhaps see hereafter what the prospect of remedy has become. The houses near the churchyard are the worst; and as for the churchyard itself, the sexton faints when he opens a grave. The small enclosure is surrounded by three roads; so that it is difficult to say how it could be enlarged. But here are hillsides in abundance for a cemetery, if the gentry of the place would set about having one. The idea is, however, too modern for the Ambleside gentry at present. It will probably be some years before they can shake off the impression that there is something irreligious and French, in burying their dead anywhere but within the shadow of the church. There are some charming detached dwellings as high up as the church, and even higher. The nearest is the house of Mr. C., the retired surgeon;—retired from such a failure of health as makes every one glad that he, who can never go out, should have such a bay-window as his, and live enclosed in so pretty a garden. From that window he commands the whole valley, with the lake at one end, and the Rydal Pass at the other, and the Langdale Pikes afar, conspicuous over the whole. A little farther along the lane is Bellevue,—a sort of bridal abode, where a young couple might fairly expect to find their first year of marriage a wondrous experience of paradise. Not much more that a year, however; for in this valley the gentlemen soon grow tired. They go off somewhere to find something to do,—some business, or foreign travel, or hunting. The ladies are satisfied enough; so well, as to be in danger of pride and exclusiveness, and indolence about leaving home: but there are really few gentlemen in the valley but the invalid Mr. C., and two or three aged men, who like the quietness. When the young or middle-aged gentry disappear, they let their houses to widow ladies with daughters, or to single ladies; and these, it is observed, rarely go away again. Thus, the society becomes, in some sort, Amazonian. When I want to make a party to meet my guests, it is a wonder if a single coat and hat can be got. Mr. C. never leaves his house: Dr. B. is crippled, and can be seen only at home, or, as a rare chance, on a fine summer's day, on the road in his wheeled chair. Mr. Wordsworth likes to see his friends at home, but does not visit. Mrs. Arnold's sons are dispersed about the world; and we see two or three of them only on occasion, for a few days. Mr. G. is always flying backwards and forwards between his home and his business in Cheshire. So, for three times out of four, our little parties are composed wholly of ladies; and they happen to be such ladies as leave nothing to be wished. Farther still along the lane is the new parsonage, a goodly house, not yet finished, where the clergyman's eight children are to grow and flourish, in full view of such a prospect as will make every landscape that their windows may command in after life flat and ugly in comparison. The lane is steep and ill-kept at present; but when the new parsonage is finished it will be improved; and I have my eye upon it for an extension of Ambleside in this direction.

Higher yet up the hill, beyond the church, is the suburb, called (for some reason unknown) Edinburgh, which has formed itself round the mill,—the bobbin-mill, whose great water-wheel is turned by the beautiful Stock beck, as it comes down foaming and frothing, from the

Stock ghyll force, (ghyll, ravine,—force, waterfall,) a quarter of a mile above.[9] There is nothing good about this cluster of houses but its position. It wants purifying, physically and morally; and, till that is done, we will let it alone.

This stream, the Stock, goes leaping, gurgling, and gushing down, overhung by trees and tormented by rocks in its channel, till it passes under the road, near the foot of the hill where we made our pause; after which it flows away in a winding course among the fields, and across the meadows till it enters the Rotha, near the Millar Bridge, which we passed on our way to Fox How. We walk over it on the road, passing the shops of S., the painter, and of the wheelwright, on the left, and of the cooper, and the confectioner, and the shoemaker, on the right. The cooper's shop and children are always neat, though flour and groceries are sold, as well as tubs and bowls, and rolling-pins; and though the children are many, and the mother always busy. She is a great needle-woman, to judge by the large piece of work,—the sheet or shirt,—one sees on her arm, whenever one glances in at her open door. Now we are in the view of the corner, round which we are to turn into the little market-place. That corner is shaded by a dark sycamore; but before we reach the sycamore, our attention is fixed by the inn,—the Salutation, whose name is a reminder of a Catholic age, when Gabriel and the Virgin looked down on the approach of wayfarers. This is the principal inn; and the range of stables is rather imposing, and the rubbing down and harnessing of horses seem to be always going forward in the summer season. And there is the civil and good-natured host; once a stable-boy himself, as he likes to tell; now a most important man in the place, and usually out on his great flight of steps, or conferring with travellers in the area in front of his house. The next inn, the Commercial, is on our right, as we turn into the little market-place; and a third, the White Lion, shows its range of back windows opposite. Round the irregular area of the market-place are the rest of the shops;—the saddler's, the butcher's, the watchmaker's, the linen-draper's, the ironmonger's, and the lawyer's and carrier's offices on the left; and on the right, the coach-office, the baker's, the milliner's, the druggist's, and the post-office; which is also the place of books and stationary. In the midst stands the dear old market-cross,[10] up its three steps,—the mouldering old stone cross, which tells of past centuries. And, casting a shadow of antiquity and solemnity over all, is the great rookery; which I make a point of passing at daybreak, in winter, unless I go to the other rookery, in Lady Le Fleming's great beeches, at Rydal. I like the noise of the creatures,—their amazing din in the February mornings, when they are beginning their building; but better still do I like their earliest morning flight,—a higher flight than I ever see them take at other times. I know now how to look for them. When it is still only beginning to be light with us, but when the sky takes the pearly or pinky hue which belongs to a winter dayspring, I look steadily up into the sky, and presently see an immeasurable flock, just at the point of vision, sailing over the valley,—sometimes winging straight for Lady Le Fleming's beeches, sometimes for the Ambleside elms, and sometimes wheeling round, as if they had time for another sweep abroad, and another chance of seeing the sun, before going to work upon their new nests.

The post-office shop is the favourite among these,—all of which yield civil and friendly treatment. The post-mistress, Mrs. Nicholson, is a favourite with us all. The post-mistress of a little country town is always the depositary of much confidence. I doubt whether anything exists, is done, or is suffered, in Ambleside, without Mrs. Nicholson being told of it: yet, never, through a long course of years, has she been charged with saying anything that she ought not. Yet, with all her discretion, she is as open-hearted as the most rash of babblers. She gives her confidence freely; but she is so innocent, so simple, and so intimately known by all her neighbours, that I doubt whether she has any secrets of her own, or ever had. I love to go there; but I keep away, if possible, at post-hours, and near the middle of the day, when she and her daughters are busy. A better time is in the early morning, before any other shop is open, when there is always one of the Nicholsons preparing the shop, and willing to serve me with postage-stamps, and spare five minutes for talking over our Building Society,[11] or my cows,[12] or any incident of the time. I never saw more perfect filial conduct than that of the two daughters, who, out of a family of thirteen, remain with their mother. H.,[13] the handsome and high-spirited one, and M.,[14] the delicate and diminutive and subdued one, are ladies of nature's making, as truly as their old mother; and in nothing do they show it more than in their tender watchfulness over her. She is somewhat infirm and suffering; and the more watchful, and the more tender are they. Mrs. N. can seldom be induced to leave home; and I therefore felt it a great honour when she lately came, with her daughter H., to see my field and my cows, and take tea with me; and as they departed, I felt that never since my house was built, had truer ladies passed its doors.

Our circuit will soon be completed now. We go straight on, past the White Lion, with the surgeon's and chief shoemaker's houses on our right, past the Royal Oak public house, past the smithy, along the highroad to Waterhead. There are a few pretty houses, set down in gardens, by the way; and one very ugly house, Fisherbeck, built for a workhouse, and looking just like it, but now let in lodgings: but the views into the Brathay valley, opening as we go, and disclosing again the little church on its height, and the overlapping hills, with the Langdale Pikes appearing last of all, engage one's whole attention, till the lake opens full and calm, and we are at the toll-bar again, and within a quarter of a mile of my host's house.

Can any one wonder that I presently dreamed of living in this valley? There was no reason why I should not live where I pleased. Five years and more of illness had broken all bonds of business, and excluded me from all connexion with affairs. I was free to choose how to begin life afresh. The choice lay between London and pure country; for no one would prefer living in a provincial town for any reasons but such as did not exist for me. I love London; and I love the pure country. As for the choice between them now,—I had some dread of a London literary life for both its moral and physical effects. I was old enough to look forward to old age, and to have already some wish for quiet, and command of my own time. Moreover, every woman requires for her happiness some domestic occupation and responsibility,—to have some one's daily happiness to cherish; and a London lodging is poorly supplied with such objects; whereas, in a country home, with one's maids, and one's neighbours, and a weary brother or sister, or nephew, or niece, or friend, coming to rest under one's trees, or bask on one's sunshiny terrace, there is prospect of abundance of domestic interest. If I chose the country, I might as well choose the best; and this very valley was, beyond all controversy, the best. Here, I could write in the serenest repose; here, I could rove at will; here, I could rest. Here, accordingly, I took up my rest; and I have never repented it, while my family and friends regard it as the wisest step I could take. I was so far cautious, that I engaged a lodging for half a year, to allow myself scope for a change of mind; but I was so far from changing my mind, that, before we were far into the summer, I was looking at any empty cottage I could hear of, which was at all likely to serve me as a permanent abode. In the midst of my search, my late host reminded me that the lowest rent would amount to as much as the interest of the sum which would build me a house of my own planning. I was struck with conviction; and immediately after, some land was offered for sale in the best possible situation. I could not get ready by the auction day, or I would have bid for the lot, which consisted of the green knoll I have mentioned before. I never doubted its being bought up instantly. But, to my amusement, and great satisfaction, this was the lot for which there were no bidders. I bought it, with two low-lying lots below it, which I obtained by some critical negotiation and exchange; and before July was out, I was in possession of that knoll and two acres of ground about it. The builder, John Newton, had received my plan of such a house as I should like, and had sent in his tender of a contract. In October, the first sod was turned; and during the winter, the building went on.

In February, I was living in the cottage under the sycamores, at Waterhead, which we have glanced at before. The windows of my sitting-room looked westwards, across the head of the lake. The winter afternoons were thus splendid, in fine weather; but, to enjoy the beauty of the early morning, it was necessary to go forth under the brightening sky. It is my pleasure at that season to go out before there is any daylight—at half past six; and I have never wished myself at home, whatever the weather might be. If rainy, I was sure to see the mists curling and rolling over the surface of the lake,—showing themselves, or letting a streak of the water be seen whenever there was an opening in the clouds above, through which a star, or a ray of the dawn could be disclosed; and, in the worst weather, there were the birds, making their February din in the woods between the highroad and the lake. It mattered little what the weather was when I stood on a little white pebbly beach, with the waves washing up at my feet, and the noisy birds over my head, making my very heart gay with their merry chirp, and pipe, and whistle, and loud song. They seemed to be trying to drown the dash and rush of the brook which was hurrying from the hills above to help swell the lake, already rising above its bounds. But, in a clear morning, when the stars were rocked on the surface of the lake, and a fragment of the old moon hung over the Wansfell, amidst the clear, greenish eastern sky, what a treat was that early walk! I was sure to see, on my return to breakfast, a sight worthy of Switzerland itself;—the snowy summit of Coniston Old Man peering over the intervening ridge, to show itself in the gray expanse of Windermere, with the first pink lines of sunrise touching its loftiest ridge. Never was there seen a colouring more soft and melting; and melting it was, for in a very few minutes it was gone;—and when I entered my sitting-room, and found it lighted chiefly by the blazing fire on which my kettle was hissing and steaming, I could hardly believe that I had seen daylight so near. But, in the afternoon, I had the very last of the daylight. While candles were lighted everywhere else in the house, I sat in the yellow glow at the window, seeing how the black pines on the rocky promontory were reflected in the orange and crimson waters, stem for stem, distinct and unmoved, while the mountains and their reflection were of the deepest purple, and a full clear planet shone with a glow-worm light in the midst of the ruddy scene. Of all the sunsets of that winter, there is one that stands alone in my remembrance. As my house assumed more and more the air of a dwelling,—that is, from the time the rooftree was on, I seldom returned to dinner at dark without having had a glance at my future home from some point or other. Its gaping doorways and window-spaces looked cold and forlorn; but when once the roof was on, I could overlook that defect from the other side of the valley. Along that other side of the valley I was walking, from Fox How to Waterhead, one bright afternoon, just at sunset; and what did I see?—my windows glittering in the last yellow rays! How home-like it looked! how completely changed in character from a shell of a dwelling to a home, merely by putting in the window-sashes! I met John Newton, and asked him about it; and he told me that he expected heavy rain, and had put in the sashes in a hurry, to keep the inside dry.

The heavy rains came, hour after hour, almost like a waterspout, with winds which made such a commotion that two panes of my windows were broken. As for the lake, it dashed and rolled all the next day, and seemed to be coming nearer in the night, so that I was not at all surprised to find a flood when I looked out the next morning. There could be no morning walk, for our house was a peninsula, which afforded only a few yards of dry footing beyond the door. Angry billows rolled over the grass-plat, up against the house walls. In the road, men were pushing themselves about on logs and planks. The little piers were all sunk, and the boat-house seemed likely to blow up. Cascades of white water were leaping and rushing down through trees, and pouring over fences into the road. Logs and faggots were drifting out from the shore, and chips were dancing on the surface. Within the house, my landlady was pulling up her carpets from the ground-floor rooms; and from the windows, the neighbours were calling to each other that no such flood had been witnessed by the existing generation. The rain was over, however, and there was a brisk wind; so that, though the lake would not go down till the tributary streams had done paying in their excess, the river and brooks in the valley would soon subside into their channels, and allow us to go and see what had happened above. By the afternoon, it was thought possible to reach a higher part of the road; and, thickshod, I went forth. Presently, I met the A.'s, all in their thickest boots, coming down to see the flood. They said the meadows in the valley were almost entirely under water. I could not turn back with them, so great was my secret anxiety about my house. It was not for long. When I reached Rotha Bridge, and looked northwards, there was my pretty gray house, high and dry on its green knoll, bright and cheerful-looking, and even with smoke coming out of one chimney. There was not a grate in the house yet; but the carpenters had made a fire under the chimney to heat their glue; and thus it was that this warm domestic token met my eye when I least expected it. Before I had finished my circuit, the wind had subsided; and when I cast my last glance at the knoll, the little column of smoke was as steady as in a summer noon.

MARCH

IT MUST be long before we could make the ground neat on and around my knoll: but we must not wait for that to institute a shrubbery and a garden. The horses' feet and cartwheels had torn up and cut my grass, round the base of the knoll, into a mass of brown mud, mixed here and there with lime;—a disagreeable sight. But our planting was finished before February was out; and much gardening must be done in March. January is the true planting month with us; but my ground could not be prepared before February; and yet my young trees have flourished, with scarcely an exception. Before the drive was finished, the laurels were set on either hand,—the range of evergreens which was to cheer the eye in winter, and bid defiance to the snow. At first these laurels were but a dotted row, with here and there a sapling of sycamore, chestnut, lime, ash, and oak interposed; but already they are a close and rising hedge, green all the year round, and showing off well the beauty of rose, lily, and dahlia in their seasons. The grandest effect at first was produced by the beeches, Mr. G. having offered me some, almost as tall as myself, from the thinnings of his wood. It was a mild, sunny day when the carts came with those young beeches, their red-budded branches swinging over the sides, and their cropped roots sticking out behind;—roots so closely cropped that, in my ignorance, I could not help doubting whether the trees could ever grow. They were planted in the wet, level ground that drains the drive; and the holes dug for them were like little wells; but they, and the variety of young trees planted with them, soon drained that level. The long red buds of the beeches duly expanded; and the trees stood the great test of the second year; and now, that bit of ground yields some of the sweetest grass that my cows ever eat.—With a view to bees hereafter, we took care to have plenty of limes; and from a regard to the birds, plenty of thorns and hollies, to secure a good winter crop of haws and berries. The hollies ought to be planted abundantly; for no tree is so unwilling to strike. It is only recently, after three years of watching, that mine have thrown up a vigorous central shoot; and put out bright green tufts at the end of every twig. But I have been fortunate in losing only a few. Wherever they stand I make all meaner growths give way to them; and in a few years, they will brighten the whole place in winter, and make it busy with flitting birds.—Where we wanted to shut out the view of the backs of the neighbouring cottages, we planted a row of larches and willows—ugly enough at first, but less so than what they hid, and sure to be soon relieved by the spread of the shrubs in front of them. The rocky parts of the knoll were not forgotten; for the house must have wood behind; so, wherever there was soil enough, we put in firs and pines, and oak and mountain ash for a relief. We had already the blessing of a full-grown oak copse, sheltering the house on its north side, and another running down the slope on the southwest. It remained to plant the little orchard;—to put in the apple and pear trees on the grassy slope to the west, below the terrace wall. Whether apples will answer well on his ground is a question of great importance to every new settler. In some places by the roadside they seem to be endeavouring in vain to grow, while in others the trees are propped up under their load of fruit. The monks of old put a pavement between the upper soil and the gravel beneath, when they planted their apple trees in districts where there was known to be gravel beneath. In our region, Nature seems to have done this paving for us; but she has too often left a too shallow soil above. How it will be on this orchard slope, time must show.

On this spot it was that the most important planting of all took place. I had asked Mr. Wordsworth whether he would plant a tree for me, and he had said he would. One fine, bright day we chanced to meet at my kind neighbour's, Mrs. D.'s, and we all agreed that there would never be a better opportunity. Mrs. D. sent to her gardener for a young oak; but Mr. Wordsworth objected that an oak was too common a tree for a commemorative occasion—it should be something more distinctive. So we selected a vigorous little stone pine, and off we went. Mr. Wordsworth struck in his spade on a spot under the terrace wall, just overhanging the little quarry from which the stone for that wall was taken. I thought it a dangerous place, sure to be run over by cats and dogs, and liable to be trodden by persons who might not see a shrub only a few inches high; but Mr. Wordsworth was decided, and in most workmanlike fashion he set the little tree, and gave it its first watering. Then he washed his hands in the watering-pot, took my hand in both his, and gave his blessing to me and my dwelling. That little tree was my daily anxiety for some time, till at last, when pondering how to fence it round without stifling it, it occurred to me to dig a flower-bed round it, which would preserve it from most of the mischances that it was liable to. It is an odd place for a flower-bed, but that does not matter. There the sacred little tree now flourishes,—slow of growth, of course, but vigorous, and no longer in danger of being trodden down.

As the March days lengthened, the valley and the hill slopes gave hints of exchanging their dull hay-colour here and there for a lively spring green; and we began to think of getting forward with the garden. In this we had effectual help from my German friend Fredrika,[15] albeit she lives at Bowness, six miles from us. When we had once settled where our flower-beds and borders were to be—how many on the north slope, how many under the terrace wall, and of what shape to make the one within the quarry, Fredrika knew how to proceed, and would not allow me to be disturbed, if she came when I was busy. Her way was to row herself in one of her three boats from Bowness to the head of the lake, stopping to eat her breakfast in the centre of the lake, and also to fish for our dinner. According to the month she would bring a booty of trout, carp, or pike, and her fishing seems to be always more or less successful. She would land in the garden at Croft Lodge, and there add some fresh vegetables to her present of fish. She would then walk the mile and half to my house, quietly put in her basket at the back door, take the heaviest tools from the tool-house, and go to work. With pickaxe, spade, and riddle,[16] she cleared the rock here, trenched a bed there, and prepared a choice border for our best plants. It was she who made and stocked my first dahlia-beds, driving in the poles with her own hands. It was she who sent me half the roses I have, and made the terrace suddenly gay the next summer, with a grand show of geraniums. When, at two o'clock, my morning's work in my study was done, I went out and worked with her till dinner-time; and then, if I accompanied her to her boat, or further, so as to take a pair of oars with her, and land at Lowwood to walk home, how sweet were those spring evenings in the meadows and on the water! How, as we cut through the lights and shadows on the surface of the lake, did Fredrika tell of her feats with her gun among the wild swans and other fowl that visited us in their passage, or answer the cuckoo that hailed us from the woods on the shore!

In the intervals between Fredrika's visits, my maid Jane and I strove to adorn our knoll in an humbler way than by my friend's lavish aid. We wanted to clothe the little quarry and other rocks with beauty,—to lodge there the white and yellow stonecrop, and Cheddar pinks, and ferns, and foxglove, and heather of various sorts; and to make the periwinkle hang down from the brow, and to lead the honeysuckle trailing up, supporting itself by the roots of the oak growing above. We accepted whatever was offered us, and then found that we were lowly enough to be pleased with the wild flowers which are yielded to the seeker by every field, copse, wall, and bank in this region. After returning thanks for the thinnings of our friends' gardens,—iris, asters, pinks, hepaticas, &c.,—we went to the weedy bridge at Clappersgate for some of the yellow stonecrop which grew there. We went with Mrs. D. to avail ourselves of permission from Lady Le Fleming's steward to take heather from an enclosure which is a sort of heather preserve. This was laborious work, so we hired Fisher's cart, with the donkey and Jack Fisher, who carried his father's heavy spade and dug up large blocks of peat soil rich with heather, wherewith to adorn our rock-shelves. But the expeditions which we enjoyed the most were those which we made by ourselves, Jane and I, with our lunch and our frail baskets, and each a trowel,—one trowel being small enough to take the ferns clean out of the crevices of the walls.

For a sample,—first, across the meadows. But we are stopped at the gate by Mother Stewart, who must be attended to at her own time or not at all. Mother Stewart, whom Mrs. Wordsworth[17] and Mrs. Arnold call a friend of theirs, and whom I humbly hope to be allowed to consider my friend too, looks so weatherbeaten to-day as to show that she has only just arrived from a peregrination; and here comes her cart, with her son in it, driving slowly, that he may not break my new crockery. Ambleside is not a place for the display of a crockery-shop; and, in furnishing my house, my only resource in this department is Mother Stewart, who itinerates with her whole family, taking orders and going into Staffordshire for what is wanted. I dare say, I am her principal customer this time; and we must now turn back to see what she has done for us. How gipsy-like she looks, with her red and blue handkerchief hanging about her face under her weatherbeaten black bonnet, and her arms akimbo, except when she takes her pipe from her mouth to speak! When her ware is all spread out on the kitchen floor, I see how good her taste is wherever I have left her an option: and I praise the chamber-ewers and basins, the water-pitchers and tea-service. But lo! the good taste is only after a pattern, I fear, for now she wants me to buy for mantelpiece ornaments some scarlet or green castles, with blue towers for paper-lighters,—articles which she holds off at arm's length, calling them in a sincere enthusiasm "most beautiful." Here is another proof of the old-fashioned character of the region. Formerly, in the days when blue and red plaster cats, and scarlet and green china owls and parrots were found in cottages, such chimney-ware as this might be seen on the shelves of crockery-shops as a chief adornment. The good cheap prints, and cast-glass ornaments, and the fine plaster busts, vases, and groups that the Italian boys have made common elsewhere, will sooner or later find their way hither. Meantime Mother Stewart might make us fancy ourselves a hundred years older than we are. Her medical ideas are old-fashioned too. She wants my opinion what to do with her young daughter, who is subject to fits. She finds no good effect from what was affirmed to her would be a cure,—binding the backbones of three sprats upon the girl's breast when she went to bed. When her wares are checked off by the list, and I have put a pen into her hard big hand, that she may make her mark, Jane sweeps away the straw, Mrs. Stewart ties up her money in a bag, and gives me her last affectionate nod, resumes her pipe, and leaves us to prosecute our walk.

As we follow the beck (Stockbeck) in the lane, we find it so full that we can imagine how the disaster happened when the two little children from yonder farm-house were drowned here in returning from school. That farm-house, halfway up Loughrigg, is hidden from us in the summer by the foliage of the ash trees at the bottom of my field, while it is a conspicuous and cheerful object in winter; but, winter or summer, I never look that way without thinking of those two children. The mother was doubtful in the morning about letting them go, but the father saw no reason for fear; and he was right; for the way was then clear. The children were desired not to leave the school till the maid should come for them; but the school-mistress, not dreaming of danger, sent them away when they had waited some time after school-hours. The fact was, the maid had found the meadow way impracticable, and had gone round by Rotha Bridge. Not fining the children at the school, she ran to the lane, found it flooded,—ankle-deep at first,—presently knee-deep. She called a man at work near, who waded in further, and found presently a little bag, and soon a little bonnet. The case was too clear. It was some time before the bodies were recovered. They had been swept into the deep channel of the beck, carried down and washed in among the trees, before the junction of the beck with the Rotha. Though I have often passed through that lane when it was flooded, it seems as strange as ever that such an event should have happened almost at my very gate,—only on the other side of a slip of field.

We leave the beck, rushing and roaring as it does in March, and cross the meadow and Millar Bridge, and wind along the foot of Loughrigg. The fences are tufted with wall-plants, which look tempting; but we will take none of them, as we can get them in every variety at Grasmere. But before entering the birch copse of Fox How, we must help ourselves to primroses from the new clearing, where they so abound as to give a yellow hue to the hillside, as seen from our windows. The blossoms nestle under every clump of suckers, and at the base of every sprout of rock. While we have our trowels in use, we take up wood anemones and sorrel, with a view to variegating the carpet of the copse,—abounding as it does in ferns and harebells, with pansies peeping out in the sunny places. The daffodils come next. For them we have not to go far; only past Fox How and Fox Ghyll,—that ideal of a country house, with the thick grass growing up to its trellised walls, and those walls completely covered with flowering creepers in the largest variety that the climate will admit; and the whole sheltered and almost overhung by the perpendicular wooded side of Loughrigg. The next abode is Mr. Q.'s, where we must beg our daffodils. Leave given, we dig diligently under the trees and on the grassy terrace, which, in another month, will present a waving harvest of yellow blossoms. But presently we stop, staying that we shall have no room for plants from Grasmere, if we go on filling our baskets at this rate.

We do not go over Pelter Bridge, but turn up to the

left, still skirting Loughrigg on its blunt end. After half a mile of miry road, between high fences, we come out upon Rydal Lake,—the exquisite little mere, with its two wooded islands sitting looking at themselves in the still waters. How every bush, and every peeping corner of gray rock is reflected in the mirror! The softened outline and hue of those graceful trees show that Spring is indeed coming on. The next time we stand here, they will be more or less green. I suppose we need not look yet for sheep upon the fells. It will be another month before they can pick a living there. Glancing round, however, we see a wild party of ragged and dirty sheep, rushing about together, as if they were scared at being at large again, or flying from the pursuit of justice, for trespass and theft in gardens, during the hungry and half-fed season which is coming to an end. May they find juicy young grass, and plenty of it, high up on the fell, that our gardens may be safe from them for another year! There they go, over the ridge, and down into some invisible dell on the other side!

Now we mount gradually, by a heathery path in the sward, seeing across the water more and more of the promontory that separates Rydal and Grasmere Lakes; seeing the pretty cottage where Hartley Coleridge lives, looking out from under its sycamores, and in its dark ivy dress, upon the little meadow and still lake before its door; seeing the Rydal quarries open in the shape of black caverns in the sides of Nab's Scar; seeing the old Roman road shining with wet, as it cuts over the promontory; seeing the infant Rotha rush from one lake to the other; seeing Grasmere open, and feeling again, as a hundred times before, that it is the most beautiful of all the lakes. What a magnificent station this Loughrigg terrace is!—the broad, dry, safe track, ascending gradually, till there is below us a grand sweep of the green hillside, down to the little white beach of the lake! Thence spreads the lake, whose margin is green throughout its whole circuit; and in the midst lies its one island,—green as emerald on its sloping side, while the steep side is crested with black pines, overshadowing a single roof. From the highest point of this terrace, what a view it is! I know none like it. The circuit of mountains shows every variety of wooded ravine, with a waterfall here and there, seen glittering in the intervals, and grassy slopes, and a few gray stone dwellings, which indicated that the scene is enjoyed by human residents. Off to the left (the northwest), Easedale opens grandly,—the position of the summits telling that a solemn valley lies among them. Immediately opposite, on the level at the end of the lake, stands the old-fashioned little church of Grasmere, with the village gathered about it. A little to the right, running due north, and mounting the long ascent of Dunmail Raise, is the road (like a mere path now to our eyes), which passes by the foot of Helvellyn to Keswick. Faint and far appear the Keswick mountains,—Skiddaw and Saddleback; and nearer, and swelling up boldly from the Raise, is old Helvellyn. That white house, somewhat nearer to us, is the Swan Inn, where Scott used to have his daily draught and chat with the landlord, when he was Wordsworth's guest, when both were young men; and where they and

Southey met, to begin the ascent of Helvellyn. Round to the right, we come again to Nab's Scar, and the Rydal woods, with the little church lifting its head from among them; and, finally, there is the infant river making itself heard and seen below. It is always hard to leave this terrace; but when at least we move off, we run down the long, steep hill of Red Bank,—too steep to be safely passed, except on foot or on horseback,—and we stop for breath at the waterfall and cistern below, which show us that we now stand but little above the margin of the lake.

And here is the wall we came to rifle. Within the space of three feet of this wall, I find six different ferns. We ply our trowels till our baskets will hold no more, even of these small plants. Having determined not to let our eyes be caught by any more plants to-day, and wondering where we shall put all we have got, we find ourselves hungry. We follow the sound of waters to the edge of a brook, and sit down on the rocks in the field above, to eat our sandwiches, and fill our India-rubber cup from the stream. Then on—briskly,—for it is an hour later than we supposed,—on, by the winding road, past the watercure establishment of St. Oswald's;—on, through Grasmere, under the church tower, over the bridge, rounding the lake all the time;—past the cottage where Wordsworth lived with his sister before he married;—up and up, passing over the Roman road, to go by a still higher, and shorter, and more beautiful cut over the promontory;—past a little tarn;—down upon Rydal quarries, where we join the mail road;—past Hartley Coleridge's dwelling on the brink of the lake, where he, standing in the porch, offers his peculiar salutation of a bow, almost to the ground, hat in hand;—past the row of noble sycamores, where we have no time to rest now, seated on the roots;—past the foot of Rydal Mount;—past Pelter Bridge again, and home,—hoping to set our plants before dark, though we have walked ten miles.

APRIL

APRIL IS a busy month in the Lake district. Besides the garden and field work of which there is so much to be done, there are the removals and the consequent sales. The 5th of April is the tax-paying day; and those who are about to change their abode, wait till that day is over, that they may not subject themselves to a needless payment of a quarter's taxes. It might be supposed that in a primitive district like ours, where the people's minds seem never to move, they would go on inhabiting the same abodes from generation to generation. So they would, if the choice were theirs: but, as we shall see, it is not so. The sales which take place in the spring and autumn, follow upon these removals; and, though the cause is often mournful enough, these auctions are the grand festive occasions of the year. We will go to one of them, and see what it is like.

It was on the 7th of April that I took possession of my house.[18] It was an occasion never to be forgotten,—the first entrance upon a home of my own. The house was not finished, neither sitting-room having a floor; but the upstairs rooms were furnished enough for residence, and the little back kitchen for cooking. There was abundance of amusement in the shifts we were put to, till our pots and pans, fenders and fire-irons came from Birmingham; and in the hurry we were in to make and put up our window blinds; and in the care necessary in going up and down stairs, because as yet there were no banisters; and in the difficulty where to seat the friends who made haste to call on me in my new capacity of resident. But there was a serious and sweet interest about the day, which remains the permanent impression. The weather was mild and sunny all day long. That particular chestnut of Mr. Harrison's, which is always in leaf earlier than any other tree in the neighbourhood, showed already a vivid green among the treetops round it. The crocuses in the grass looked gay; the sorrel among the roots of the oaks in the copse was most delicate; and as the sun went down behind the pines on the ridge of Loughrigg, the yellow glow which he flung across the valley was rich and mild. Evening was come, and my room had no bedstead. I began to wonder whether I really was to take possession on this long wished-for day, when, in the last yellow light, I saw two men coming down the hill, from the cabinet-maker's, carrying some weight between them. In an hour's time, we had made our beds,—the maids and I,—and the new blinds were drawn down, and the kettle was steaming and singing, and the steady-burning lamp gave a sense of stillness such as should, on occasion, hang about a real home. Long after others were asleep, I sat in the light of the fire, feeling what it was to have entered upon the home in which I hoped to live and die; to work while I could, and rest when I could work no more, if I should indeed live so long. The next sweetest thing was the morning's waking—the rousing up to the first business of a new life.

The weather is as fine as yesterday. That is well for the sale in Troutbeck, and for J. and me, who mean to attend it. We wait only for the post, and before eleven we are off for our walk of a dozen miles. We have hopes of obtaining at the sale some of the many household articles we yet lack; and at all events, we must look after a little pig at Mr. W.'s farm in Troutbeck. It was not my intention to enter upon even that much farming, but J. had set her heart upon it from the time she saw the field. I found her, one spring afternoon, hovering about the slope, where, as she showed me, we could have a perpetual series of vegetables. She was willing to engage that the eye should never be offended with yellow cabbage leaves, and strewed gooseberry skins; and ended by saying, that if we had but a kitchen-garden and a pig, she should have nothing more in the world to wish. This was irresistible. I suspected that she was mistaken, and that she would find ere long, that fowls and a cow were indispensable to perfect earthly bliss; but I was willing to let her try for happiness on her own terms. The kitchen-garden was already trenched, manured and stocked; and now we must see Mr. W.'s fine breed of pigs, and choose one for our new piggery. We must go by the most beautiful way, and get our first sight this year of the

Kirkstone Pass. It is a pass that few venture through in winter, for fear, not only of the drifting snow, but of the insufferable north wind, which, rushing up the pass, seems to pierce one's very life. In April, it is cold enough; but, as we have to go in that direction, we must try for a sight of the sea from the highest inhabited house in England,—the white public house at the entrance of the pass, to which the honour of being the highest inhabited house in England is awarded by the best authority—the Ordnance Surveyors, who have put up a board on the house signifying the fact.[19] I once went up with a nephew and niece, to sleep there—partly to be able to say that I had spent the night on such a perch, and partly for the sake of the morning view. The good dame is clean and tidy; but the double windows are small, and scarcely a few inches will open; and, though such closeness may be necessary at such an elevation, it is anything but wholesome or agreeable. What warmth is necessary was shown by a question which the dame came in to ask while we were at tea, and which made us laugh most uncivilly. She asked whether we "preferred" sheets to our beds. The custom of the house evidently is to wrap up in blankets or rugs, in order to sleep, even in August. Well: to this house we are first to mount—taking our time for the steep and almost continuous ascent of three miles and a half. How steep it is! How soon we look down into the church tower, and see the valley mapped out below us, and find the lake spreading and lengthening, and little Blelham Tarn now glittering beyond it, over the nearer hills—and the Langdale Pikes rearing their crests above the Grasmere range—and line behind line of ridges, grayer and fainter, extending westwards to the sea!—that is if we look behind us. If before us, the Kirkstone mountain swells up, bare and hard; the height which, as Wordsworth tells us, echoed "Joanna's laugh;" "and Kirkstone tossed it from his misty head."[20] And now, we see the house, sitting down, as it were, at the entrance of the pass. How prodigiously steep the road looks, winding up over the heath—without fence, or tree, or shrub—spanning the torrent, but otherwise wholly wild!

We are almost breathless when we reach the house. On the morning after our night's rest in this place, the mist was so thick we could not see a yard before us. Now, how clear it is!—cold, blue, and clear,—with a whitish line of sea on the horizon; a line which might be taken for a strip of clear sky, but for the smoke of a steamer, coming out from behind a promontory. This wide view is very fine, but I prefer the other which we are going to see: so let us be off! We leave our baskets in the porch, order bread and cheese and beer to be ready for us against our return in twenty minutes, and run on down the pass, against the cutting wind.

There is the Kirk Stone, which gives its name to the pass; the block which, from a certain point of view, seen against the sky, is very like a little church. What a mass of *débris* it is that it surmounts! It has struck me, when standing between this point and the lake,—Brothers Water—which now opens upon us at the bottom of the pass, how we have before the eye in one view, the various results of the action of nature in a mountainous region, and especially by the agency of water. There are tarns among the hills on the right; Hay's Water, where the angler goes for a day of solitary sport; and Angle Tarn on Place Fell: and these tarns gratify, not only by their beauty, but by the sense of use which attends the perception of their beauty. Their use is to cause such a distribution of the waters as may fertilize without inundating the lands below. After rains, if the waters all came pouring down at once, the vales would be flooded: as it is, the nearer brooks swell, and pour themselves out into the main stream—as now the little torrents are feeding the beck in the midst of the pass, which rushes down into Brothers Water. Meanwhile, the springs are busy in the same way above, emptying themselves into the tarns. By the time the streams in the valley are subsiding, the upper tarns are full and begin to overflow: and now the overflow can be received in the valley without injury. While always ready for this occasional work, nature is also eternally busy at more regular processes, which do not show from day to day, but are very striking after a course of years. She disintegrates the rocks, and now and then sends down masses, like the Kirk Stone itself, thundering along the ravines, or to bridge a chasm, or to make a new islet in a pool. She sows her seeds in crevices, or on little projections, so that the bare face of the precipice becomes like that above Brothers Water yonder, feathered with the rowan and the birch; and thus, ere long, motion is produced by the passing winds, in a scene where once all appeared rigid as a mine. She draws her carpet of verdure gradually up the bare slopes, as in those swelling grounds above Hartsop, where she has deposited earth to sustain the vegetation. She is for ever covering with her exquisite mosses and ferns every spot which has been left unsightly, till nothing appears to offend the human eye, within a whole circuit of hills. She even silently rebukes and repairs the false taste of uneducated man. If he makes his new dwelling of too glaring a white, she tempers it with weather-stains. If he indolently leaves the stone walls and blue slates unrelieved by any neighbouring vegetation, she supplies the needful screen by bringing out tufts of delicate fern in the crevices, and springing coppice on the nearest slopes. She is perpetually working changes in the disposition of the waters of the region. The margins of the lakes never remain the same for half a century together. The streams bring down soft soil incessantly, which more effectually alters the currents than the slides of stones precipitated from the heights by an occasional storm. By this deposit of soil new promontories are formed and the margin contracts, till many a reach of waters is converted into land inviting tillage. The flats below us, and all the greenest levels of the smaller valleys, may be seen to have been once lakes. And while she is thus closing up in one direction, she is opening in another. In some low-lying spot a tree falls, which acts as a dam when the next rains come. The detained waters sink, and penetrate, and loosen the roots of other trees; and the moisture which they formerly absorbed, goes to swell the accumulation, till the place becomes a swamp. The drowned vegetation decays and sinks, leaving more room, till the place becomes a pool, on whose bristling margin the snipe arrives to rock on the bulrush, and the heron wades in the water-lilies, to feed on the fish which come there no one knows how. As the waters spread, they encounter natural dams, behind which they grow clear and deeper, till we have a tarn among the hills, which attracts the browsing flocks, and tempts the shepherd to build his hut near the brink. Then the wild swans see the glittering expanse in their flight, and drop down into it; and the waterfowl make their nests among the reeds. This brings the sportsman, and a path is trodden over the hills, and the spot becomes a place of human resort. While nature is thus working transformations in her deeper retreats, the generations of men are more obviously busy in conspicuous places. They build their houses and plant their orchards on the slopes which connect the mountains with the levels of the valleys: they encroach upon the swamps below them, and plough among the stones on the hillsides—here fencing in new grounds, there throwing several plots into one: they open slate-quarries, and make broad roads for the carriage of the produce; they cherish the young hollies and ash, whose sprouts feed their flocks, thus providing a compensation in the future for the past destruction of the woods. Thus, while the general primitive aspect of the region remains, and its intensely rural character is little impaired, there is perhaps scarcely a valley in the district which, any more than this pass, looks exactly the same from one half century to another. The little lake below us was doubtless of a different extent, form, and character from what it is now, when the accident happened which is believed to have given it its name. Two brothers set out to cross it on the ice, as the shortest way to church, one Sunday, in a long-forgotten time: the ice broke near the middle, and they were never seen more.

Such sales as we are about to attend—(and it is time that we were turning back, after having once more fixed in our memory every feature of this noble pass)—show that changes among the people proceed no less certainly, while more rapidly, than among the scenes they dwell in. Once upon a time every household had nearly all that it wanted within itself. The people thought so little of wheaten bread, that wheat was hardly to be bought in the towns. Within even the existing generation, an old man of eighty-five, was fond of telling how, when a boy, he wanted to spend his penny on wheaten bread, and he searched through Carlisle from morning to evening before he could find a penny roll. The cultivator among the hills divided his field into plots, where he grew barley, oats, flax, and other produce, to meet the needs of his household. His pigs, fed partly on acorns or beech mast, yielded good bacon and hams; and his sheep furnished wool for clothing. Of course, he kept cows. The women spun and wove the wool and flax, and the lads made the wooden utensils, baskets, fishing-tackle, &c. Whatever else was needed, was obtained from the pedlars, who came their rounds two or three times a year; dropping in among the little farms from over the hills. The first great change was from the opening of carriage-roads. There was an inducement then to carry grain and stock to markets and fairs. More grain was sown than the household needed, and offered for sale. In a little while, the mountain farmers were sure to fail in competition in the markets, with dwellers in agricultural districts. The mountaineers had no agricultural science, and little skill; and the decline of the fortunes of the statesmen (estatesmen) as they are locally called, has been regular and mournful to witness. They haunt the fairs and markets, losing in proportion to the advance of improvement elsewhere. On their first losses, they began to mortgage their lands. After bearing the burden of these mortgages till they could bear it no longer, their children have sold the lands: and among the shop-boys, domestic servants, and labourers of the towns, we find the old names of the former yeomanry of the district, who have parted with their lands to strangers. Much misery must always intervene during this process of transition. The farmer was tempted to lose the remembrance of his losses in drink when he attended the fairs and markets. The domestic manufactures he carried with him—the linen and woollen webs, woven by his wife and daughters—would not sell, except at a loss, in the presence of the Yorkshire and Lancashire woollens and cottons, made by machinery. He became unable to keep his children at home; and they went off to the manufacturing towns, leaving home yet more cheerless—with fewer busy hands and cheerful faces—less social spirit in the dales—greater certainty of continued loss, and more temptation to drink. Such is the process still going on. Having reached this pass, it is clearly best that it should go on till the primitive population, having lost its safety of isolation and independence, and kept its ignorance and grossness, shall have given place to a new set of inhabitants, better skilled in agriculture, and in every way more up to the times. It is mournful enough to a resident to meet everywhere the remnants of the old families, in a reduced and discouraged condition; but if they can no longer fill the valleys with grain, and cover the hillsides with flocks, it is right that those who can should enter upon their lands, and that knowledge, industry and temperance, should find their fair field and due reward.

When we leave the Highest House, after our luncheon, and turn through the gate for Troutbeck, we begin to see how the country-side makes a festival of such a breaking up as we have already told the story of. There is the family from the High Stock farm, climbing the hill to drop down into Troutbeck, by the shortest way. It is the first time this season, that they have ventured over the bog. And look at the fiddler, coming down from the opposite ridge, in hope of being wanted for a dance in the evening! And now, when looking down into the deep, long trough of the Troutbeck valley, we see how much it has lost of its wonted quiet. Its primitive dwellings have poured out their inhabitants, to make yonder crowd, far below, which marks the place of the sale. As we draw near, my heart fails me. I see the old man, with his downcast face, and the old wife, with her apron often at her eyes. Their children should have removed them yesterday. But they would not go, I am told, and they boast of their children's doings in the great towns, as they fill the jugs of beer on yonder table, and set on another bottle of whiskey. How the auctioneer walks to and fro, to collect the bids, restless as a beast in a cage, rather than majestic as a southern auctioneer in a pulpit. There—there goes the old carved chair—the straight, highbacked, black chair, so curiously carved, with its date, 1607, half disclosed among the old vine pattern! It is bought in at once, evidently for some moneyed person—probably some London gentleman, or West End cabinet-maker; for these old carved chairs are the fashion in London now, and agents go through the dales to buy them up. Ah! now the old cabinet is going; and this, at last, is too much for the humbled owner.[21] Why, even I cannot bear it. J. has found a party of friends to join. I shall deliver over the purse and the whole business—pig-buying and all—to her, and go home.

And here I am again in quiet, half way up the heights, with that finest of all the views of Windermere opening before me, which you Americans say, is so like their North River, near West Point. It is not so beautiful as that, but it is exquisite in its way. For three miles to come it will be before me at every turn, till I have descended to its brink, and left it behind me, a mile from my own home.

MAY

WHAT A MORNING it is! My early walk shall be to Stockghyll Force, even though my breakfast should be delayed by it for a quarter of an hour. Near as that waterfall is, it is not every day, nor every week, that one can take one's walk there in the dewy hours. If the ground is all wet elsewhere, one finds pools in that path; and in frosty weather, the first ascent is rather too perilous. I found that in the winter, when I scrambled a few yards over a convex mass of ice, thinly covered with snow, which completely enveloped the road. I then fell, and could by no means get up again. Every attempt to move, ended in my sliding further to the edge of the little precipice; and I was not disposed for a plunge into the tumbling stream below. I dare not say how long it was before I could obtain a hold for either hand or foot. But now, while there is dust on the roads, and the trees are in their tenderest green, is the very time for a dry foot-walk to the fall. Ha! what was that flitting before the window as I dress? Is it possible that the swallows are here already? I fancied I saw one in the meadows, two days since. Yes,—there is another,—and a third,—skimming over the field, and flitting up to their nests under the eaves, now and then. They left eight nests last year; and now, soon we shall be seeing the little pert heads peeping out of the hole at the side of the nest, as we come up to the porch. The very sight of their swoop gives one the strongest sensation of summer!

As I go forth and return, the least agreeable object is the bare and torn slope and base of the knoll, where the grass was cut up and ground to pieces by the builders' carts. I have tried in vain to obtain sods to lay down. The gardeners say there is no such thing to be had for love or money. I was inexperienced enough in the ways of the district to think of taking a cart to the mountain side, and cutting what sods I wanted,—though the grass there is mossy and coarse, and not of a good sort to introduce into my field. But Mr. Wordsworth stopped the enterprise, by telling me that the mountain grass is the indefeasible property of the statesmen, and can be touched by no one else. Moreover, he said that it takes a hundred years to restore, fully, the pared part of the pasture. Thus, the only resource left to me, was to tread in hay-seed. J. obtained an apronful from the hayloft at the inn; but it will take very long for the grass to grow at all; and then it will be mixed and coarse. Well, it is good for us to have some one point which we cannot carry; and I must make up my mind to this great blemish.

It is rather a strange way to the waterfall,—this only way, through the stable-yard of the Salutation. It is crowded with ostlers, rubbing down their horses;—horses as yet sleek, and in good condition; but destined to be worn to skin and bone with fatigue, by the end of the tourist season. I pass under the rookery,—now more noisy than the whole town beside ever is. As I leave the cawing behind, the gush of the water becomes fuller, and the twitter of a myriad of nestlings more loud and gay. Next comes the creaking of the large water-wheel of the bobbin-mill, on the other side of the stream. It is a pretty picture,—the slow turning of the red-brown wheel in the deep shadow of that bank, while the sun peeps up high enough to fling flecks of light through the trees upon my path; but I am glad to leave it for the closer retirement of the wood beyond. How fine are the reaches of the brown and foaming steam;—brown in the shadow, but a clear green where the mounting sun touches it in some open angle. The feathered banks now rise very high; and soon after the wheel is out of hearing, the waterfall announces itself by its continuous dash. Up, up, leads the path to it, ending precipitously under a perpendicular rock, where there is room for only one pair of feet to stand; and the only guard is the projecting ash which overhangs the depth below. And there, before me, with nothing to obstruct the view, is the Force; which I think one of the most beautiful of the district; and not the less beautiful for being only a mile from home, and open to everybody. It is divided by a projecting rock from top to bottom; seventy feet, I am told, and the symmetry of the two portions is the distinctive beauty of the fall. Through all their four stages, from ledge to ledge, the two portions precisely correspond; and they are equally inclosed among high, wooded banks; so that the whole is a finished picture, though untouched by art. The sun has just reached it, as I hoped it would; and that faint prismatic touch on the crown of the fall is what I chiefly came to see. I know now that the early May morning is as good as a September sunset for seeing Stockghyll Force; ("the fall in the ravine of the Stock brook.")

While I have been up here, the town has been awaking and coming abroad; and as I return, I meet an angler here and there,—one pushing his way through the underwood below, in search of a good station above a pool of the stream;—another already fixed under the shadow of a tree whose roots are swept by the waters;—and one or two more, with baskets at their backs, and long rods lowered under the branches, hastening to the higher fords and falls, up in the fells. In the road near home, one artisan or labourer after another touches his hat, or gives me the greeting of the morning. But what has happened at home? J. and M. are watching for me on the terrace; and here they are flying down the drive, evidently with some news;—and not bad news.

This was a curious incident that my maids ran to tell me; an incident which has remained mysterious from that day to this. They had found lying on the slope, on the north side of the house, a pile of sods, which had evidently been put over the wall in the night. They were of the finest grass, neatly rolled and piled. Our first idea was, that a neighbouring gardener had mistaken my inquiry for an order, and had involved me in an expensive purchase; but the gardener knew nothing about it, and could not imagine where such sods were to be had. Then we turned our thoughts to Mr. S., in the next field, with whom some civilities had passed about a fence; but, in the course of the morning, Mr. S. called to us over the fence, to ask where we got our sods, as he had inquired for such in vain. Fine as they were, they did not cover much ground; and in two or three nights more another load was deposited in the same place. We could not undertake to watch the northern slope by night; but we did, on the third occasion, watch the gate and entrance,—I to a late hour, and my maids from an extremely early one, as they had to let in the varnishers before four o'clock; and again, in the same place, lay another load. After an interval of a week, a large quantity,—probably a wagon-load,—was found, and finally, a fifth portion, which sufficed to cover every bare spot, and left some grass over. Under this last pile lay a letter,—studiously vulgar in its external appearance, and with bad spelling within; but, from the straightness of the lines, and the evidences of a good hand which peeped through the disguise, obviously written by some educated person. It pretended to be from two poor poachers, who affected gratitude to me for having written against the game laws, and begged to show it by thus secretly presenting me with what I most wanted for my garden, as I could not "coax" my own grass to grow. I have never been able to learn what kind neighbour devised this benevolent joke. Every acquaintance that I had in the valley gave me a serious assurance that he or she knew nothing about it; and, as I said, the incident remains a mystery to this day.

The sales were not all over yet. A remarkable one took place towards the end of this month of May. The people might be seen flocking towards a house which I now discovered for the first time, though it stood near the road, past the old Roman camp, along which I had walked almost every day for months. The dwelling had been so concealed in a thicket of evergreens, that it was only by looking down upon its gray roof from the heights, that its existence could be recognized by strangers. Here had lived and died an old clergyman, who took life so much as a matter of course as to have made none of the ordinary preparations for dying. He died at the age of eighty-six, without a will; and great were the embarrassments in consequence, about the distribution of his property, and the letting of the house,—as it could not be clearly ascertained who was entitled to receive the rent. There was no appearance of his having felt any serious call to his pastoral vocation; or, indeed, to any other. He took things easily through life;—most things, if not all. The discontent of his parishioners made him angry; and he was surly under their occasional hints to him to resign; but, on the whole, his life seems to have slipped away in a sort of holiday mood, which the strictest can hardly quarrel with wholly. Hartley Coleridge, and other men of some note, were, from time to time, pupils of his; and it was no uncommon thing for them to find, on coming to school, a closed door, chalked with an inscription in the master's hand; sometimes "Gone a fishing;" sometimes "Gone a hunting;" and now and then with an invitation to the lads to follow him to such or such a place. As he grew older and more remiss, he met with more mortifications; and at last, he received a wound to his feelings from the gentle and kindly postmistress herself; who certainly never in her life intended to hurt anybody. He went into her shop, and told her, testily, that the people were at him about resigning; and that it was no use of the people plaguing him about resigning; he did not mean to resign;—he was not thinking of resigning, and he would not. "Well, now, sir," said the kind woman, "I'se right glad to hear that." The old man brightened up; somebody was on his side. She went on, "People say we could not be wus off for clergy than we are, taking in the neighbourhood; but I'se right glad to hear you won't resign; for, what with Sir Richard and his drink, and Mr. ——, with his doings, we should be even wus off than we are now." When the compliment came to this, the old pastor could hear no more; he bounced out of the shop. He had not much more to bear, nor any long time now in which to feel his loneliness. During this month of May, his gate stood wide to let his coffin pass. A few of the evergreens were cut down, under universal assent, to let in air and light upon the dwelling. The secluded chambers were now open to everybody; and those who attended the sale, when they looked abroad through the gaps in the thicket, and saw the gleaming lake, and the velvet meadows, and the wooded steeps of Loughrigg, could not but wonder that, in such a scene, any man could so enclose his dwelling as that he could see nothing. Since that month, times have changed with that dwelling. An open-faced, and open-hearted mother lives there now, with her beautiful daughters; and, not only for its free hospitality, but for its care of the sick, and the orphans, and the ignorant, it is more like the pastoral dwelling now than it ever was before.

It must have been an association of contrast rather than resemblance, which made me earnestly desire, after this, to visit the home of Robert Walker, so widely known through Wordsworth's memoir of him,[22] and explore the valley where he dwelt. The image of Robert Walker is familiar to all readers of Wordsworth. They see him marrying on £5 a-year and a cottage, and then fulfilling the duties and charities of his curacy at Seathwaite, for sixty-six years. They see him in his coarse, blue frock, with its black horn buttons, his wooden shoes plated with iron, and his spinning-wheel, which he plied in the church, while he taught the children of his parish; or trudging through the snow, with his package of yarn upon his back, going to the nearest market-town to sell it, and buy necessaries for his flock of children. They see him in his pulpit, fervently addressing his parishioners, on Sundays and weekdays, and helping the poorer and more distant of his flock to their Sunday dinner of broth, sometimes made from the supply of meat for the whole coming week. They see him helping his flock in shearing their sheep and making their hay; and, from time to time, refusing to leave them for a more lucrative cure; and proving that, when his salary was raised to £17 a-year, he needed nothing more, because, through his industry and economy, he could lay by something for the placing out of his sons in the world. This was he, who, throughout the neighbouring valleys, was called "The Wonderful;" and the wonder of whose deeds has not yet abated.

I wished to see for myself the scene of this man's life and labours, after the contrasting scene of the hunting and fishing pastor's life had closed in my immediate neighbourhood. My friend, Miss D., felt the same desire; and we went together. We took a car to Coniston, nine miles, in order that we might reach Seathwaite in the best manner,—by dropping down upon it from Walna Scar, which can be crossed only on foot. It was a glorious noon when we dismissed the car, and began to ascend the moorland. We left behind us the bright and prosperous environs of Coniston, and a wide extent of hilly country, subsiding into the low blue ridges of Lancashire; and when we now and then turned, we saw below us a reach or two of the Lake of Coniston,—gray, and reflecting the dark promontories in a perfect mirror. On our right towered the Old Man,—the mountain in whose interior men are busy digging out copper, while the only traces of human existence visible to us, were the tracks along and up its slopes,—paths leading to the mine,—and a solitary house, looking very desolate among its bare fields and fences. Soon, however, when we had crossed one or two of the grassy undulations of the moor, we came upon a party of peat-cutters, with their crate, and their white horse, which looked absolutely glittering in the sunlight, amidst the browness of the ground. The next trace of man which we met, was in a little stone bridge spanning the rushing brown stream, the outlet of the tarn called Goat's Water, which has always water enough to make foam among the stones in its channel, and in winter is a torrent. Before us is a pretty steep ascent, with a well-marked track, and, as soon as we began to pant, and to complain of the heat, a breath of cool air came to us over the ridge, warning us to turn and bid farewell to the scene behind us before a new one was disclosed.

What a disclosure it was when we had gone a few steps further! There were the highest summits of the district,

Scawfell and Bowfell, with craggy steeps interposed between them and the eye. There was the sea, over the ridge, and with a high horizon-line, blue in the light of noon; and faint and far might be discerned the outline of the Isle of Man. All around us were fells, sloping down to the Duddon, and completely inclosing the little circular vale of Seathwaite, into which we were now to descend. These fells were, some of them, and especially the one on which we stood, green and smooth; others were brown with heather, or half-covered with wood, or broken up with gray rocks. Below us we saw,—not the Duddon, for it is hidden in a deep, rocky channel,—but the vale so well known through Wordsworth's description of it, in his notes to his Duddon sonnets.[23] Down we went into it, first by the green track across the fell, and then by a steep, stony road, which landed us at last among the farmsteads of the vale, and the gray stone cottages, each overshadowed by its massive sycamores or light birch, and surrounded by its field-plots.

Of course, our first inquiry was for the church and Robert Walker's tomb; and we were told to follow the road above the brook till we came to Newfield. A sweeter walk than this,—the two miles from the ridge of Walna Scar to Seathwaite Church,—can scarcely be found; nor a more complete contrast than between the wildness of the moor, and the rich, broken ground of the vale, with its wooded and rocky knolls, its full stream, prosperous homesteads, and fertile fields. When we reached the church, we found it little loftier or larger than the houses near. But for the bell, we should hardly have noticed it for a church on approaching; but when we had reached it, there were the porch, and the little graveyard, with its few tombs, and a spreading yew, encircled by the seat of stones and turf, where the early comers sit and rest till the bell calls them in. Here we now sat and rested, looking, as it were, into the minds of those who, in the last century, occupied the same spot, and looked upon the same scene, although listening for a voice long since hushed. It was in 1735, or 1736, that the wonderful pastor entered upon this cure; and he left the world just as I was entering it,—in 1802;—a link sufficient to make me feel the interest of a contemporary mingled with that of a retrospect into a past century. His tomb was before us as we sat; and the grave of his wife, which, as a descendant tells us, "he could never pass without tears." The loss of his aged partner was the blow which shattered him at the last. "He never preached with steadiness after his wife's death. His voice faltered. He always looked at the seat she had used. He became, when alone, sad and melancholy, though still, among his friends, kind and good-humored." Close by their tomb stands a little dial, on a whitened post, to tell the time to the neighbours who have no clocks; but it looks very like a monument to the diligent pair who worked while it was day, and have been removed, like all else, by time.

Just outside the churchyard wall is a white cottage, so humble, that we doubted whether it could be the parsonage; yet the climbing roses, and glittering evergreens, and dear lattices, and pure, uncracked walls, looked as if it might be. We walked slowly past the porch, and saw a kind-looking, elderly woman, who told us that it was indeed Robert Walker's dwelling, and invited us in to see the scene of those marvelous charities of sixty-six years. Here it was that the Sunday messes of broth were served. Hither it was that, in winter, he sent the benumbed children in companies from the school in the church, to warm themselves at the single household fire, while he sat by the altar during all the school hours, keeping warmth in him by the exercise of the spinning-wheel. Looking abroad, we saw that there is a schoolhouse now; and we admired the healthy looks of the children about the doors. While examining the gravestone of the pastor, we were accosted by an elderly man, who told us that he was the grandson of Robert Walker's sister. This, the present pastor, mourns over the change of times, and is offended at it. Mr. Walker's pride was in allowing no dissenter to meddle with his people, and in being able to say that "he had not one dissenter of any denomination whatever in the whole parish." Now, the Wesleyans have opened a chapel at Ulpha, which draws away some of the flock; and others have ceased to come to church since the attempts to get copper from the neighbouring hills,—the miners enticing the people to diversion on Sundays. The old stocks are gone, the present curate observes; and the new families are different. There used to be from seventy to ninety worshippers in the mornings, and from fifty to seventy in the evenings; and now there are seldom more than seventy. Thus do "possessions vanish, and opinions change,"[24] even in this stronghold of the parish priest! It is a blessing to us that he has bequeathed an example which teaches us the insignificance of possessions, and unites, with regard to itself, all opinions.

JUNE

JUNE 21ST : the longest day. Of all days of the year, that the longest should be that on which I must forego my early walk! But there is so much before me to-day, that I must husband my strength. There is the walk to Bowness; and rowing and fishing for the rest of the day. As I throw up the sash at six o'clock, and see how cool the shadows lie under the eastern heights, and how dewy the garden is, it seems a pity that I cannot start off at once, and accomplish the walk before the sun grows too tyrannical. But the mail will not pass from three hours yet; and I must not go without my letters. It does not follow that I must remain within doors. I will gather a glorious bouquet for F. M.[25]

The grass is dewy. What a pity not to mow the two pieces that want it so much,—the plot at the end of the terrace, and that in the quarry! J. brings me the scythe and whetstone, and says she thinks there are green peas enough for a small dish, if I like to carry some to Miss M. So, off she goes to gather them, and such gooseberries as she can find, while I mow my grass. The harebells wave so prettily on the little bank under the oaks, that it grieves me to cut them down; but that slope must be kept sunny and warm; and the grass is too tall. Down they all come! The crisp fall of the grass under the scythe in the dewy morning, is as sweet a sensation as the sweeping sound. There is a heap of fresh food for my tenant's cow; and the quarry will presently yield another. What a sweet place this quarry is,—the honeysuckle climbing up by the jutting roots of the oak, over the face of the rock, and ferns and rock-weeds sprouting out of every crevice, and heaths tufting the ledges! And what wealth of roses in the parterre in the middle! Few are full blown yet; but nothing is prettier than a bouquet of buds. Ah! J. has left me little to do by the time the mowing is finished. She says there is such a basketful that, if I please, she must go with me to carry some of my load. Well; she may go half-way. She may go as far as Calgarth. I must call on the L.'s, and we shall have a rest there. And now to breakfast!

Not yet! As I am wiping the scythe at the tool-house door, I see a great commotion in my neighbour W.'s garden; and M. comes to tell me that his bees are swarming with the swarm that we are to have. Our bee-house has long been ready, and the smell of paint quite gone; and now J. is rubbing our new hive with sweet herbs and honey. There it goes, with its clean white cloth; and before I have done breakfast, it is properly placed on its stand in the bee-house, and all alive with inhabitants. I hope they will have a happy life. We have done what we can for them in surrounding them with flowers, and beds of sweet herbs; but there is a better resource for them in the mountain heather. In six weeks' time, Loughrigg will be growing crimson and purple with heather blossom; and it is certain that the bees do stretch their flight that far, and some say, even to the higher slopes of Wansfell,—which is a long flight for them. I wonder bees are not universally kept in such a district. As I have to pay £1 for this swarm, they must be less common than they need be. My hive must swarm well next year, that I may give my maids a stock of bees. It will be a pretty source of interest and of profit to them.

"The mail is in sight ma'am." Then we may go in five minutes. We must give the H.'s that much time to sort the letters. It is still early enough for pleasure in our walk, we find when we reach the road, and see that the dust is still damped down by the dew. My letters and newspapers are ready for me; and there is no proof-sheet, or other business which need spoil the completeness of my holiday. Here is a whole day to be passed without touching pen, book, or thimble! It now occurs to J. and me that the walk will not be half a mile further, and that it will be much pleasanter, if we leave the highroad, and go up Wansfell, to follow the track through its wood to the lane above Low-wood. It is a toilsome ascent at first,—stony and hot and close; but by the time that we come out upon the brook, a sweet air blows upon us from the lake. We sit down on the low wall above the clear pool, and enjoy the dash of the little fall, and remind each other that for a long way now, our path lies under the trees. Between the trees, as we proceed, noble views open upon us of the two valleys at the head of the lake,—now reeking in the heat of the sun, and the air flickers between our eyes and the pale Langdale Pikes, now standing out clear and sultry, under a sky from which every remnant of mist seems melted away.

At the end of our shaded path there is a gate, and we come out upon the bare heath; but the breeze is more than a match for the sun, and we grow cooler as we advance. Who would have thought of finding a spring and cistern, hung with water-weeds and half hidden by ferns, in such a place as this? It seems more appropriate to some retired lane, than to a bare mountain slope. Now we begin to descend,—into the field, through the paddock, past the old-fashioned farm-house, down and down into Troutbeck lane, and down again into the highroad.

After another mile, we are at Calgarth gate. How could Bishop Watson contrive to be otherwise than happy here? He built the house, he planted the woods, and he blessed the whole neighbourhood by planting the hills around, so that the Calgarth woods are the glory of the district. Is it possible that, in the midst of such privileges, a man and a clergyman should be disturbed and querulous, because he was Bishop of Llandaff, and not Bishop of some higher and richer see? Far happier is the present tenant of the mansion, who desires nothing more than to spend his life in rowing about the lake. It is a pity that he is to succeed to a baronetcy. His station, and its requirements, will be purely embarrassing and irksome to him. As long as he can carry out his pet theory, that twelve o'clock is the middle of the day, and have his breakfast, with his children round him, at four in the morning, and his dinner at ten, and his supper at five in the afternoon, and be in bed at eight; and hammer away at his boats, and spend all his fair weather on the water, and not be required to wear stock or cravat except at church, he is happy; and, in as far as his inheritance of a baronetcy interferes with all this, it will be a misfortune to him. Here he comes, under the trees, bareheaded, his coat hanging on his arm, his shirt open to the waist, and the sleeves rolled up to the shoulders; his plush pantaloons half-covered with square patches, so clumsy that no tailor could have put them on. It must be a specimen of his own mending. What a good face it is, amidst all this oddity! And what a charming voice and address and tone of conversation! How strangely come such a voice and address from one with such a weather-beaten face, and such a mop of grizzled hair! He told me once that one of the afflictions of his boating-life is, that sounds comes so far and so clear as they do over calm water. He hears conversation in boats distant from him half the width of the lake, and sometimes such conversation is about himself;—about who he is, and where he came from, and what a queer fellow he is. He often has to row himself out of earshot. And F. M. makes the same complaint,—hears herself pointed out as the Lady of the Lake,—a foreign lady, who fishes and shoots, and the like. What could possess the Bishop to build his house down in the hollow, and with its back to the lake? How its pink plastered walls are discoloured by damp; and how much one hears of rheumatism from the inmates! And here, where one would think it hardly possible to get out of the way of a noble view, the front windows command little more than a sloping field!

Here J. may rest herself before returning home; and, as the lady of the house is absent, I ask leave to show J. the portrait of Bishop Watson, and his celebrated library. She never saw so many books in one collection before and will never again think so much of our library at home. Here come the children! They desire me to go to Bowness by the short cut through their field and the woods, and say they will go with me and carry my basket and bring me out at Hayrigg, within a mile of Bowness. Away we go, therefore, walking between hedges of tall grass, nearly ready for the mowers, and then winding through the woods where the wood-sorrel clusters about the roots of the old oaks, and blue-bells dye all the shadows, while a few daffodils remain in the sunny places. How cool is the pale-green light under the young beeches; and how the white butterflies play about their smooth stems, and follow one another up among the branches! Is this the path,—almost in the water? Yes; but it is firm white shingle, and will not wet our feet. This must be charming after sunset; but the sun beats hot from the lake at present, and we are glad to turn up the ravine behind the boat-house. A steep ascent, beside the tumbling brook, brings us out upon the road.

This *is*, after all, the finest view in our whole neighbourhood,—from the lofty mountain-peaks in the north, down over the valleys, down over the spreading Calgarth woods, and along the whole lake, from end to end, with all its bays and promontories, and alluvial bottoms, and steep skirting sides, and wooded islands, and seats of the gentry, and farmsteads of the statesmen,—with the white sails of pleasure-boats gliding hither and thither, and the plodding steamer seen far off beyond the Ferry House. Is it most beautiful now,—all verdure and gleams and deep shadows,—or as I have seen it in January, when, at sunset, there was a bar of red-hot snow on the ridge of Wansfell, and the islands lay purple in the crimson lake, the Calgarth woods standing so still as that not a single twig let fall its burden of snow? Each season decides in favour of itself.

And now, to Bowness! After passing the hotel and shops, I must take my way through the churchyard, for the sake of the old yews and firs, all garlanded with ivy. I know of no churchyard more distinguished by its growth of funereal trees, and their black shade is eminently welcome on a hot day like this. The square tower and long nave of the church seem to tell of its age. So this is one of the good works of the supposed murderer, King Richard III.! In 1485 he granted a warrant for five marks (£3 6*s*. 8*s*.) towards building this church, and its style is Norman accordingly. Now, a few yards more from the gate under the yews, past the great ash, which is the advertising station of Bowness (how its trunk is stuck over with handbills!), and I am at my friend's door. There is Carlo's bark! He and his mistress are on the watch for me.

There is claret and water on the table. While I am resting and refreshing, we lay our scheme for the day. I meant to call at the parsonage, where one may always hear something of Mrs. Hemans[26] (who was guide and friend to the curate in his youth), and where I love to see the most old-fashioned parsonage I know of; and I wished to pay my respects to the aged daughters of Bishop Watson, who are curious and interesting specimens of the literary ladies of the last century, of whom we have very few left: but F. M. tells me I shall not go to-day. It is too hot, and both houses are too far off; I must come another day for these purposes. One visit, however, she does not oppose my making, but flushes with pleasure at the proposal;—to her landlord's shed, to see how her new boat gets on. It is just at hand, and a cool place. So we go, after desiring to have dinner at two o'clock. Carlo runs before us, to see the curious boat in which he will have to sit so still, that he may not turn his mistress and himself over into the water. It is a curiosity—this new boat,—of mahogany, thirty-three feet long, and only twenty-six inches wide in the middle. It will be a pretty sight—the shooting of this arrow-like skiff over the smooth lake,—with the one graceful rower and her demure friend Carlo seated in front of her. She vows I shall never set foot in it. She is not a whit afraid for herself; but she will admit no one but Carlo into so nicely balanced an affair. What grace there is in her freedom of action! Who would have thought of boat-building being a graceful operation? Yet now, when she cannot hold her hand off the work, how beautifully she uses the hammer, and rapidly makes a row of copper-headed nails shine along the side!

While waiting for dinner, and having taken note of any new fishing-rod, boat-model, or fowling-piece hung against the wall, or any new miniature of my friend's painting, or work-box of her construction, I get her to give me the literal English of some passages of Humboldt's KOSMOS,[27] which seem to me wrongly rendered in all our published translations. She confirms me, and I am truly glad; for it is painful to suppose Humboldt inconsistent with himself, or timidly complying with popular prejudice. Meantime, Carlo waits upon us,—opens or shuts the door, rings the bell, and even sings when desired, or when bribed by a mouthful of our dinner. Was ever anything more ridiculous than a handsome dog on his hind legs, looking up to the ceiling, and modulating his whine and howl into a doleful song? Dinner done, and the young peas much praised, down we go to the boat, not to return till, perhaps, midnight; and, therefore, carrying with us biscuits, a bottle of claret, and glasses. F. M. takes the oars first, as I shall have my turn by-and-by. We wander for an hour down and across the lake, visiting particular points of view,—passing Storr's Hall, putting in near the Ferry, and then betaking ourselves to the shades of Curwen's Island, till the sun shall have sunk lower. And what could we do better than moor our boat in this little cool cove, where the birch and ash hang over almost into the water? In such a place as this it was that Wordsworth, being hoaxed by a wag, accosted my friend in a way which somewhat astonished her. Having been assured that she was a gipsy, he naturally felt some curiosity about her; and, one hot day, when she was lying at the bottom of her boat reading, in one of these coves, he came up, and asked questions about her origin and supposed wanderings. Her replies did not remove his fixed impression; and it was with extreme surprise that he soon after met and recognised her in an evening party.

The hours slip away as we lie couched among the ferns, reading our newspapers, or amusing each other by narratives of our wide travels. If F. M. tells me of the Pyrenees or the Danube, I tell her of the Mississippi, or Pharpar and Abana, the rivers of Damascus, or of adventures in Nubia. And then we walk round the island, which is a mile in circuit, or play duck and drake from the white pebbly beaches, on the still waters. At length, we agree that the shadows are deep enough under the wooded steep to the west; and, as in another hour it will be moonlight, we may now set about our fishing.

Carlo looks on demurely while F. M. arranges her lines, and I take charge of the oars. We first go under the western shore, and float among the islands, where we have the waters pretty much to ourselves. For two hours we hardly speak. I row gently, dipping as softly as I may; and F. M. starts with delight at every pull at her trolling lines. It is not with her as with a man of eminent name who was one of our party on such a night as this. After long expectation, he cried "Halloo!" and drew in his line with an anxious smile, finding on his hook only my glove, which he had somehow conveyed overboard with his line. Instead of this, F. M. draws in trout upon trout, till the silver store gleams in her basket in the rays of the moon. How she loves to see pencils of white light breaking along these shadowy straits between the islands! Her spirits rise as the air becomes balmier, and the lake more still; so that we seem to have it to ourselves! And when we emerge into the full moonlight, and put out into the wide expanse, her joy breaks into music. Leaning back, with her hands behind her head, and looking up into the sky, she pours forth German songs, one upon another—never for a moment, however, forgetting her lines, but starting up at every pull, and being still capable of some regret when she finds her prey to be a pike and not a trout. At length, it is long past eleven, and we must go home. Her kindhearted landlady has a little clear fire in the kitchen, where she broils us a supper of trout in a trice. And then the moonlight is so bright in my chamber that I decline a candle.

There would be no excuse for idleness for me, or any one living in a region where my occasional holidays can be such as I have enjoyed this day.

JULY

THIS IS THE DAY that my young nephew and niece (at present my guests), and I had fixed for setting forth on an expedition to Calder Abbey and the extreme northwest lakes of the district, returning by Derwent Water, and under Helvellyn. But, when we made our plan, we forgot that this was Rushbearing day.[28] The young people will probably never see a rushbearing anywhere else; for there are few places, and those extremely retired, where the custom subsists; and, moreover, the Wordsworths ask us to go to tea at Rydal Mount, after the spectacle; and my

Fig. 6. The Rushbearing at Ambleside, circa 1835 (from a sketch by J. Redaway)

guests would rather, if need were, lose the old Abbey, which will yet abide for their whole lives and many more, than the old poet whose days cannot now be long in the land. So we have put off our trip for one day, and can still spare three for it.

In ancient times, as old chronicles tell us, the parishioners everywhere brought rushes to strew the churches with before the Feast of Dedication. The stranger now looks in vain for the rushes: but the gay garlands are still carried, and placed in the church: and then, in this village, the children are entertained by Mr. H., whose gate is opposite mine. We cross the road, and enter the grounds early, that we may see the last of the preparations made. How admirably adapted the field is for such a spectacle,—two green hillsides sloping down to the level where the tables are placed! Cousins[29] and his men are still fixing the trestles, and laying the boards which make the tables. We are not the first of the spectators to arrive: a crippled gentleman and some aged ladies are seated on chairs under the trees: and lo! over the wall beyond the lawn, and glancing among the trees, are the gay garlands, showing us that we are scarcely too soon, after all. Now the gates are thrown wide, and here they come,—the head of the procession entering, winding a little way through the shrubbery, and then turning in upon the grass, and filing off on either side the long row of tables. S. observes how like a Catholic procession it is,—how easily one might fancy one's self looking at a Neapolitan church festival. To my eye, it looks like a Catholic procession in England; and that is all. I have been told that it was the late curate who introduced these curious symbols,—the triangle with the dove, the Virgin and child, and several more which ill befit a Protestant procession. He was at that time a Puseyite,[30] and is now a Catholic priest: yet his handiwork among the Rushbearers remains. A lady, who has a terrible fear of heresy, asks me what I think of the show. I tell her that it seems to me curiously popish for our country and time, and inquire if it is true that the symbols I point out to her are of recent introduction. They are. I could, as I tell her, look on them with veneration, if they were a mere perpetuation of an ancient observance; but that I dread the effect of introducing a more ritual piety among children growing up in a society where the gross vices of rural life are very prevalent. Her replies are strange. First, she speaks of these symbols being good, because they are holy and venerable; and in the same breath she says it does not matter what the symbols are, as the children are too ignorant and dull to know or care anything about them. All the while, no one knows better than she, that the brothers and sisters of some who are carrying the garlands and hanging about the outside of the gates, listening to the music, and longing for the tea and the buns and the fun, but excluded because their parents have sent them to the school conducted by the Independents, and connected with their chapel. The parents declare themselves perplexed what to do, between the warm and inviting chapel and school on the right of the road, and the shadow of the church, and the great proprietors on the left: so, some of them send half their children to the church-school, and half to the other; and, if there happens to be an odd number of children, it is said by jesters that they send the middle one for six months to one school, and the other six to the other. The amazement of my young guests at such a state of things is great; but they were born and brought up amidst the enlightenment of a populous midland town, and could have no idea of the ignorance about the liberty of conscience which exists in such nooks of the island as this, where dissent is called schism, and schism is regarded as an unpardonable crime. Yet, what a lesson might we not draw from the fact of the diversities of belief within our valley! Let us see. We have High Church, Low Church, and Middle Church families; Catholics, both in and out of communion; Independents, Unitarians, Quakers, Swedenborgians, Wesleyans, Plymouth Brethren, and some who belong to no Christian sect at all. This should surely be a lesson to us all not to lord it over the humble, or connect advantage or disadvantage with modes of belief. But this is one of the matters in which we are a century or two behind the southern parts of our island. While we are watching the children enjoying their feast of buns and tea, a gentleman,—a stranger from the South,—obtains an introduction to me. His kindly zeal on my behalf makes me laugh, when I discover what his object is. He thinks there is nothing like plainness in asking when you mean to know a thing: so he inquires if it is true, as he has been told, that I make a point of making all my marketings on a Sunday. I tell him that there is not even an oven open on a Sunday in Ambleside, much less a shop; so that I could not make purchases, if I wished it; and that, in brief, I never in my life attempted to buy anything on a Sunday. "I thought so,—I knew it would end so," said he, in vast indignation at some neighbouring critics, who had made a small mistake. I told him, further, that I am not accountable to anybody for my own views and use of Sunday; but that I consider myself bound to afford my servants every facility for attending worship as much as they please, and that their freedom is provided for accordingly. It would have amused this gentleman, if I had told him of certain anonymous letters and copies of verses,—very coaxing and flattering,—entreating me to join the church,—not for my own sake, but that of the church; as if church-membership could be entered into for such a reason! Such are some of the curious incidents of an old-fashioned state of affairs like that which subsists in our quiet corner.

At Rydal Mount, we see again a few of the faces which we met in the field below. Ah! where are there pleasanter festivals than these summer tea-drinkings at Wordsworth's? The few assembled are those one likes to meet,—a few visiters or wayfarers, who are proud and happy to be there. Doors and windows stand open, and we go out and come in as we like. If we sit in a corner beside Wordsworth, and mention a mountain peak, an eagle, or any secluded dale, we may be blessed with an outpouring of his knowledge or feeling on subjects that he and we like best. How bland, how earnest, how kind, and even how lively are his discourse, and manner, in one of these outpourings. Old,—old beyond description as he looks,—how full of vigour and clearness are his conversation and his voice! His age may show itself in his silence,—in his uncertainty about rousing himself: but one sees no sign of it in his discourse. And then, his exquisite wife,—the beloved of us all! What a pleasure it is to have one's turn with her! She too can help us about the eagles and herons, and the secluded dales. She can tell us the date, forty years ago, of their last seeing a Rydal eagle; and she is behind none in the enjoyment of life at the Lakes: a life whose only fault is, as she thinks, that it makes us too fond of this world:—a thing which, it seems to me, may safely be left to nature; for there are, as far as I know, few instances of unwillingness to die, when the time really comes. It generally seems to be, then, the thing we most wish for.

I beckon S. and F. to follow me, and step out of the window to show them the garden and terraces. From the mossy and grassy platform before the house, the view is one which can hardly be surpassed, if seen, as now, when the sun is sinking in a summer evening. The rule in our district, that each one of us thinks his own situation the best, would certainly give place to a vote in favour of Wordsworth's, if it were not for the drawback of the long ascent to it; a serious matter to a resident much given to long walks, and apt to be very tired at the last mile. But, at this moment, that is nothing: and the scene before the eye is accepted as unrivalled,—the full survey of the Rotha Valley, with Windermere glittering at the end, surmounted by the Fromes's Fells; and, on the right, the peep into the Rydal Pass, where the exquisite Rydal Lake juts into view. We must see more of this last department of the landscape; so we leave the platform, and cross the green slopes and little dells of the garden, and wind between the espaliers and under the fruit trees, and come out upon the two terraces formed by the poet, and truly fitted for his meditative walks when he was composing. Here, the beds are quite covered with periwinkle, blue and white, whose blossoms he must often have seen waking up to the morning sun, and whose shining leaves must many a time have glittered to the moonbeams in his sight. At the end of the upper terrace, we pass through the summer-house, which is all lined with fir cones. Its further door opened: what a scene bursts upon us, from this perch on the breast of Nab's Scar! It is made up of the old elements,—lake, islands, wooded steep, craggy peaks, and dappled mountain-side; but in a new and most rich combination. There is no use talking about it: we can but gaze, and lovingly carry it away.

Before the west has faced, the moon is up to light us home, and we must be gone; for we have a toilsome day before us to-morrow. "Well, F., what is it?" I ask of my nephew as we rapidly descend the hill, and are under Lady Le Fleming's great beeches, where the rooks are settling themselves for the night. "You look very full of something." F. and his sister had found out the moment we entered the study this evening, that they had seen the poet before. They had seen an old man in a Scotch cap and green spectacles and plaid cloak, cutting ash sticks out of a copse by the roadside, for half-a-dozen cottage children who were about his heels; and as he walked on, whittling his poles, the little creatures were pulling his cloak and asking him questions, and he was talking to them all the way as he went. This, they now found, was Wordsworth. "O yes," said I, "I could have told you that before, if you had asked me. It is exactly Wordsworth's way." Whatever may have been his contemplative pacings on his terraces, such as this are his walks below.

Well, we have seen Calder Abbey, and a good deal more. Our trip was mainly on foot,—F. carrying one knapsack and I another, and S. a basket; but while our way lay along the highroads, we occasionally hired a car to save time and fatigue, reserving our strength for the mountain passes. Thus, looking forward to the Abbey as our evening treat, we jogged on at the base of the mountains, overlooking the tract between them and the sea, where feudal lords and monks settled themselves before they had obtained access to the heart of the district. On we went, past homesteads, each over-shadowed by its sycamore clump—that luxury, introduced within two hundred years, but now so common as to make us wonder what was in their stead before;—past wayside cisterns, where the waters from the hills are flowing in and swimming out again the whole year round; past fields which expand and brighten as Eskdale opens out towards the sea; past Santon Bridge, where the Irt runs to the bay under an ivy-mantled bridge, through meadows and scattered woods; past Gosforth, a stirring and rising little town, where new dwellings, built of the red stone of the neighbourhood, are rising on every hand; up the ascent whence there is a wide view of coast and sea; and there, as I had secretly hoped, was the Isle of Man visible, lying afar. It was only a softly pencilled outline this afternoon, and not as I have seen it when the wind was east, so clear as that the shadows were seen filling the hollows of its hills. Only a shady avenue of beech and ash now lay between us and Calder bridge.

It is but a mile further to the Abbey; and, as soon as we had had tea at the Bridge inn, we set forth. Having gone through the village, and past the bare, new red church, we entered upon a scene so quiet that a monkish feeling stole over us before we caught a sight of the ruins. Nothing is heard along this shady road but the stroke of the woodman's axe, or the shock of a falling tree, or the whirr of the bustling magpie, or the pipe of the thrush by day, or the hoot of the owl in the dusk. A squirrel hied across the road before us, and where the sunshine streamed into the tent of a spreading beech, a pair of white butterflies chased each other with a dancing flight round its trunk into the lucent green shadow; but no rude sights or sounds marred the repose, sacred in our minds to the old Cistercians who trod these ways, in peace, while all the world besides was at war.

At the end of a mile, we looked about for the ruins, which we knew to be on our right hand. We saw a tempting avenue, and though we would try it: so we ventured upon opening the gate, and advanced under the chestnuts, limes, and beeches, till we perceived somewhat under their sweeping branches, which showed us that we were right. The greensward at the outlet is so bright, as to have the effect of a gleam of mild sunshine, even on a shady day, or after sunset; and, springing clear from this sward, rise to the left the lofty pointed arches of the old ruin, in noble proportions, disclosing beyond a long perspective of grassy lawn and sombre woods. The Abbey is built of the red sandstone of the neighbourhood, now sobered down by time (it was founded in A.D. 1134), into the richest and softest tint that the eye could desire. But little is known of it beyond its date and the name of its founder, Ranulf, son of the first Ranulf de Meschines, a Norman noble. The church was small, as the scanty remains show; and the monastery, which looks like a continuation of the same building, could not have contained a numerous company. From the fragments of effigies preserved, it appears that some eminent persons were buried here; but who these knights and nobles were, there is no record available to tell, carefully as these memorials were wrought to secure the immortality of earth.

The eye is first fixed by the remains of the tower, from whose roofless summit dangles the tufted ivy, and whose base is embossed by the small lilac blossoms of the antirrhinum; but at last the great charm is found in the aisle of clustered pillars. Almost the whole aisle is standing, still connected by the cornice and wall which supported the roof. Luxuriant honeysuckle and ivy load these remains with verdure and luscious bloom, climbing up till they grow down again on the other side. We wandered in and out among these pillars, and into the sombre corner where the tall ash grows over towards the old tower-wall, making a sort of tent in the recess: we looked into every niche and damp cell in the conventual apartments, and went down to the red and tufted and broken river banks, and watched its stream leaping and rushing along in its deep channel, under the overarching trees, and said to each other, how well the old monks knew how to choose their dwelling-places, and what it must have been to the earnest and pious among these Cistercians to pace their river bank, hidden in the shade, and to attune their thoughts to the unceasing music of the Calder flowing by. We felt ourselves happy in seeing this place in the evening. It is a fine thing to see the shadows flung upon the sward, sharp in the broad sunshine, and to have the eye caught by the burnish of the ivy, and the sense soothed by the shade of the avenue: but the scene is sweeter, when there is just glow enough in the west to bring out vividly the projections and recesses of the ruins, and when the golden moon hangs over the eastern mass of tree-tops, ready to give her light as the glow dissolves, and when the rooks are winging their way to settle for the night in the nearest wood.

What a contrast was the next evening! We were lying, at about two hours after noon, on the shingle at the head of Ennerdale Water, somewhat uneasy as to whether we could obtain a guide over Blake Fell to Scale Hill, at the end of Crummock Water. The distance was only six miles; and on the map the track looked clear enough: but I was resolved to allow no risks to the young people under my charge, and I refused to proceed without a guide, though it was hard to say what we could do, if we failed to procure one. The waters grew grayer and rougher while we waited: but we thought no more of this, than what the wind would be refreshing during the ascent, and the heat was at present intense. It was soon announced to us, that a guide would await us at the distance of a few fields: we considered our affairs comfortably settled, and set off up the Fell, all in good spirits and security. The heat was still very great; so we took our time, and lagged behind the guide, though he carried our knapsacks and basket. He was a quiet-looking elderly mountaineer, who appeared to walk very slowly;

but his progress was great compared with ours, from the uniformity and continuity of his pace. In the worst part of our transit, I tried the effect of following close behind him, and putting my feet into his footsteps, and I was surprised to find with what ease and rapidity I got on.

At first, we stopped frequently to sit down and drink from the streams that crossed the track, or flowed beside it: and during these halts, we observed that the blackness which had for some time been appearing in the west, now completely shrouded the sea. Next, we remarked, that while the wind still blew in our faces,—that is, from the northeast,—the mass of western clouds was evidently climbing the sky. The guide quietly observed that there would be rain by-and-by. Next, when we were in the middle of the wide Fell, and we saw how puzzled we should have been to find a path, while winding among the swampy places, even in the calmest weather, we pointed out to one another how the light fleeces of cloud below the black mass swept round in a circle, following each other like straws in an eddy. Soon, the dark mass came driving up at such a rate, that it was clear we should not get through our walk in good weather. The dense mist was presently upon us. On looking behind, to watch its rate of advance, I saw a few flashes of lightning burst from it. The thunder had for some time been growling afar, almost incessantly. The moment before the explosion of the storm was more like a dream, than perhaps any actual experience I ever had. We were walking on wild ground, now ascending, now descending,—a deep tarn (Floutern Tarn) on our right hand, our feet treading on slippery rushes, or still more slippery grass: the air was dark as during an eclipse, and heavy mists drove past from behind, just at the level of our heads, and sinking every moment; while before us, and far, far below us,—down as in a different world,—lay Buttermere and the neighbouring vales, sleeping in the calmest sunshine. The contrast of that warm picture, with its yellow lights and soft blue shadows, with the turbulence and chill and gloom of the station from which we viewed it, made me feel this the newest scene I had witnessed for many a year. I had but a moment in which to devour it; for not only did the clouds close down before my eyes, but the wind scudded round to the opposite point of the compass, throwing me flat as it passed. Within a few minutes, I had several falls, from the force of the wind and the treachery of the ground,—now, in a trice, a medley of small streams. It was impossible to stop the guide, much as I wanted to ask him to look back now and then, to see to the safety of my companions in the rear. In the roar of the blast, and the crash of the thunder, and the pelt of the hail, I might as well hope to make the elements hear. So it was necessary to keep up my pace, that he might not stride away from us entirely; my companions making a similar effort to keep up with me. Through stumblings and slidings innumerable they did this,—the lightning playing about our faces the while, like a will-o'-the-wisp on the face of a bog. The hail and rain had drenched us to the skin in three minutes. The first hailstones penetrated to the skin. They were driven in at every opening of our clothes; they seemed to cut our necks behind, and they filled our shoes. Out hats were immediately soaked through, and our hair wringing wet. The thunder seemed to roll on our very skulls. In this weather we went plunging on for four miles, through spongy bogs, turbid streams, whose bridges and stones were covered by the rushing waters, or by narrow pathways, each one of which was converted by the storm into an impetuous brook. When we had descended into a region where we could hear ourselves speak, we congratulated one another on our prudence in not proceeding without a guide. Without him, how should we have known the path from the brook, or have guessed where we might ford the streams, whose bridges were out of sight? Two horses, we afterwards found, were killed on the Fell in that storm: and we should never have come down, we were persuaded, if we had been left to wander by ourselves. As we sat at our tea, in curious masquerade fashion, at the hospitable Scale Hill inn, dressed in such odds and ends of clothes as the people could spare us while our own were drying, (our very knapsacks being wet through,) we thought over our last two days of travel, and felt as if the calm sunset at Calder Abbey were enhanced in its charm, when looked back upon through the storm on Blake Fell.

AUGUST

THE SEASON has arrived when our district is in its richest beauty; but when it yields the least pleasure to the resident gentry. The fatigue of life at the Lakes during August and September is such that all of us who can leave home go to the sea-coast, or to the Continent (when there are not revolutions in every kingdom there) or to the Isle of Man, or to play the tourist ourselves in Scotland or Ireland, or to visit family and friends. The railway is not to be blamed for our fatigues. They existed before the railway was planned. Wordsworth and his comrades,—the poets who are strangely called "the Lake School," though they differ from each other as much as poets well can,—could have told, any time within the last quarter of a century, how strangers can intrude themselves, on the excuse of admiration of genius. As more authors have retired hither, and as the works of the veterans become better known, the nuisance increases: but it is an old grievance. People who call themselves gentry prowl about the residences of celebrated persons who live here for the sake of quietness, waylay the servants to ask half a hundred questions about the habits of the household, ring at the bell to petition for autographs, stare in at the windows, take possession of the gardens, thrust themselves into the house with complimentary speeches; and there is seldom a season when some of them do not send to a newspaper, or to a correspondent who ventures upon putting it into a newspaper, an account of all they see and hear, and sometimes that which they have merely imagined. About the end of July, therefore, family after family of residents departs. Some let their houses; and those who remain at home may thus enjoy pleasant intercourse with intelligent strangers. In other cases, shutters are closed, and garden gates are locked; or the bustle of white-washing and cleaning may be seen going on, during the absence of the family. Those are the days in which such of us as remain at home love and cherish the early morning hours, as the only opportunity for a quiet walk. At the earliest hour, one can never be sure of not seeing a party on the terrace, or in the field, staring up at one's window: but, once beyond one's own gate, the roads and meadows are clear enough for pleasure till eight o'clock. So early as that, we meet jaded horses and a sleepy postilion coming from Patterdale or from Keswick—tired already because they can get no sufficient rest, night or day, during these two months. Sleek as horse and man are in spring, they look sadly harassed and reduced before October. So early as this, the little market-place is full of bustle, with omnibus and coach setting off; and the rubbing down of every horse in the stables is going on within sight,—that nobles and gentry may pursue their journey after breakfast. The poor cooks at the inns are half crazy with hurry and heat, and fatigue. Travellers were arriving till midnight, wanting supper: and other travellers,—pedestrians, and those who go by the early coaches,—have been served with hot breakfasts since five o'clock. All the day, and half the night, is broiling and stewing, and roasting and boiling going on, though the hottest season of the year. Well may the wages given to these cooks be the amazement and ambition of younger functionaries in private houses, whose business is done when they have sent up three meals in a day, and who have the cool of the evening to themselves. Every bed in the town is yielding up its occupant, and no one could believe how many beds are supplied in so small a place. In one season, when I let my house to the Dean of L——, and he had good rest in its best room, the Bishop of L—— was actually compelled to sleep on a mattress laid on the floor at the chief inn. Since that, some of the residents have done what I do not like to think of. After having given up their beds to travellers, and slept in sheds, they next gave up the sheds, and slept under trees. The nights were warm and clear when they did that: but ours is no climate for such a risk as this; and I hope it will not happen again. This was after the European revolutions, which closed the continent to all but adventurous English travellers.

The meadows are the place for early walks at this season. There is no dust there. Strangers do not know the intricacies of the knolls, or how to find the little falls or windings of the streams. The drawback about the walk is that one must return by the market-place;—must slip into the town by the back way (a pleasant way enough), and pop in at the butcher's to bespeak his mercy,—to remind him of one's constant custom throughout the year, and ask if it is not hard that now, when we want to be hospitable, and when we believe we have provided a dinner,—sufficient, however, homely—we should find ourselves without enough to go round. We were promised a fine piece of sirloin; there comes a piece of two ribs. We had engaged a leg of mutton: there comes up little more than a shank. We had bespoken a goodly dish of trout: we are allowed only two.

About the fish, the butcher smiles. He has nothing to do with that. About the meat, he looks grave. He is very sorry: but what can he do? He can only parcel out his resources as fairly as he can, and try to be sufficiently provided next year. He assures me that he has no comfort of his life at present. People cut him up as he has to cut up his meat. He must say he wishes the residents had some resources of their own to rely on at this season: and he tells me that at a certain country inn, three miles off, five dozen fowls per day are killed and eaten. And this reminds me of what Lady R. told me of her method of proceeding, when called on to receive eighty-four chance strangers in the course of three months,—to give them more or less entertainment in her secluded valley. Bacon and eggs, eggs and bacon,—this is what she relies on, if butcher and fish-cart fail. Her guests,—be they nephews and nieces, or bishops and countesses, must make up their minds to bacon and eggs, if they come to the Lakes. So I promise the butcher to think of keeping pigs and fowls to an extent which may relieve him of my demands at this season.[31] A neighbour of mine was wishing, the other day, that we could get the Queen here, and lead her among the dales;—put her and her husband on ponies, and feed them on bacon and eggs. No luxury but trout from the streams: no triumphal arches, no attending magistracy, no bands of music; but instead of these, the rainbows which span the waterfalls, the wild goats on the fells, and the gush of waters hurrying down from the tarns above to the meadows and lakes below. We have no doubt she would like it; for she has something of a mountaineer spirit, and loves to spend a night in a hut (as it is called) of her own among the Scottish wilds.

The mention of this to nephew and niece at breakfast sets us longing for the coolness and stillness of a mountain town. We declare that, one of these days, we will go into hiding in Easedale, and leave the strangers to prowl about here, and do without us as they may. "Some day," says one. "What day will that be?" "Any day but this," we agree. "We must be industrious all the morning." No such thing happens. Looking out, we see the clouds of dust and the whirl of carriages on the road. We see blue and pink muslin gowns and summer bonnets moving about in the meadows: and the telescope discloses three sketching parties within view. Of all these people, some will certainly be coming here. We shall be balked of our industry if we stay at home. Let us be off into hiding!

F. runs down to the inns, to try for a car to carry us four miles, to Grasmere church; or perhaps five, to the brink of the meadows, while S. and I dress in light walking trim, fill the flask with the whiskey which is appropriate to tarn expeditions; order the hard eggs and beef sandwiches, and send to the gardener's for fruit.

The car is obtained; and before an hour is over, we have passed Grasmere church, and left the dusty road, and are within the sound of the brawling stream which comes down from the tarn. At that stream, we dismiss the car; and in a moment we seem to have stepped back into June, with its milder warmth, and its quietness, and even its haymaking. What a contrast is life here and where we were but an hour ago! The few people who are making hay on these levels,—these perfect levels between abrupt mountain sides,—live in yonder farm-house,—that secluded place, niched in among stone fences, canopied over with massy sycamores: and for many weeks together, they see no face but those of the household; and their monotonous lives are seldom varied but when the autumn or spring sales take place, and they cross the rampart under which they live for once to meet their fellows, and to hear the voice of mirth, and to dance to the fiddle, and to find they have social capacities.

It was from such a dwelling, in this very dale, that a farmer and his wife, not many years ago, went over into Langdale, to attend a sale. It was by that path that they went, and were to have returned. It looks an easy path, winding by the ravine; a path hard to miss, broad enough, and not very steep. So says F.: but I tell him that it is impossible to tell in August, among these mountains, what any place on them would be like in snow. The children sat up long that night,—the elder ones. They,—the elder ones,—were too young to be duly apprehensive. They saw the snow falling all the afternoon: when they looked out in the evening, they found a heavy drift at the door: so heavy a one, that the eldest girl laid the baby in the cradle, and set to work to get in fuel, lest the wood-house should soon be blocked up. When at last she lay down to rest, she had no fear. It was too late for her parents to return that night: but perhaps they had remained in Langdale. Those who live secluded, in a position of danger or inconvenience from climate, become patient to a point of apathy. A whole family of men and boys will sit round the fire in bad weather, without employment or ideas,—without fret or worry,—waiting till the weather mends. Just so these children stayed within, waiting for their parents' return, till they were so hungry and so cold, that something must be done. I think they had food and fuel on which they held on for two days. Then, a boy was sent,—and it was some good way,—to the nearest house. A stir was made at once. The women went and fed and warmed the children; and the men ran round to summon other dalesmen, and all turned out upon the mountain. They followed the track into Langdale,—found that the farmer and his wife had set off in good time on their return, on the same day, refusing to spend the night in Langdale, because the children would not know what to do without them. Back turned the searchers, with heavy hearts: for now they knew what to expect. The snow was partly melted; but some tracks were found—lost—and found again. At one point, the snow was so trampled, that it was thought some doubt or difficulty had occurred here; and somewhere near, then, might the missing ones be looked for. But darkness came on before either man or dog had made any discovery. At daylight, the search was renewed; and at last, the barking of a dog brought the searchers to a spot where the woman's body lay at the foot of a precipice not more than fourteen feet high. Her skull was fractured. At a little distance, quite away from the track, lay the man, dead from mere cold, to all appearance. It was thought that they had separated a little, to explore; and that the woman was returning to her husband,—probably guided by his voice, when the precipice, lying between, proved a trap, in which she perished. The funeral was attended by the whole population of the neighbouring dales; and the people's hearts were so touched that they took the children home. But not the less do they attend the sales, and yield to the temptation of a dance, in all weathers, and under heavy risks. The social faculties will not be denied.

And it is well that they will not. In my opinion, there is no comparison between the family of a dalesman who lives too high up the fells for intercourse with his kind and that of a farmer under the sycamores in the levels below. In the last case, you may meet some strange whimsies. You may see in a rude chamber, where the planks of the floor are gaping and there is no ceiling,—only the dark rafters,—a muslin frock hung up, trimmed with lace and satin ribands, and stuck over with atrocious artificial flowers, red and blue, with a morsel of tinsel in the centre of each bunch: and you may hear a girl of such a family talking eagerly on her way to church on Sunday (as we did) about whether Charles B. admired her most in her diamonds or her emeralds. You may see much time spent in learning to dance of an itinerant master; and you may hear of sad follies and errors which ensue from the merry-makings at the sale or in the barn: but, I think, if you have ever been high up, in the most secluded of the mountain hollows, you will think the blank ignorance and apathy there the worst of all. The man leaves home now and then: and, even if he gets drunk, three times a year or so, he hears people speak, and receives ideas. His wife has become scarcely able to speak. You could with difficulty understand her; and her gestures and voice are savage and almost alarming. Her son carries his feet as if they were made of lead. If a traveller appears, the lad stares with round eyes and open mouth; and when he resumes his work, looks as if the aim of his life had been to learn to be slow. In the old days, there was occasionally a wolf to hunt; an eagle to circumvent, and bereave of its young: and many a Border war to which the dalesmen were summoned, for a foray or a campaign. Now, there is nothing:—only to keep a few sheep, and to grow a few oats; to eat the meal, and then grow oats again. It is surprising that the cleanliness of the dwellings is kept up as it is:—the more so because the people are dirty in their persons. There is, I am assured, hope of amendment in this—in the lower dales, if not in the higher mountain dwellings. Where there are families enough within reach of a common centre to furnish a dozen children or upwards, the inhabitants entertain a school-master on "whittle-gate" terms: that is, he puts in his whittle (knife) among the provisions of the family; is boarded by the farmers in turn: and we may hope that one of the lessons he will enforce will be that "cleanliness is next to godliness." He will praise the purely clean slate floor, and the white deal table, and the shining pots and pans; and then point out how little trouble it costs in comparison to keep hair and teeth clean, and to do justice to the skin, where there is a natural bath of the finest kind in the nearest rock basin and gushing stream.

Up to such a dwelling we have to go now,—and past it,—and beyond where there are any dwellings at all; beyond where even sheep are to be seen. The stream will guide us. That is the beauty of seeking a tarn. You may miss a short cut, and make a circuit: but you cannot miss your tarn, if you follow the stream which comes from it. The broad waterfall is our object for a great part of the way;—the ledge over which the water spreads, and offers a curtain of froth and a fringe of spray which may be seen far off in all weathers. We will not go too near it, but hold the path above, where the ferns make a show of fencing us in on either hand. We are such babies as to lead the sheep after us by baaing as we go; and it is droll to see how puzzled they look, and how they stare round them, as if not quite sure that they are right. But we must leave off that now; or we may lead them astray among the heights where they may bleat in vain for shepherd or mate. How they stand gazing after us. If they are here when we return, we will escort them down again.

Now, up this heathery slope,—and over this bit of bog,—and up, up, that indistinct path yonder, and we shall enter that purple hollow where lies the tarn. Did you ever consider, F. and S.,—what tarns are for?—what special service they render? Their use is to cause such a distribution of the waters as may fertilize without inundating the lands below. After rains, if the waters all came pouring down at once, the vales would be flooded: as it is, the nearer brooks swell, and pour themselves out into the main stream, while the mountain brooks are busy in the same way above, emptying themselves into the tarns. By the time the steams in the valley are subsiding, the upper tarns are full, and begin to overflow; and now the overflow can be received in the valley without injury. That is the office of these little mountain lakes.

Now,—do you begin to feel it? Does not some breath of coolness steal out of the purple hollow? You observe what precipices gird it about: and now, at last, you see the dark gray sheet of water itself. Did you ever see anything before which conveyed to you such an impression of stillness? Let us lie down on the grass on the brink, and see how unmoved the shadows lie. See here! look at these diamond drops, sprinkled over the herbage. Parched and hot as all is below, see how a cloud has here come down,—stooped in its course, to brighten the verdure in this recess. It seems almost a pity that no lamb followed us hither: yet how would it start at the echo of its "solemn bleat," as Wordsworth calls it,[32] and how it would listen for the sheep-dog's bark, or anything that would relieve it from the depth of silence here! Can you fancy a yet more impressive retreat than this, not far from us? It is said that on the glassy surface of Bowscale tarn, round which the rocks rise darker and higher than here, no sunshine touches for four months of the year: and now and then the stars may be seen at noonday. We cannot see that here: but look, look!—that is a sort of dawn breaking on the deep gray of the water,—those converging silvery lines trembling on the surface. Do you see how it happens? The wild-drake has taken the water on the opposite shore; and this way he comes with his brood behind him. Yes—here are more dimples in the mirror,—from some restless fish or fly. And after all, we are not alone! Some one is under that mass of rock, angling. F. says it is a woman. If so, it must be F. M.[33] It is F. M.: and now the rocks have to echo our laughter at being thus respectively frustrated in our search after solitude. But our friend has caught fish enough for one day; and now she must sit down to dinner with us, and help us to pity the Ambleside people, who would be glad enough of such a seat as ours, amidst dews and shadows, and fresh waters, and not a sound but of our own voices.

SEPTEMBER

THERE THEY GO, across the meadows!—the sportsman and his dog! Ah! they are turning towards the lake. I thought so; for, if they want stubble-fields, in which to search for partridges, they must go to some of the more open country to the south. They will go by steamer, probably, a few miles down the lake, and then turn into the newly-reaped corn-fields. In hardly another county in England than this, would it be Michaelmas Day before one saw partridge-shooting. Not that I can say I ever saw it here at all. Ours is not a district for game,—till, indeed, you come to the great castles which lie off the skirts of the mountains, where corn-fields spread down gentle slopes, or lie level under the warm, autumn sunshine. In them, you may see, for the first of this month onwards, groups of gentry,—members of parliament, noblemen, and other friends of the host,—enjoying a holiday from the cares of government and legislation, and amusing the ladies mightily with their likeness to children out of school. The childishness of men's recreations is a subject of never-failing wonder and amusement to women. Women can be childish too,—as when condescending to fancy balls, and making a business of the preparation for them: but this is not so inimitably amusing as the solemnity and complacency with which men lay out large amounts of money, and maintain servants, and devote their best abilities for the time to the pursuit of sport,—whether it be racing, hunting, or shooting. The shooting-dress is as serious a matter of concern to an hereditary legislator, who has been sitting, night after night, helping to rule the destiny of a nation, as her ball-dress ever was to a girl just from school. The servants are as care-laden as government officials; and there is reason for that. While poachers and game-keepers murder each other, more or fewer every year, while game-keepers are in such terror lest the game should fall short, as to commit suicide rather than meet their employer when some of their pheasants' eggs have been stolen, it must be a serious lot in life to be in the service of a sportsman. But when these considerations are not immediately in sight, there is something extremely ludicrous to middle-class people, whose lives are filled with genuine interests—with the real business and natural pleasures of every day—in seeing the elaborate preparation for sport made by grown men, the importance which it has in their own eyes, and their supposition that it is equally grand in the eyes of women and middle-class people.

It is not that such observers do not themselves like recreation, and what, in a general sense, is called sport. We might be ashamed for ourselves, of the elaborate preparation for the first of September, which we see the most pompous men condescend to; but we like to start off on a country expedition,—on a gipsy tea-drinking,—or a nutting-party; and can dance at a harvest-home as merrily as anybody. If there is childishness in such things, it is true childishness—merry and social and unpremeditated. And the expedition of yonder sportsman in the meadows is of the natural order. There is nothing fine about it; he and his dog go off by themselves, not knowing or caring whether any one looks after them; with no solemn gamekeeper awaiting them, and no anxiety at heart about reputation to be won or lost in the stubble. I question, by the way, whether they will bring anything home; but they will have the pleasure of the expedition at least. And when in England was there ever a lovelier day?

Some reconciling associations hang about hunting that are wanting about shooting. Hunting is so ancient! and it had so genuine and respectable an origin in the necessity first, and then the benevolence of rescuing the inhabitants of some district from the ravages of wild beasts. The excitement of the chase once experienced, and being found delightful, one does not wonder that it was protracted when "wild beasts" had given place to mere "wild animals," and these again to a deer, carried in a cart to an appointed spot, and then let out, to be chased by the eager dogs and horsemen in waiting. But the existing practice of shooting is comparatively modern. In one of Smollett's novels (Sir Launcelot Greaves),[34] it is mentioned as an extraordinary thing that one of the personages shoots a crow flying; and we are told by Wood, the antiquarian, that the first person who ever had to do with a setter dog—the first who ever taught a dog to sit, to catch partridges, was Robert Dudley, Duke of Northumberland—son to the great Duke of Northumberland. By the way, I am following this day a custom of just the same date, which is usually considered an ancient one. A month ago I ordered a goose for this Michaelmas Day; and it is safe in the pantry. It was Queen Elizabeth, we are told, who ordered our Michaelmas dinner, three centuries ago. It was on the feast-day of the warlike St. Michael, who put down the devil so valiantly, that Queen Elizabeth was sitting at dinner, eating roast goose, when news was brought her of the defeat of the Spanish Armada. This racy sauce made the dish so delightful to her that she had roast goose for dinner every Michaelmas Day, so long as she lived; and, of course, all loyal subjects of the monarchy must do the same, till St. Michael and Queen Elizabeth are forgotten. In our county and Lancashire, the peasantry call the particular goose of this day, "the goose with ten toes," a peculiarity which seems puzzling enough; but an antiquarian has kindly explained that point also. The last word of the old church service, which the people used to hear without understanding, on Michaelmas Day, dwells still on the ear, or did, when the ten toes of the Michaelmas goose were spoken of: "Tua, nos quæsumus, Domine, gratia semper præveniat et sequatur: ac bonis operibus jugiter præstet esse *intentos*."[35] Ploughmen, and other labourers, who are fed by the farmers, take it ill if they are not supplied with roast goose on this day; and some even stipulate for it when hired. And no one can wonder at this, if the people really believe the saying they often repeat, "If you eat goose on Michaelmas Day, you will never want money all the year round."

A sudden fancy here seizes me and my guests—the lad and lass who have already seen something of the peculiarities of the district under my guidance. Our own goose will keep, and we should like to see one eaten by people who believe that they are thus securing a sufficiency of money for the year round. We could not very well intrude ourselves in the house of any neighbour; but if we scour the country, we shall fall in with a harvest-home, or a ploughman's supper at some farm-house in the dales, where we shall be welcome as spectators. I am for trying Langdale; there are so many farms in that vale, and the people at Millbeck know me so well, that I can obtain from them any information that is procurable at all. We will go by Skelwith and Bleatarn, and make this our nutting expedition too. We will carry plenty of bags and baskets, and ride as far as Skelwith Bridge. The doubt is about getting home. These harvest suppers are late, and the vale is six miles off. F. says there is a fine moon; and S. reminds me that it is Saturday, which may stop the jollity at midnight.

Still, ...[36] Well, we will carry our nightcaps; and we will tell the servants to give us up if we do not appear by twelve o'clock.

Sunday.—We have been agreeing over our somewhat late breakfast, that our expedition was a charming one. Some things about it were so new and strange, that we have an impression on our minds of having been in foreign parts. I suspect it is rather that we have had a dip into a past century. We dismissed our car when we came to the woods where hazels abound; and then we plunged into the depths of the shade. It was very pleasant; the gush of the waterfalls—first Skelwith, and then Colwith—being just far enough off to soothe the sense, and to calm the spirits, which are apt to rise high on a sunny autumn day. On we went, sometimes catching at a high-swinging bough, clustered with nuts, sometimes thrusting ourselves into a thicket of hazels to explore a nook, where certainly nobody had been before—this year, if ever; sometimes keeping a great booty to ourselves, to surprise our comrades with presently, sometimes calling to them in glee, to come and help. At last, we came to the final fence, and must emerge upon the bare wild,—part heath, part bog. This passed, we came upon the lane—the very steep descent which leads us down upon Colwith, where there were more woods, and another booty of nuts. I only hoped that the black dog would not be at his post—the dog which is set as a guard upon the waterfall—or, rather, upon the fees for showing the waterfall. That dog is a constant trouble. I never want to see the fall better than it is seen from the road; especially when, as now, I am on my way to Dungeon Ghyll, which shames most of our falls. But, the moment a party appears upon the bridge approaching Colwith, the dog starts off to the farm-house upon the hill; and then comes the girl, breathless, with the key upon her finger, just to be told that we do not want her. It was so yesterday. We assured the girl that it gave us concern to have brought her down from her employments half-a-dozen times to no purpose, having only twice given her a shilling. She smiled,—did not own what it was that made her always appear at the opportune moment, but caressed the dog so affectionately and approvingly, as to convince us that he puts a good many shillings per annum into her pocket. Few things in this district are more painful to me, than to observe the moral mischief wrought by the fees of strangers, all along the road, during the "tourist season." It ruins the children. They lounge in the roads and lanes where there are gates to open, bask in the hedges, quarrel in the ditches, when they ought to be decently at home, or busy in the field with their fathers. They scramble for money, and grow greedy and selfish, without having any of the excuse of town children, who suffer from want. A writer of power tells us how, when following two bare-footed, ragged, hungry-looking children in London, who were gossiping as they walked, he heard the one say to the other, "Once I had a halfpenny;" and then came the story of the single halfpenny, which made an event in a life.[37] Here, the children in the by-roads receive many pennies in a day, during three or four months of the year, and sometimes silver; and they scramble for the coin thrown to them as if it were the bread of life that it is to the cellar-born child in a large town. Something even worse may be seen. A lubberly boy lies on the grass, basking in the sunshine, and bids the little, pale girl—his sister or playmate—watch the gate. When a car comes, she opens the heavy gate with difficulty and toil. A penny is thrown. He signs to her to pick it up, and bring it to him. He sees entreaty in her eyes, though she dares not refuse to come. He wrenches the money out of her hand, pockets it, motions her to her hot station again, and composes himself to sleep till the next wheels are heard. This was pointed out to me by a friend, who saw in this little anecdote an illustration of the lot of woman, wherever woman can be made to work. The tourists may have brought much good into our district; but we owe to them the great evil, that the children on the by-roads have the hurtful experience of profuse gains during a short season, of an employment which is more like begging than work.

The scenery grew wilder at every step for the next mile or two,—over heaths, and past little Langdale town, where there are rushing springs and rude sheepfolds below, and opposite, stretching up the mountain slope, the old pack-horse road, once the only road to Whitehaven. We held on and up towards the ridge which separated us from the vale, which is the scene of Wordsworth's "Excursion." "Behold! beneath our feet a little lowly vale." Who is there that cannot go on with the quotation—that does not remember the urn-like shape of the vale, the "two green fields," the "moorland house," the cuckoo "shouting faint tidings of some gladder place?"[38] There was the little tarn, like a circle of light in a dark place, shining as it does amidst its enclosure of sombre hills. The moorland house is still the only one; but there are more trees by many hundreds that when Wordsworth fixed his Solitary there. Plantations of larch stretch this way and that, and must make it a "gladder place" for the cuckoo when the bright green tassels come out on every spray. This was the place for us to dine; somewhere on the breast of the steep where the Solitary was desired to climb, for the good of body and spirit. We saw two children high up, where we were sure there must be a capital view of the whole recess, so we made for that point, and the creatures were so rooted to the spot by amazement, that there was no fear of their flying. They were gathering bleaberries,[39] and, as we were in no hurry, and could not have the sport of gathering bleaberries every day, we set to work to help them; and then bought all they had, and made them sit down to help us away with our dinner. There is little to be learned from children here. Between the breadth of their dialect, and the slowness of mind and speech of these mountaineers, it is difficult to obtain information from them. These children, however, could tell us that harvesting was going on in Langdale. As we looked down upon the oat-fields below us, we saw that there could be no harvest here yet, in this vale "uplifted high among the mountains,"[40] but the half hour's descent into Langdale would, we knew, make all the difference in climate and in seasons. It was time now to be going; so we made for the lowest of the surrounding ridges, a sort of gap, where the wonders of the head of Langdale began to open upon us. A most impressive assemblage of mountains it is, closing in a fertile expanse, whose fields run into nooks between the spurs of the mountains, and where a farmstead here and there peeps out from under its canopy of sycamores. There is no lake in this dale, but it looks as if it must at one time have been all water. The spurs thrown out by the mountains now meet and now alternate, so as to make the levels sometimes circular and sometimes winding. Except just at the head, the dale-farms are on the rising grounds which skirt the levels; and cheerful and pretty they are, each of gray stone, on its knoll, with its clump of trees about it, and ferns scattered all round it, and sheep browsing on the fells above, while, in spring, the ewes and lambs nestle near the shelter of the dwelling. After reaching the levels at the head of the dale, I led myself and my comrades into the same scrape that I had twice before fallen into. By following the road that winds through the middle, we came upon the beck at a point where there is no bridge. As before, it was decided that it would be too troublesome to go back; and we must just wade through barefoot. The water was delightfully cool and pleasant, but the stones were terribly hard and sharp. These misadventures and vagaries are, however, what dwellers among mountains must not care about; and, once shod again, we found we were no worse. Another half mile brought us to Millbeck, and there, the sight of the well-known long table assured me that we had come to the right place at the right time. The harvest supper was to be this evening; and the geese were already in preparation. We presented our bleaberries and shining nuts—accepted an invitation to stay—and, to avoid being in the way meantime, set off to visit Dungeon-Ghyll Force—half a mile off on the mountain side.

The name might lead a stranger to fancy that some noble's castle was in question. But, in the language of the country people, a fissure or cavern in the rock is called a dungeon. Ghyll means a fissure also; so dungeon is emphatically a fissure by name, and it certainly is so by nature. When we reached the spot where the dark chasm yawned, and the waters were loud, my young companions wondered how the sight could ever be got at, or whether they were to be satisfied with the sound. At first I left them to puzzle it out, but when I drew to the verge, the laugh was against me. The broad, stout ladder which I had always found here before was gone—rotted by wet, and broken to pieces by stress of tourists—like some other things in the district. We could not think of being baffled, so we tried the descent, and found a footing in the rock. There it was, the waterfall in its cleft, tumbling and splashing, while the light ash, and all the vegetation besides, were in motion, as they are everlastingly, from the stir of the air. Looking up, we saw how a bridge was made at a vast height by the lodgment of a block in the chasm. We were fortunate in being there just at that hour of the autumn evening when the sunlight gushes in obliquely, a narrow, radiant, translucent screen, itself lighting up the gorge, but half concealing the projections and waving ferns behind it. The way in which it converts the spray into sparks and gems can be believed only by those who have seen it.

What a contrast was the scene we returned to! What a noise of mirth and feeding! How the beef and bread disappeared when every bone of each goose was picked! And the pies and cakes—how they melted away out of sight! The people here keep no beer in the house at ordinary times; because of the watching of the excise when they serve refreshment to strangers, lest they, having no license, should furnish any excisable article for pay. But now, how the beer-jugs went round! The men were thirsty with their harvest-home labours, and, they said, with shouting the tidings along the vale: so they drank heartily, not intemperately, however, for they cared more for the dance than the pleasures of the table. While the elderly men sat in the porch, and on the benches outside the house, smoking their pipes, and comparing all the harvest-homes they had known, the lads and lasses, the fiddler and a drummer that they had by some means caught, adjourned to a loft for the dance. "So, you call this dancing!" said F., evidently thinking that though he had intended asking some of the lasses to dance, he could not rival the sport he saw. The thumping was like a desperate attempt to bring down the building; and the stronger the thumping, the louder was the drum; so that the fiddler wrought till the perspiration ran down his face, without making himself much heard. I was beginning to find this intolerable, when the host beckoned me away, telling me that I might like to see what some of the young people were doing with our nuts.

We looked into the back kitchen, where a great fire

was burning on the hearth, in the wide chimney common in old farm-houses here, and there was a girl on her knees in the heat, with two or three other girls and lads behind her, all intently watching a row of nuts laid just within the fire. They were telling matrimonial fortunes. If a nut, named after a lover, bounced, he would prove faithless. If a pair burned quietly away together, it would be a happy marriage. If they cracked and started off from each other, there would be discord. We little supposed, when we gathered these nuts, what power of hope and fear, pain and pleasure, lay within their shells.

We were entreated not to think of departing before the fun was over. It would not be late, the host assured me, as the Sabbath was near, and a guest was willing to carry us in his cart three miles or more on our way home. It was only for the lad and his sister to walk home in the moonlight those three miles, which they would like better than riding, if they had merry company. The fun was over early. At a quarter before twelve the son of the principal guest, a substantial statesman, much looked up to in the dale, went to the fiddler and said, "My father's respects, and he will be obliged to you to lend him the fiddlestick." The hint was taken. Before the clock struck twelve, we had departed; and we left very few behind us. After a jogging ride of four miles, and a silent walk of two more in the mellow moonlight, we found ourselves on our own terrace, taking a loving look of our solemn circle of mountains, while the servants were waking up at the sound of the door-bell, and preparing to let us in and light us to bed.

OCTOBER

THE GLADSOME SEASONS of the year are now over. From this time till the very end,—till our Christmas festivities begin,—we prepare ourselves for gravity and for composure under the most serious incidents of our annual life. People who live in towns, or in an average climate, and to whom the change of seasons is almost insensible, may smile at so solemn an announcement of the disappearance of summer and its pleasures; but there are circumstances attending the advent of late autumn with us, which suggest and require a certain sobriety of spirit. The season, not only of gales and floods, but of disease and death is drawing on, and nothing is more impressive to a new resident than the spectacle of the sickening autumn; nothing more trying to the mind and heart than the inability to convey to others one's own conviction that the visitation is invited by ourselves,—that it is our own fault that so many of our little society suffer and die as they do. I could not bear this a second year; and in my walks during the shortening days, my thoughts were occupied with what could be done to rouse my neighbours to consider and act in defence of their health and their life.

These walks are in themselves as sweet as any in the year. It is, to be sure, rather mournful to see the last of the swallows assembling on a housetop, in that sort of commotion which shows that they are planning to follow those that went last month. We know that they are here now only because the wind has been south for the last few days;

and that as soon as it gets round to any quarter less directly opposite, we shall lose them. Well, the twelve nests that they have put up under my broad eaves shall be left untouched, that I may see the gay creatures again in seven months. This same south wind brings out the last faint odours of the year; and it calls up the gray mists which I see rise from the valleys, and breathe out of the mountain clefts, and sail away, still rising as they go, till they settle round every peak, and spread and join, until we feel ourselves roofed in with mist; and all below is seen in the singular clearness of a dewy atmosphere. If a stronger wind comes to open the sky again, how rich and ruddy is the landscape! The further woods and nearer hedges and thickets are gay and glittering. The holly berries begin to show, and the large scarlet hips on the briers, and the shining, clustering blackberries, which we cannot help eating as we go. The scarlet and green berries of the nightshade look so tempting that I wonder we do not hear of more mischief from them among the children, who are out everywhere gathering blackberries for sale. Here are sloes[41] in plenty, covered with bloom; but most people have so many damsons[42] at home, that few care to corrode their tongues with sloes. Among the roots of old trees, we still find a primrose here and there; and the slender heath-bell (often miscalled harebell) wanes over a layer of dead leaves. One likes to call this delicate flower by the pretty name of the harebell; but I believe it is settled that the blue hyacinth is the real harebell, called so because its roots are a favourite food of the hare. Among the remnants of the passing year, we see the cheerful spectacle of preparation for another. The plough is in the field; and the last glow of the October sun brightens the gray horse on the distant slope, and enables us thus to see the brown horse also, and the man and the plough which we might otherwise have overlooked on the dim hillside. In the midst of the deep quietness of an autumn day, when the passage of the squirrel over the dead leaves, and the fall of the acorn, and the hum of the bee above the latest blossoms are marked sounds, how suddenly, and with what a sweep comes upon the ear the cry of the hounds and rush of horses, as the hunt rushes across the landscape! How the scarlet coats shine behind the coppice and gleam across the stubble! Not many scarlet coats, however, but a good many country costumes,—the gray homespun, the drab, and the Sunday dress of some of my neighbours, I think I recognise. Yes, there is A——, and there B——, and C——, one a builder, another a shopkeeper, making a frolic of the hunt, heating themselves in the sun by an unwonted ride, and likely, I fear, to heat themselves more perniciously at night with drink and revelry. There they go, out of sight, and soon the last echoes of the hounds have died away.

There is something in these autumn, as in early spring days, which exhausts one's strength. One looks round for a resting-place after a very few miles. I must ask for a seat in this old farm-house: the seat and the draught of milk are graciously given. My thoughts being turned on the health of the district, it is natural to observe how entirely all conditions of health were overlooked, while those modes of living grew up which are still followed by the country people. The door here is not high enough for man or woman to enter without stooping; the window is on the same side, and there is a dead wall opposite. If there is too little access to the outer air elsewhere, there is too much in the direction of the chimney. The chimney is a large recess, six feet high, and capable of containing three or four persons sitting on each side the fire, which burns on the hearth. A large provision of meat hangs in the smoke; and well smoked the meat is likely to be, judging by the soot which hangs upon everything within the recess. The wicker, plastered sides are almost as sooty as the beam and chain from which the boiler is suspended. It is said that the country custom of men sitting bonneted within doors, arose from the need of keeping their heads covered from the soot and draught, and even the dirt of the chimney. The fire is of peat; and when the autumn and winter storms pour rain and blast into the wide funnel of the chimney, the soot is brought down in oily streams, which it almost turns one's stomach to see trickling on the walls. The chambers are no nicer. The "bower," the room of the master and mistress, is extremely small; over the pantry, and a little larger. The loft, where everybody else sleeps—children, servants, and all—has no ceiling; no furniture but the great chests where the oatmeal, the malt, some dried meat, and the family clothes, are kept; no sheets on the beds, but rugs and blankets for warmth; and, probably, no partition but a rope carried across the loft, on which are hung the clothes in wear. If there is a partition, it is probably of upright boards, through which everything must be heard, and anything may be seen. The young men may wash their faces and hands at the pump every day, for what I know; but from what one sees when their collars are open in warm weather, it seems that they dress as their neighbours, the pitmen at the collieries, do on Sundays,—put on a clean shirt over a skin which has not felt the touch of water for half a year or more. The elderly woman, now on the settle, nursing the infant (her grandchild) is ill; and she tells me, with a sort of contempt, of the advice the clergyman gave her, while waiting till the doctor came round. The advice was, to put her feet in warm water and go to bed. I asked her if this was not good advice. She says that, in the first place, putting her feet in warm water would send the blood to her head; and, in the next place, that it is thirty years since she washed her feet, and it shall be another thirty before she does it again. Seeing me of another way of thinking, she tells me that she had a daughter who washed *her* feet once; and she died under the age of twenty-five. The infant is now to be washed, however, and I am glad to see it. The mother, having brought me a basin of milk, sets about washing the babe, and does not omit the feet. I remind her, however, that she has forgotten the arms and hands. She says the babe must wait awhile for that; it was a good way yet from six months old. She informs me that, if her child had its arms and hands washed before it was six months old, it would grow up a thief, and she would not like that. Thus do all our superstitions and old sayings work in favour of dirt.

Intemperance and dirt usually go together; and never did I see intemperance and all sensual vice so prevalent as here. It is clear to me, that the discomfort of the houses has much to do with this fearful liability. The young men come home from work to an overcrowded dwelling; a room full of bad smells and the noise of children, and with scarcely space to turn round. What wonder that they go to the public house! Coming home late, their sleeping-place is in a hot room, where six or seven people are huddled together, already too close for decency, and breathing noisome air. Pondering these things,—remembering how good are the wages and how constant is the employment here—being aware that there is no poverty, but that the difficulty lies in the unwillingness of proprietors to build cottages, or to facilitate the building of them by others, I made up my mind, that the true way to improve the health and morals of our neighbourhood was, by putting the people in the way of providing wholesome dwellings for themselves. There was no time to be lost. Already, since my arrival, had grave after grave been dug in the overcrowded churchyard; and one valuable life after another had sunk before my eyes. Benevolent people were giving wine, and broth, and luxuries to the sick, and consoling the repentant, and warning the profligate, but no one seemed to think of the shorter or surer method of taking in hand the *causes* of sickness and debauchery. It was worth trying whether something could not be done.

From the Sanitary Commission in London it was easy to obtain reports and other documents, which would teach us the best methods of draining and constructing new houses. When these had arrived and been well studied, our builder, John Newton, and our house carpenter, T. C., and his wife, came to tea with me, to talk matters over. It makes my heart ache now to think of that evening; to think how, all unknowing of the future, we sat in happy consultation, perceiving hope and encouragement whichever way we looked, and trusting that in a few years we might see the place regenerated. Never was there a fairer field for such a reform. Nature has made everything ready to our hand. She has given us the slopes on which our little town stands; the gullies, which may carry away its drainage; the wholesome soil under our feet; the rocks, which may serve as the foundation of our dwellings; the copious flow of streams from the hills, and the brimming rock-basins, which offer the purest water in abundance to all who need. It is not Nature's doing that the people have dung-heaps against their walls, and filth soaking into the foundations; and ditches uncleaned through all the heats of summer; and dead dogs and cats thrown into the beck; and cabins built against the damp earth of a cutting, where no air can blow through the dwelling; and so little care to bring the fresh waters among the dwellings, that the women have to toil up the hills, with tubs on their heads or pails in their hands, to bring down the smallest quantity of water that will suffice for household purposes; or that the churchyard is so putrid—so filled with the untimely dead, as that the sexton faints when he opens a grave, and the surgeon reports that he cannot cure the fever cases which occur in the vicinity of the churchyard. These things are not Nature's fault: those of us who live according to her laws find this the healthiest place we have ever dwelt in;—nor can we blame fortune for it either, while the mechanics of the place can and do pay rents for unwholesome cabins, which would be high for cottages of the first order. Neither nature nor fortune is to blame for the spectacle of aching rheumatism by the fireside, ricketty infancy on the threshold, loathsome scrofula in the workshop, consumption coughing the night away, fever tossing on the bed, and death collecting old, young, and middle-aged, within the fatal boundary of the churchyard. On these things we took counsel and agreed. We agreed that the want of the people was of sanitary knowledge, first, and then of guidance in improving their condition. My guests pledged themselves to support me in every effort to supply these needs; and, if we could succeed in forming a building society, to be faithful to the methods of draining and building laid down by the Central Sanitary Commission in London.

On the first summons, the people came together in the school-house. They knew already how glad they would be to have better dwellings, and that for many years they had asked for such in vain, while land could always be found for sites for gentlemen's houses. They could easily see the principle of a building society: how, if twenty men could lay by a shilling a week, it was a pity that all should wait twenty weeks before any one could have the use of a pound; whereas, if they put their money together in some safe place, one man could have the use of a pound at the end of one week, while the twentieth would be as well off as before. They could easily see how, if thirty or forty persons who desired to possess a good cottage, paid a certain monthly sum for a certain term of years, they might, in constant succession, be made possessors each of such a dwelling, till, at the end of the term of years, all should be served. The question was, how the land to build on was to be obtained. Some few who desired to be members had land of their own. As for the rest, I had good news for them. An opulent friend of mine, who saw the importance of the case, had empowered me to purchase any piece of land suitable to the purpose, which might at any time be on sale. She would either take ground-rent for the portions to be built upon, let or sell it by the half acre, or quarter acre, or as might be desired. My benevolent Quaker neighbour, moreover, reminded me that the best portion of such ground would be in request for gardens till wanted for building on; and that, if not sought for this purpose, he would himself pay a handsome rent for any cultivable portion. All now went on rapidly to the critical point of establishing the society. The people chose their trustees and their committee, made a wide inquisition into the terms and proceedings of similar societies elsewhere, and framed their rules. We got the rules certified by the government actuary, to place our society under the protection of the law; and when that was done—which was not till after many weeks,—met with happy faces to transact the business of the first pay night. Some things had happened which had spread gloom over the whole place; but they tended to encourage our project, and we were all looking forward to the completion of our term of thirteen years as one which would testify to a vast change in the health, morals, and fortunes of Ambleside. If we lived to the end of thirteen years, we hoped to see a hamlet of thirty or forty wholesome dwellings adjoining the hillside. We hoped that the labouring man would have the comfort of privacy in his lodging, and whole families the enjoyment of decency in their dwelling. We hoped that the young married couple might go to a home of their own earning; actually their own, without any rent to pay; and that the governess and the shopman, and the maid-servant might, before middle life, find themselves the owners of a property yielding rent which, laid by to accumulate, would go far to provide for their latter years. Such hopes appear to us now as reasonable as ever, but to be certain of this we must await the lapse of the thirteen years.[43]

During the weeks required for the maturing of this project, there were other things to be done. The people who were sighing in disease, and groaning under bereavement of those they loved best, still did not know how to seek and promote health. But they were willing and anxious to hear what was known. They came together, week after week, to hear how true it is that "we are fearfully and wonderfully made;" to hear the stories (of which no one ever tires) of the plague-visitations of former centuries, and of the ravages of cholera in our own time: to hear what the conditions of health are, and how far our life is truly in our own hands; to hear how drunkards die by abuse of the stomach and nervous system; and how, by abuse of the nervous system and the brain, lunatic asylums are filled. Under the hearing of these things they would sit immovable for an hour and a half at a time. Under the hearing of these things the notorious poacher and night vagabond would turn white, and sink his head upon his knees; and the young tippler would stagger out and faint upon the threshold. Matters have mended since then. We have a local Board of Health, which watches the drains, and pounces upon every nuisance; and meetings have been held, and large subscriptions have been made for building a new church,—partly for the sake of a new place of burial. Some of us are hoping, however, that there may be enough of delay to place us under an expected Act of Parliament, whereby we may be compelled to choose our burial-ground away from places of human resort;—some sweet breezy spot, perhaps, among the hills, where the dead need no longer be the fatal enemies of the living.

Some of my neighbours have still other hopes also. Seeing how we all like to meet in the evenings of the winter half-year, when no strangers are in the place, and the shop-keepers can put up their shutters early, we begin to think of expanding and varying these meetings in the school-house, and if we do so, it may happen that while some existing dwellings will have ceased to command rents, and will be assigned to the pigs, or demolished, the ale-houses may be exhibiting their attractions to empty benches.

NOVEMBER

IF THIS IS the gloomiest month of the year throughout the British Islands, it is eminently so in our district; at least the latter half of it, when St. Martin's Summer is over, and the wintry gales and floods come upon us. It is our fever month; and the fever is very threatening this year. Of all the men in the place, of those who could least be spared, John Newton was first down in it. He was to have come to me about some Building Society business, but sent one of the children to say that he was unwell, and must keep his bed for that day, but hoped to come on the next. He did not, however. In my walk before daylight, I did not now, as usual, meet him going forth, apparatus in hand, to sweep a neighbour's chimney; or, playing with his rule, evidently meditating some building scheme. I used to think him the most active man in the place, by the way in which he went forth in the morning—cheerful, wide-awake—while some other men moved slowly, as if they cared for the cold; and one, now and then, was so tipsy, that it was mournful to see his attempts to touch his hat to me, and to walk straight while in my sight. At first we were told that Newton had caught cold; but it came out in time that he had been out hunting, and that implies conviviality after the sport. It was soon evident that it would be weeks before he could leave his bed. At the same time, Edward H., a young carpenter, lay down in the fever; and for thirteen weeks his mother and sister were watching him night and day, getting little rest but in an easy-chair, during all that time. It was very affecting to hear the poor fellow in his delirium, incessantly talking of the sanitary matters on which he and his neighbours had been receiving new knowledge. May that new knowledge do something for us before another year; for our state this year is terrible. In D.'s, the fishmonger's, low, damp cottage, the children are down in scarlet fever; and there are four cases of fever in houses next the churchyard—cases with which the surgeon declares he can do nothing. In two of the houses, the lower rooms have to be shut up on account of the putrid dribble from the burial-ground which trickles down the walls. If we, who live in airy, dry houses, built on the rock, our wells always swimming with the sweetest water, feel some depression from the gloom and heaviness of the season, what must it be to those who are spending the passing weeks in the sick room!

It is good to cheer ourselves with out-door spectacles as long as the Martinmas Summer allows. The grand spectacle of the season is the Martinmas hiring—the half-yearly engagement of farm-servants, both lads and lasses. Those who wish to be hired, stand about the market-cross, with a sprig of green, or a straw in their mouths. The days are short now; but before it is dusk, the young women move off to see the shops,—a grand sight, however few they be, to the dwellers in the dales. The young men follow them; and now begins the great match-making of the year. Each youth invites his sweetheart to the dancing-room, and plies her with cake, and punch or wine, little regarding the expenditure of his half-year's wages in such a cause. Jealous quarrels, and sometimes desperate fights take place in the intervals of the dancing; and it is said that the women fight sometimes almost as well as the men, when on behalf of a lover. Strange and fearful as this appears, we must remember how rare are these occasions of excitement, and that the monotony of a year, or at least of a half-year, has to be worked off this night. There is little doubt that some weddings will follow; but for many months, only unbroken dulness has preceded.

On occasion of such meetings as these, offenders against domestic morals are liable to be punished by a sentence of public opinion. Unfaithful husbands and wives, and men who beat their wives, are made to ride the stang. The stang is the pole on which loads are hung, when carried on men's shoulders. It is the ancient "cowl-staff." "Where is the cowl-staff?" cries Mrs. Ford, one of the Merry Wives of Windsor, when about to despatch Sir John Falstaff to his ducking among the dirty clothes, in the ditch on Datchet Mead.[44] Delinquent husbands here have as much cause to dread the stang as the fat knight. They are liable to be hoisted on it among the savage jeers of the crowd, and to be carried through and through the town, till they are half dead with shame and fear. It is a terrible sight, this punishment by lynch-law[45] in our old-fashioned district. If the coward who beats his wife, succeeds in hiding himself, a substitute is placed on the stang, who incessantly proclaims, in a ribald rhyme, that it is not himself who is the delinquent, and who it is that he represents. This is, perhaps, our greatest barbarism. There is another which revolts one's feelings too; but it is common throughout the kingdom, and may be said to be borrowed from London:—the Guy Fawkes celebration, on the fifth of this month. Those who are busiest in the preparation for it, probably know least what it means; and it is to be hoped that those who have most reason to know—the Catholic residents—care less for it than some of their Protestant neighbours do on their account. To boys, and other holiday-lovers, Pope-day (as they sometimes call it), is a funny holiday, with a bonfire at the end of it. For some time before, we have to look to our fences, our old trees, our outside shutters, our palings, our wood-piles; for keen eyes are on the lookout for drooping branches, hedge-stakes, loose pales, unhinged shutters, unprotected casks, and everything that will burn. Such booty is secreted, and watched as hidden treasure. On the morning of the 5th of November, we meet a Guy here and there, in all frequented places—a boy dressed up in paper ruffles, and paper mitre, old clothes, and a horrible mask, with a dark-lantern in one hand, and a spread bundle of matches in the other—all ready for blowing up the King and the Parliament, little as he knows about either. Some people give half-pence, and somebody always bestows a tar-barrel. As soon as it is dark, the gentle little Catholic lady who lives just outside my gate, and the kind-hearted Catholic gentleman on the other side of the valley, who does some helpful act for somebody every day of the year, may hear the far-off shouts of the crowds who are met to light the bonfire. If they look out, they may see the bright flame on three or four conspicuous points of the high-grounds, looking yellow under the silver stars, or turning the November fog into a ruddy, rolling cloud. If I were a clergyman or schoolmaster, I would take this matter in hand, explain to the people how terrible the story of the Gunpowder Plot really was, how much too serious to have ever become a jest and a festival, and how fit now to be practically forgotten in our intercourse with our Catholic neighbours, and out of respect for their feelings. It would be an excellent thing if we could transfer the merry-making to the date of the Catholic emancipation; but I fear that even yet our society is not able generally to enter into the full enjoyment of that great event. Leaving such scenes, there are still tranquil pleasures to be had as winter is about to lower on our mountain tops. One of the most interesting spectacles in the high uplands, is a Sunday harvesting, here and there. I never saw this anywhere else; and in this region it appears a remarkable exception to the general strictness of observance. This month of November, was called by our Saxon ancestors, wind month; and there are special winds which the husbandman has reason to dread, if the weather has compelled him to leave his oats or barley out on the uplands till now; and it seems to be granted among us that a genial day is not to be lost because it happens to be Sunday.

I have said that this is the wind month of the Saxons. In some parts of this district we have a wind of our own; on the signs of which, the husbandmen in certain valleys keep a careful watch. This is the celebrated local gale called the Helm wind, which comes to us over Cross Fell. The mildest breath of east wind ascending the fell which bounds us on the east, becomes cooled when it enters the cap or helm of the mountains, and rushes down to displace the warmer air of the valleys to the west. It roars fearfully in the fissures and ravines of the range; but the great conflict has to come. When it becomes rarefied by the warmth it finds at a certain distance down the slopes, it begins to rush aloft again, encounters the current from the west, discharges the moisture it carries on again reaching the cold region, and thus presents the appearance of a singular sky. The sudden cloud it emits (called the Helm Bar), seems pulled into wisps—indeed, the whole heaven seems pulled into wisps—by the contending currents. In the calmest weather, if it be growing colder, the husbandman casts a glace at the eastern heights, and is easy if all be clear. If, while not a breath of wind seems to be stirring, a little cloud forms on the ridge, and spreads north and south, he says "the Helm is on," and dreads the event if he has produce out in the fields, or fruit left on his trees. Down comes the blast in a few minutes—here unroofing a house, there whirling away a stack into the air, and scattering its contents far and wide, tearing up trees by the roots, blowing the astonished horseman from his saddle, and upsetting a laden cart into beck or ditch. The Bar sometimes opens, and discloses a stratum of higher clouds, perfectly motionless; while fragments of itself are torn off, and whirled this way and that in the opposing currents. It is said that this wind blows sometimes for nine successive days without a moment's lull; by the end of which time, I should think those who live near its range must be well-nigh distracted, for its sound is that of a roaring sea. There is a high average of health in the valleys subject to the Helm wind; but the injury done to vegetation is great. People find their spirits rise, they say, under its invigorating influence, even while they see such grain as is out, and the last foliage of the year, turned black and beaten down by this cataract of air.

Stranger tricks than these are played by the elements in a region like ours. Nature sends us spectres to scare the ignorant, and puzzle the wise. Two persons, whose word no one would dispute, once saw on Souterfell, a man with a dog pursuing horses at so prodigious a rate, as to be altogether astounding; and not appearing for a moment only, but traversing the whole length of the mountain, disappearing at the further end. The witnesses agreed that the horses must have cast their shoes in such a gallop, and the man must have broken his wind, and died of the exertion; so they went early the next morning to pick up the horse-shoes and the man's body, if they could find it. They found nothing but a range so steep, that neither man nor horse could traverse it at any pace. For a year this incident burdened their minds; when twenty-six more persons were placed in their predicament of witnessing a wholly incredible thing. For upwards of two hours, and till darkness shrouded the fell, troops of horsemen were seen riding along the mountain side, in close ranks, and pretty rapidly; and frequently the last but one in a troop galloped on to the front, and there put himself into line. Everybody knew that the thing could not be real. The supposition which first presented itself was, that this was a refracted and multiplied image of some troop of horsemen, soldiers, or others, who might be riding somewhere within the range of the light. But it never could be ascertained that they were such; and the length of time which elapsed, the two hours occupied by the passage of this equestrian host, would still have remained unaccounted for. The facts were formally attested by a sufficiency of witnesses; and they remain to be explained. Similar appearances among our mountain districts, towards the close of the last century, were confidently pronounced by some pious persons, to be the rebuke of Heaven for our war with America. Others, however, thought we were rebuked enough by a more substantial instrumentality than these aerial armies.

But to revert to commoner incidents of the region and the month,—now is the time to enjoy the last sweetness of sunny rambles before looking for the sublimity of winter. The stillness of the woods is gone. Already the regular, alternate strokes of the woodmen's axes are heard, succeeded by the crash and shock of the falling tree. In the coppices, the young men are cutting down the underwood which has stood its sixteen years—the oak, ash, alder, birch, and hazel, which must now be brought down for use. Little or no charcoal will be made; for the wood is wanted for the bobbin-mill at Ambleside, where some of the Yorkshire and Lancashire mills are supplied; and for hoops, which will find their way to Liverpool; and for hurdles and corals, and the peculiar kind of baskets, called twills. When we pass a dwelling which is blessed with an orchard, we may see the inhabitants busy collecting the last of their walnuts, and of their apples, and of the damsons that purple the trees on which they grow. The voices sound cheerful from among the trees, whose yellow leaves come dancing down at every shaking of the air. At regular intervals sounds the flail from within the barn. The fowls are exceedingly busy about the barn-door, while so much grain is scattered about; and the sparrows are on the watch for what they can get. A few more birds are lingering with us, flitting among the hips and haws in the hedges. If we wander on to the spring-heads, or stand to watch the flow of the beck among the stones in its channel, we may see the jerking wagtails, now perching on a stone, and now actually wading into the coldest water, in search of the maggots which they will never allow to become insects. If we wander further, and enter or coast any of the deer-parks of the district, we shall see the robin perched on some point of the paling, letting the passing air ruffle the scarlet feathers of his breast; and if we look up into the belt of trees, our eyes are met by that somewhat pathetic sight, the deserted nests among the leafless boughs. To the boy, this may be a gay sight, promising the sport of speckled eggs hereafter, and furtive climbing, and all the delights of birdnesting; but to older persons, it is a mournful sight, reminding us of the hushed songs of the vanishing year. The wood-pigeons may, however, be heard on calm days at this season; and also a much more remarkable sound,—the cry of the stag wooing the hind, amidst the thick-fallen leaves in the depths of the wood.

If one mount higher, even to the ridges, while the calm Martinmas weather permits, we may come upon something as interesting as anything the district can disclose,—an assignation of Science with Nature. In the wildest scenes of Nature, Science here finds a quiet field. A rain-gauge is seen on the most desolate spot of the least known ridge, carefully secured against the force of the gales. I know of five such; and I have seen the aged shepherd who has them in charge, proceeding on his monthly round of visitation. As I watched the tall old man with his staff, passing out of sight on the vast mountain slope, I thought that knowledge and wisdom were as appropriate and beautiful here in the wilderness as anywhere else on earth. These solitudes are no scene for the busy handiwork of man, in their toil for bread and convenience; but neither are they a tomb "where no knowledge or device is found."[46] Alas! these words, sounding in one's mind at the very farthest point of a mountain ramble, carry one's imagination back to the dreary graveyard below, and the sick who are lying all round about it. There was little comfort to be had by hovering about there, and asking how all went on. The mere sight of John Newton's house almost decided his fate, to my expectation, so foul was the stable-yard at the corner of his dwelling, and so did the causes of unhealthiness abound in all its surroundings. Yet it startled me when the surgeon told me that he thought he could not get through: "I will not say that he cannot live," he declared, "but I own I have no expectation of it." It was even so. Clear as his mind was throughout, quiet and tractable as he was in illness, so as to beguile his wife and friends with hopes to the very last, he was cut off in his vigour, arrested in the midst of many schemes, removed from his tribe of nine children, whom he left destitute, and taken from us just when he had become the most important man in the place, to the general health and improvement. It was a heavy blow to many; and the harder to bear, because there was no natural call to him to die thus early. But for such gross violations of the laws of nature as we are guilty of here, and in most places where men congregate, he would have been living now, and a great misfortune would have been saved to us all. The day of his funeral was most dreary. I went, though the rain was coming down like a waterfall. The procession was long; for the club of Odd Fellows, to which he belonged, all attended, according to custom. I did not like the spirit-drinking on assembling, nor the levity of manner of some of the members,—encouraged, perhaps, by the obligation to attend frequent funerals, as the brethren die off; but it was some comfort to know that by the rules of the Society, the widow and children would not be allowed to come to actual want. I saw the coffin lowered into the putrid hold dug for it, and watched the last of the train away, before I left the sodden churchyard, where he and I had agreed that it was murder to survivors, and a disrespect to the dead, to deposit more corpses. There I left him, with the wintry downpour splashing upon his grave. Since that, my other agent and comrade in sanitary matters, T. C., has sunk; and I hardly know where to turn next. But such bereavements must quicken our zeal.

DECEMBER

"THE LAKES in winter!" exclaim our southern relations and friends, with a shrug or shudder which conveys compassion, and a sort of contempt. They do not understand us when we say that the winter is the season that we best love. We should not perhaps say that the month of December is our favourite month; and we admit that the quietude of our valley in winter has as much to do with our pleasure as the beauty: but, take everything together, it is the dearest time of year to us. As for me, I stand up for the beauty of the season here, in comparison with the midland counties. My early walk is now charming. It is a bright thought to me when, waking in the morning, I know what o'clock it is before striking the lucifer match by my bedside. It is six, or a few minutes after. Sometimes, I will not let myself look what the weather is till I am dressed, and must decide how much to wrap up. If it is gusty and rainy, it tells its own story upon the window-panes. It all is still, I draw back the window-curtains in a sort of suspense,—generally, however, having some notion of the state of the weather from the feel of my cold bath. If the stars are bright, one's heart dances. Perhaps there is a fragment of moon hanging over Wansfell,—the last gibbous symbol of the month: and if so, I cross the meadow to have the golden spectacle before me from the other side of the valley. As I cross the little bridge, I cannot but stand a minute to see how the morning star looks in the water below,—whether still as a duplicate planet, or shivered into silvery fragments by ripple or gush, according as there has lately been rain or drought. Sometimes I almost think I like the stormy mornings as well. To struggle on against wind and splashing rain, in a thoroughly waterproof dress, is really pleasurable when it happens in the morning, when one has no fear of being benighted, when one is unfatigued, and is going home to breakfast by a bright fireside. How cheerful looks the breakfast-table by firelight, the daylight strengthening every minute, and one's whole frame in a glow from exercise, and one's mind all awake for the work of the day! The third case in regard to weather—that in which there is neither star nor storm, but still cloudiness—has its own interest. In such weather, all is clear below the cloud-canopy, which seems indeed shut down like a firmament. There is no mist upon the meadows, nor wet in the roads; and if it were light enough to see the mountains, they would be seen with a clear outline. The smoke from the nearest chimney goes straight up. The dead leaf on the spray, suspended by a single dry fibre, hangs as still as if it were in a vacuum. But if there is no motion, there are more sounds than usual,—every one being reverberated as in a vault. The rooks, flying from their nests to feed in the meadows, make a prodigious noise. The robin in the path seems desperately in earnest, from the loudness of his twitter; and so does the far-off cock, crowing to rouse his little world. Most wonderful then is the church clock, or the passing bell, the solemn tone, so seldom heard thus far, coming clear and full through the still air. Such weather is the time for extending one's walk to the heaths, which may soon become too boggy for winter walking. The furze still scatters its golden blossoms over the most dreary spots; the plover whistles in the dry places, and in the marshy ones the snipe may be seen balancing itself upon a bulrush. Every village has its sportsman; and here one may be sure of meeting one's armed neighbours, as eager now for snipe as they were, and will be again, for trout in June. In passing the copse, on my way home, I may catch a note, here and there, somewhat sad, of the thrush. In more open countries, the larks may now be heard, not singing, but in confabulation: but we have no larks. Those who have the privilege of living in valleys with rock boundaries, fit to contain eyries, must be content to forego something that is enjoyed in less beautiful places; and what we have to forego is the presence and song of the lark, and of some other small singing birds. What we have instead is the spectacle, seen from a mountain-peak, of the dun hawk, sailing or wheeling a little way below, about to swoop, perhaps, upon the chickens in one's own fowl-yard. A few miles away, where the ridges subside into open plains, the larks live in the furrows, as in the south; but in proportion as we approach the great rocky centre of the district, with its deep ravines and small alluvial basins, the smaller birds give place to the hawk, the buzzard, and the raven; and, within this century, the eagle.

The romance of the ancient eyries has passed away. The shepherds are no longer driven desperate by the loss of their lambs, so as to risk life and limb in scaling the crags, as they used to do in Borrowdale and Eskdale. No heroic dalesman now stands out from among his fellows, in the yearly enterprise of robbing the eyrie, as long as the old birds cannot be reached. Such a hero was a great man in his day; and all the people of the dale would come to hear his story of what the eyry was like; and what a strewing of bones (bones of lambs and fowls) he found there; and how fierce were the young, so that he had to kill them, instead of bringing them down alive for a show, as he had intended. If he made the attack somewhat earlier, so as to bring away the eggs, he had, from every neighbouring shepherd, five shillings for every egg: a price which, considering the value of money in those days, proves how mischievous a foe was the eagle. No more than two eggs, however, were found at one time. Nobody undertakes positively to declare that no one pair of eagles is left in the district, but I imagine such is the fact. Mr. Wordsworth's last view of one was prior to 1813. There are rumours every year on one having been seen here or there; but the romance of that kind of warfare is as completely over as that of the Border wars. Another romance is dissolving form year to year, and will soon be heard of only as matter of history, like the buried villages in Morecambe Bay:—the passage of that same bay by the sands. The two brisk rivers, the Ken and the Lune, carry down soil, with which they meet the seatide in the estuaries, so that the area between Lancaster and Farness is in course of being filled up; and a wide space is left by the retiring tide, across which travellers take their way, to save space and time. They are finding, however, that the railway saves their time, without exposing them to the dangers belonging to the Oversands Road, as it is called. But the country-people cling to old ways; and there are enough who still go by the sands to turn our attention that way when the strong southwest winds of December blow up the Channel, and drive the sea into the Bay. I believe there is still a coach which goes over seven miles of the sands at the safest hour:—an hour, of course, varying daily. But the way to enjoy the transit most is by going with the guide, whose experience is greater than anybody's, and who can tell, by the way, all the traditions of the place. He can show the spot where the remains of a buried village were seen at the beginning of the last century; and others where it is conjectured that several villages stood which are named in Domesday Book, but of which no vestige remains. As the guide leads the way on a clear day, winding among shifting sands and changing channels, showing how safe all is made by the poles which are erected here, and the furze bushes stuck in there, it is all very pleasant, amidst the freshness of the sea-breeze, and the spectacle of the lights and shadows on the screen of mountains round. The sense of insecurity no doubt heightens the charm. But very different is it when the wind changes suddenly to the southwest, hastening in the tide,—even heaping up the waters below; or when a firm bank is discovered to have become a quicksand; or when the poles have disappeared; or, worst of all, when a fog comes on. Then it occurs to the traveller what dead are about him, and, perhaps, under his feet. He remembers the story told by Gray, the poet, in his letters from his lake tour:[47]—how an old fisherman in his cart, with two grown-up daughters, and the old wife on a horse, set off to cross the sands, which they knew as well as any of us know our own neighbourhood: how a fog came on, and the water rose under their horses' feet: how the old man would go a little way to see, and did not come back: how the wife would not be persuaded to leave the spot, but wandered about bewildered: how, when at last they turned back, and trusted to their horses, it was too late, and the old woman was washed away, and the girls saved only by the horse actually swimming with the cart, in the strong instinct of self-preservation: and how the poor daughters were found, quite wild, clinging to the cart, unable to tell their story for days afterwards: and how the ebb-tide told the story by leaving on the sands the bodies of the old people. There are others to be remembered, too;—the three men who sank at one moment, in a soft part of the sands, where they had always found good footing before; and the traveller who went down erect upon his horse, and who is buried somewhat like the Indian chief in his mound on the Missouri;—only that the one is under the margin of the sea, and the other above the brink of the great river. It was only the other day that a countryman had a narrow escape, sinking up to the neck in a quicksand just before dusk. As it happened, somebody saw his head, and saved him. Within an hour, the head would not have been remarked in the closing twilight. The guide used to be paid £10 a-year by the Prior of Cartmel: a large sum in ancient times, and much increased by presents from pilgrims. The office was virtually hereditary, and, I believe, is so still. The payment has long been increased to £20 per annum, and it is now paid out of the Queen's revenues, she being Duchess of Lancaster. In another generation the office will probably become a sinecure. Meantime, when we have a strong southwest wind blowing up from the Furness Fells, we think of the sands, and hope that no one may be crossing them.

There is as much romance as ever hanging about our slate-quarries. Here and there on the mountain sides, in every direction, are the black holes where harbour some of the liveliest interests of the region. Below these holes, and on each side, are the heaps and dangerous slopes of *débris*, which show the extent of the quarrying done within. The quantity required is immense. Not only are the floors of the kitchens and cellars throughout the region laid with purple slate, but the whole ground-floor of all dwellings but those of the gentry; and the greenish slate which comes from Tilburthwaite is wanted universally for roofing; and large quantities are sent to a distance. The work goes on, summer and winter; and, fearful as some of it is in all seasons, in winter it is perhaps as perilous as any but seafaring employment. It almost takes one's breath away to look up, on the calmest summer day, at the dark, stupendous, almost perpendicular Honister Crag, where the clouds come to rest, and to see the quarrymen at work among the slate, looking like summer spiders, hanging quivering from the eaves of a house. In winter, what can they do among such blasts as come rushing among the peaks? They are liable to be puffed away as the spiders would be if you took the bellows to them. This last winter a man was blown like a straw, from the heights down to the rocks of the stream in the vale below. In some places where the slate is closely compacted, and presents endways a perpendicular surface, the quarryman sets about his work as if he were going after eagle's eggs. His comrades let him down by a rope from the precipice, and he tries for a footing on some ledge, where he may drive in wedges. The difficulty of this, where much of his strength must be employed in keeping his footing, may be conceived; and a great length of time must be occupied in loosening masses large enough to bear the fall without being dashed into useless pieces. In many places, however, the methods are improved; and the quarries are made accessible by roads admitting of the passage of strong carts. Still, the detaching of the slate, and the loading and conducting the carts, are laborious work enough to require and train a very athletic order of men; and there they are now, in hourly risk of December storms, which almost blow the breath out of their bodies on the steeps, while sending down formidable slides of *débris* into the vales below. It is because the best slate is found near the top, that these dangers are incurred; and the consequence is that we have among us a set of men capable of feats of strength, and an endurance of toil now rarely heard of elsewhere. The most stalwart knight who ever came hither of old, with his full armour and battle-axe, to fight against the Scot, never carried a heavier weight, or did more wonders in a day, than these fine fellows. When two or three of them emigrated a year or two since, among a crowd of passengers from the manufacturing districts, the difference between the two sorts of training showed itself on their coming in sight of the mountain peaks of New Zealand. Not only did the low-country women, but their husbands from the towns and the plain, shed tears at the sight of what looked so terrific to them; they wept and wailed that they had ever been induced to come to places so wild. At the same time, the Westmoreland men were all spirit and joy,—refreshed by the sight of mountain crags after months of flat ocean, and not fearing about getting a living, if once in a mineral region. In this region, some of them live in slate-built hovels, many hundred feet aloft; while others ascend and descend many times between morning and night. Formerly the slate was carried down on hurdles, on men's backs; and the practice is still continued in some remote quarries, where the expense of conveyance by carts would be too great, or the roads do not admit of it. Thirty-two years ago, a man named Joseph Clark, made seventeen journeys, including seventeen miles of climbing and sharp descent, in one day, bringing down 10,880 pounds of slate. In ascending, he carried the hurdle weighing 80 pounds, and in descending, he brought each time 640 pounds of slate. At another time, he carried in three successive journeys, 1280 pounds each time. His greatest day's work was bringing 11,776 pounds. He lived three miles from his place of work, too. His toils did not appear to injure him; and he declared that he suffered only from thirst. It was believed in his day, that there was scarcely another man in the kingdom capable of sustaining such labour for a course of years. It appears, however, that the region has always been celebrated for cases of longevity and of bodily strength. When Kentmere Hall was built, Hugh Hird, a Trout-beck man, lifted a beam which ten of the workmen could not move; and when sent by Lord Dacre on a message to the King (I forget which king), he ate up a whole sheep for his dinner, in the presence of the royal household. They had let him order his own refreshment, and this was what he ordered, under the name of "the sunny side of a wether."[48] He probably thought that if he did the work of ten men, he deserved the food of the same number.

Early in last December the weather changed. A black frost set in which lasted till New Year's Day. I remember one year when we could gather twenty-eight kinds of flowers in one garden on Christmas Day. I had rather have this frost than such unseasonable weather; but it was very severe. Our bulbs,—hyacinths, tulips, and crocuses, were all duly potted before it came on; and were standing their allotted six weeks at the bottom of a dark closet, receiving a sprinkle of water once a fortnight. All was done to secure our February show of flowers, and it was well; for the frost left us none without. One grievous thing it did,—it cut short the life of our neighbour, Hartley Coleridge.[49] I have mentioned where he lived,—in a lodging on Rydal Lake. He was frail, as all who saw him well knew; frail in resolution, and subject to the mischiefs which befall those who cannot take care of themselves. One night during this frost he was fatally chilled, when he ought to have been warm at home; and when once in bed, he never rose again. Everybody was kind. All who knew him loved him. I knew him little; but there was something profoundly affecting in his fate.—I went one day to see the skating on Rydal Lake. Nothing could be gayer than the scene. The orange sunset sent a glow over the ice. Brightly-dressed ladies walked on the margin. Young ladies were taking rides in chairs, impelled from behind by their skating brothers. The mountain sides echoed back the shouts of fun and pleasure with a metallic sound, which told of the sharpness of the air, as much as the exhilaration of the shouters. I could not bear it. I was standing on the grassy slope before Hartley Coleridge's cottage. The blinds were down, and all looked blank there; and I had been told that he could not live. There was something less painful in his funeral. I set out for Grasmere churchyard, four miles off, in driving sleet and bitter cold; but before I descended upon the vale of Grasmere, all was clear and bright. I took my station by the churchyard wall, at the base of which the Rotha was rushing, full, clear, and green. The sun cast a gleam upon the lake—a gleam which penetrated the dark shadows from the impending heights. It might be said to cast gleams also among the graves, so green were the sides next the sun. All was solemnly closed in by old Helvellyn, ghostly in its new-fallen snow. The small, light coffin, like that of a child in appearance and obvious weight, was followed by some who seemed truly in there places there;—Derwent Coleridge,[50] with his benevolent countenance, so welcome, no doubt, beside the death-bed; and the sorely-grieved landlady, in her deepest mourning, weeping as if she had lost a son; and Wordsworth, who had also done his duty to the departed—the duty of admonition while it could avail, and of tenderness when it was needed. How old he looked that day. It was impossible to look on him, and not dread the approach of the time when he, the crowning honour and grace of our mountain abode, must be given up by us, and probably laid under this very grass.

This was a somewhat mournful close of the year at Ambleside. But, wherever men live, there is always variety of moods enough to secure every observance having its due. Christmas was kept as usual. Every window and every apartment shone with holly, and every table steamed with good cheer; and singing and dancing broke into the nights. And when the last day of the year came, the housewives were as superstitious as ever about letting nothing be thrown away. The very dishwater stood till the next day, lest the good luck of the new year should be thrown away with it. Truly, to live in Ambleside, is like going into retreat in a former century.

CHAPTER THREE

FROLICS WITH THE HUTCHINSONS[51]

THE HUTCHINSONS have appeared in the *Journal* before.[52] We all remember the singing group, and the Memoir which Mrs. Howitt gave us.[53] It is pleasant to me now to connect them with our lake scenery—to think that our valleys have resounded with their harmonies. Mrs. Howitt wrote to me that the Hutchinsons were coming to Kendal; and I forthwith settled in my own mind that they must sing to us at Ambleside. Everybody about me wished to hear them; and they wished to come, so the whole affair arranged itself easily enough. The large room at the White Lion[54] was engaged, and filled with benches, so as to hold the greatest possible number—200. As the time drew near, however, I met a shake of the head whichever way I turned. Everybody was sure that many more than 200 people would want admission. People were coming from Bowness, Grasmere, Hawkshead, and even Kendal; and if they should be turned

Fig. 7. The Hutchinson Family, circa 1846 (a sketch by Margaret Gillies, from the *People's Journal*)

back from the door, how could they be expected to bear it patiently? And then the heat was excessive. Everybody was afraid of it. But what could be done? Here was the largest room that could be had; and the Hutchinsons could not stay to give a second concert. Such was the state of things—the tickets almost all sold—everybody wanting to go, and everybody dreading the heat when the Hutchinsons were to arrive—on Tuesday evening, June 16th. I had advised their coming by Newby Bridge from Lancaster, so as to finish their day's journey from Liverpool by the Windermere steamer. A trip by steamer from end to end of Windermere is the prettiest finish of a summer day's journey that can be imagined.

It was as lovely an evening as any during this glorious June of 1846. As I stood on the shore at Waterhead, waiting for the steamer, I endeavoured to look upon the landscape with the eyes of a stranger, and thought that if I were then seeing it for the first time, it would appear to me the true paradise of this world. The soft ruddy evening light on Wansfell, the purple hollows of Loughrigg, the deep shadows on the western side of the lake, pierced by lines of silver light—the white gables of the houses at Clappersgate, peeping from the woods which skirt Loughrigg—and the little grey church on its knoll in the centre of the Brathay valley—these made up such a vision of delicious colouring that I imagined my friends on the deck of the steamer saying that never, in any lustorus evening of a New England autumn, had they enjoyed a richer feast to eye and mind. Then came the steamer, rounding the point from Low-wood. There seemed to be but few passengers on deck—no sign of any band of brothers, with a sister in the midst. They were not there; and I had only to hasten home, lest they should arrive some other way. Before I had been at home many minutes, I saw from my terrace a barouche coming rapidly along the winding road, with one bonnet and several grey caps in it; it entered my gate, drove up to the porch; and I found myself among hearty American friends once more.

The first business to be done was to go down to the White Lion, and see the room. When there, we could only agree, like other people, that the room could hold only 200 and that it would be dreadfully hot. Then the brothers and sister stepped on the platform, and tried the fitness of the place for music. What those few notes were to others I know not. I saw afterwards that a number of people had on the instant gathered in the street; and a little friend of mine observed that he had now heard music that he thought beautiful. As for me, long years of solitary sickness had passed since I last heard harmony, or anything that I could call music, except one song in my sick room from Adelaide Kemble:[55] and this was almost too much for me now, in full health. It thrilled through me, as if I were a harp, played on by the wind. It seems to me that I never before heard such harmony, such perfect accord, as between those four voices. I believe the echo never sleeps in the ear of those who have once heard it.

The next day, Wednesday, was reserved for a glorious country holiday; and it turned out a day of pleasuring without alloy. Rare as is the event of a pleasure day without alloy, for once it was so. A party of seventeen persons, aged somewhere between seventy-six and twelve years, met on the shore of Grasmere—about three miles from my house. We had three boats, and in them—rowed by ladies, children, young men or servants, as the fit took us—we crossed to a shady, shingly spot, before the greatest heat of the day came on. There on the shingle, some lay down, and talked, or played duck and drake, while others dabbled in the cool ripple, or dipped their heads, and let the water stream from their locks. Abby Hutchinson, the youngest of her parents' sixteen children, and therefore called "the baby," dropped asleep for a few minutes, with her head upon a stone—her sweet face looking as calm and innocent as any baby's. Other young ladies pushed off in a boat, to practise rowing, and came back relived of the toil by a spirited little fellow of twelve who wielded their oars manfully. Then off went one or another of the Hutchinsons, rowing away suddenly, as if for his life, and coming back no less vehemently. It was a gay little party, on the margin of a clear lake at the bottom of a basin of mountains—mountains all green to the summit—dappled with woods and slopes, gay sunshine and deep shade. In the midst of the lake was its one island, green and bare, except on the side where a pine-grove casts its shadow on the waters. On the opposite margin was the village of Grasmere, with its old church—its low and square tower showing itself from among the trees. Immediately behind it arose Helm Crag, the most beautiful summit in all the neighbourhood for form, light, and shadow. To the left branched off the mountains, now grey and purple, which encompass Easedale. To the right ascended, winding round the skirts of Helvellyn, the road to Keswick. Scattered nearer at hand, among the nooks and on the slopes of the hills around the lake, were dwellings whose aspect might tempt wandering spirits of earth or air to stay and rest amidst Nature's peace. In this scene was our morning passed.

Then came the merry dining; the spreading of the table-cloths on the grass; the finding rocky seats to eat on conveniently; and the grouping (as if they could not help it) of the Hutchinsons to sing, their breath of song stirring up the quietest spirits of the party, like a breeze breaking the glassy calm of the lake; and then the lazy rest after dinner; broken by the arrival of a fourth brother of the Hutchinsons', bringing letters and newspapers from Liverpool, by the last packet. When each on his separate stone had read his letters and dispensed his public news, all who were ready for enterprise, and not afraid of the heat, began to climb in the direction of High Close. What a scramble was the first part! Tempted by the shade of a wall, we went straight up the face of the hill, where the grass was as glossy and slippery with the dry weather as so much satin, and for almost every step forward, we slipt one back. After a few laughs, some sensations of despair, many slides, and universal vows to return another way, we all reached the road, half-way up the ascent, and from thence all was easy. Cool airs soon came to us over the ridge before us: we got some water at a farm-house, and then attained our object. We stood in a field whence we commanded the finest view in Westmoreland. Far to the left streched away Windermere among the lessening hills. Nearer to us lay Loughrigg-tarn, a round little lake, on higher ground, though beneath us. There it lay, blue and clear, under the dark slopes of Loughrigg. Immediately below us spread Elter Water—looking like a group of ponds amidst greean meadows. To the right stretched Langdale, the winding, narrow valley which is overhung at the further end by the glorious Langdale Pikes; our landmarks amidst the billowy hill region in which we live. Last of all, arose Bowfell,—the mountain mass which closes in the whole. Such is the mere outline of the scene which, sprinkled over with dwellings of every kind, from the great castle on a promontory of Windermere, to the grey hut on the mountain side—with farmsteads, hamlets, mills, cottages—a chapel here, a bridge there, a sheep-fold below—such is the scene which is rightly called the finest view in Westmoreland. The Hutchinsons will never forget it. They noted down the names in their tablets, and the features of the scene in their minds. In the midst of it all, however, sweet Abby, looking herself as fresh as a daisy, had in her hand a basin of clear cold water for the benefit of the thirsty.

After returning to the boats, the next thing was to row across to Grasmere, as we were to go a mile beyond the village, to a friend's house in Easedale, to tea. That was an evening to be remembered. Our venerable hostess sat, in her beauty, under a shady tree, happy among her happy guests. The tea-tables in the shade looked cool and tempting. We were in a garden, in front of a white cottage—an elegant, rambling cottage, all covered with roses, whose porch was almost one mass of blossom and spray. The sun let us alone under our trees, while it shone every where else, making the wild and sometimes dreary Easedale, one scene of light and greenness. Soon, the Hutchinsons grouped themselves, as if by some irresistible attraction, and sang piece after piece, to the rapture of their hearers. Those who have heard them sing *The Cot where we were Born*, the *Ohio Boatmen*, and the *Excelsior*, may conceive something of our delight. And,—of all things to be doing—they were next teaching us to play *Fox and Geese* on the green below. They themselves played with great humour; and in the midst of our fun, I saw that all the servants of the house were looking on from a corner of the terrace, and not a few labourers from outside the gate. It was dim twilight when we arrived at home, after our merry drive of five miles; but Asa Hutchinson was not so tired—nor Abby neither, but that they would help me to water my parched dahlias and young fruit-trees. They worked with me at the pump, and in carrying water; and I shall think of them as my dahlias bloom and my fruit-trees grow. Next moring at breakfast, too, the farmer-spirit awoke in Asa as he saw the mower enter my field. He sprang up, wishing he "could get a chance to mow a bit:"—a wish easily gratified. My own little scythe was brought out; and he and his brothers—and again Abby—trimmed the grass round my young pear-trees. They reminded me that they were farmers, as if to account for the prank, in which however they had my entire sympathy.

This was the day of the concert. The evening before, a neighbouring gentleman had kindly and beneficently offered that his lawn should be the scene.[56] His servants should move the benches, put up the platform, attend at the gates, and save all trouble. In the morning, the hot weather melted away all doubts. It seemed clear that all parties—those who could not be consulted and those who could—would be best pleased to be sent to a shady spot in the open air, where any number of people might hear without any crowding. The Hutchinsons themselves begged that all the townspeople who liked might hear them, those who could not pay, as well as those who could. That concert will never be forgotten by any who were so happy as to be present. The Hutchinsons enjoyed it more than any they have given in this country. Abby left her bonnet in a rhododendron bush out of sight; and the family group came up a green slope from a thicket below. The little platform was erected under the deep shade of spreading sycamores. In front and on either hand were collected a larger audience than any house in Ambleside could have contained; and among them were some who could not have enjoyed the pleasure elsewhere; an invalid lady, who lay on the grass; and an infirm old gentleman, whose chair was wheeled into the circle. There was row behind row of the tradespeople, servants and labourers of the neighbourhood; and in the centre, behind all, the parish clerk—zealous in the psalmody and all the other good objects of the place, and most active in promoting our concert. He deserved the enjoyment which I am sure he had.

And now, when I am most anxious to convey some impression of this festival, I am least able to do so. How is it possible to give an idea of the soul-breathing music of the Hutchinsons to those who have not heard it? One might as well attempt to convey in words the colours of the sky or the strain of the nightingale as such utterance of the heart as theirs. One can only observe the effects. There was now hearty laughter, and now many tears. Nothing can be said of the interior emotions which found no expression. Everybody congratulated everybody else on having come. A young servant of mine, who went all in high spirits at the prospect of an evening's pleasure, cried the whole time—as did others. At the end, when every heart was beating in response to the brotherly greeting and farewell offered in the closing piece—*The Granite State*—the parish clerk sprang up and called for three cheers for the Hutchinsons, which were given by as many as had unchoked voices. I think no one could have come away without a strong impression, consciously or unconsciously entertained, of the good and beauty of a free nurture and exercise of our human powers. There must be many among us with powers, of one sort or another, equal to those of the Hutchinsons. If we could be wise, and take courage to follow the lead of our natures, it cannot be but that many of us might be as free, as simple, as happy, as beneficient as they—as able as they to speak to hearts, and to awaken souls.

As for me—I crossed the road to my own gate in a mood which the Hutchinsons described to me as theirs when I entered the room where we met for the last time:—"We are happy and sad," said they. I was happy and sad; and, I dare say, so was everybody who was at that moment returning home from that green spot under the trees. The most moving thing however was yet to come. When they had dressed themselves for a night stage to Patterdale, and had supped, and said farewell, and seated themselves in the carriage, they stopped the horses on my terrace for yet another minute, and sent forth a sweet and most mournful chorus of farewell to me, in notes swelling and dying away in the still night air. I was "happy and sad" as I turned in to my solitary lamp. I could not let the glass-door be closed, late as it was; but again and again I went out on the terrace to look for more stars to light my friends' way over the mountain pass, and to watch the summer lightning—not without some impression that their sweet strain of farewell was still floating over the valley. To me it can never die away into silence.

The Knoll, Ambleside, June 20th, 1846

Postscript. Mr. Hartley Coleridge was present at the concert; and the effect on him of Abby Hutchinson's singing of the *May Queen*[57] may be judged of by the following sonnet, which he permits me to append to this paper.

TO ALFRED TENNYSON.

I would, my friend, indeed, thou hadst been here,
Last night, beneath the shadowy sycamore
To hear the lines to me well-known before
Embalmed in music, so translucent, clear,
Each word of thine came singly to the ear,
Yet all was blended in a flowing stream.
It had the rich repose of summer dream,

The light distinct of frosty atmosphere.
Still have I loved thy lines, yet never knew
How sweet they were—till woman's voice invested
The pencill'd outline with the living hue,
And every note of feeling proved and tested.
    What might old Pindar be—if once again
The harp and voice were trembling with his strain!

CHAPTER FOUR

OUR FARM OF TWO ACRES[58]

TERRAIN AND TILLAGE

HALF A CENTURY ago there was a good deal of sauciness in the temper and manners of people who had the management of land. The great landowners were introducing improvements; the small farmers were giving up an unprofitable game; and the large farmers—trusting in the Corn-laws—claimed to have their own way, did not care to study their art, unless they lived near Mr. Coke or the Duke of Bedford, and laughed at everybody who attempted tillage on a small scale.

This sauciness brought out William Cobbett,[59] with his strong spirit of antagonism, to contradict every insolent saying, and almost every received maxim of the class; and he broadly and positively declared that a cow and pig could be kept on a quarter of an acre of land. He explained in detail how this might be done; and a great number of

Fig. 8. The Knoll, Ambleside, with cows in foreground, circa 1856 (from Martineau's *Autobiography*)

people have followed his instructions, finding, for the most part, that though the thing might be practicable for one year, or occasionally at intervals, it is not true that, one year with another, a cow and pig can be kept on a quarter of an acre of land. Since the repeal of the Corn-laws great changes have taken place in the general mind as to what quantity of land will and will not repay the efforts of the husbandman. The prodigious improvements which have been introduced into agriculture have benefited small properties as well as large; and the same science and art which render it good economy to expend thousands of pounds on the tillage of a large farm enable the intelligent husbandman to obtain from a few roods[60] an amount of value which nobody but Cobbett dreamed of in the last generation. We do not know that the regular "small-farming" of a former century has as yet revived among us; the competition of the holder of thirty or fifty acres with the tenant of a thousand: but the experiment of making the most of two or three acres is at present one which attracts a good deal of attention. There are few signs of the times in economy and social affairs more thoroughly worthy of the interest it has excited.

There are two classes of persons, broadly speaking, to whom this experiment is of consequence—the husbandman who lives by his land, and gentry, especially ladies, who happen to have a little ground attached to their dwellings, from which it is just as well to derive comfort and luxury, or pecuniary profit, as not. Two remarkable and very interesting statements have been published on the part of these two classes; and I, the present writer, am about to offer a third, in order to render the presentment of the case of miniature farming complete.

John Sillett,[61] the Suffolk shopkeeper, who forsook the shop and took to the spade, recovering his health, and maintaining his family in comfort on two acres of land, has given us his experience in his well-known pamphlet of seven years ago, on "Fork and Spade Husbandry." The great extension of Freehold Land Societies[62] affords to a multitude of townsmen in England the means of leaving town-industry for rural independence, as John Sillett did, if they choose to work as he did; and it seems probable that a future generation may see a revival of the order of peasant proprietors in this country which was supposed to have died out for ever. As to the other class to whom small-farming may and does answer, we have just been presented with an agreeable description of their case in the little volume called "Our Farm of Four Acres, and the Money we made by it." In my opinion the book is somewhat too tempting. The statement, each one no doubt perfectly true in itself, will require some modification when taken to represent the first six years, instead of the first six months of the experiment; but the narrative is so fresh and animated—the example of enterprise and energy is so wholesome, and the scheme of life is so wise, that the book must be a real boon to a class of society which sorely needs such aid;—the class of gentlewomen who have not enough to do. We hear a great deal of the penalties of an unnatural mode of life endured by single and widowed women in confined circumstances, who pine away their lives in towns; and we see many who do not suffer from poverty, losing health and energy for want of interesting occupation. If that book should induce only one in a hundred of these languid women to try a country life, with the amusement of a little farming in a safe way, it will have been a blessing to our generation.

John Sillett's experiment was one of fork and spade husbandry exclusively. That of the ladies on their Four Acres was an experiment of grazing, almost exclusively.[63]

Mine is one of an intermediate order. I do not derive the subsistence of a household from my two acres; nor do I keep cows and pigs on the easy conditions of a plentiful allowance of grass and arable land, with the resource of a Right of Common, to serve at every pinch. I am obliged to keep a considerable portion of my little plot in grass; but my main dependence for the subsistence of my cows is on fork and spade husbandry. Thus, like the ladies, I keep cows for comfort and luxury, to which I may add the serious consideration of creating a subsistence for a labourer and his wife; while, with John Sillett, I obtain the value of the ground and animals chiefly by tillage, instead of merely gathering in the expensive commodity of grass. The case is this:—

I bought a field, in order to build myself a house, in a beautiful valley in the north of England. The quantity of land was somewhat less than two acres and a quarter, of which more than half an acre was rock. On the rocky portion stands the house, with its terrace and the drive up to it, and little oak and sycamore and ash copses behind and flanking it. An acre and a quarter was left in grass, which I at first let for grazing for £4 10*s*. a year. Enough ground was left for a few vegetable and flower beds, which the women of the household took such care of as they could. At the end of a year from our entrance upon our pretty house in the field, the state of things was this. The meadow was a constant eyesore; for the tenant took no sort of care of it. His cow was there, rain or shine, without shelter or shade, and usually ill, one way or another. The grass was lumpy and weedy. Sheep burst in through the hedge on the south boundary, that hedge being no business of mine, but belonging to the tenant on the other side. It was a broad, straggling, weedy hedge, which harboured vermin, and sent showers of seeds of pestilent weeds into my garden ground; and as sure as my cabbages began to grow, the hungry sheep—sharpset as they are in March—made their way in, and ate off a whole crop in a night. It cost me from 6*l.* to 10*l.* a year to hire an occasional gardener, by whom the aspect of the place was barely kept decent.

At the same time, my household were badly off for some essential comforts. The supply of milk in our neighbourhood could never be depended on; and it failed when it was most wanted—in the travelling season when the district was thronged with strangers. During that season, even the supply of meat was precarious. Fowls, hams, eggs, butter, everything was precarious or unattainable; so that housekeeping was, in the guest season, a real anxiety.

Becoming nearly desperate under difficulties which townsfolk scarcely dreamt of, I ventured upon the experiment—more bold twelve years ago than now—of using my own patch of land for the production of comforts for my own household. I have made this explanation because I wish it to be clearly understood that I did not propose to *make money* by my miniature farming, and should never have undertaken it with any such view. I could not afford to lose money. The experiment must pay itself or stop. But, here was the land, with its attendant expenses; here were our needs and discomforts; the experiment was to make the one compensate the other. At the end of twelve years, I find that the plan has been unquestionably successful, though some of the estimates of the first two or three seasons have been modified, and an average of agricultural mishaps has occurred, as if to render the enterprise a fair specimen. It has, on the whole, been sufficiently successful to attract a great deal of notice, and influence some proceedings in the neighbourhood; and, therefore, as I conceive, to justify my adding one more illustration to those which already exist of the benefit of making the most of a small area of land.

The first essential was a labourer. I obtained one from an agricultural county, as spade husbandry was a thing unheard-of in my own neighbourhood. He brought his wife; and his wages were at first 12*s*. a week, out of which he paid the low rent of 1*s*. 6*d*. per week for his cottage; a model cottage which I built, with the cow-house adjoining, for 130*l*. These stone dwellings last for ever, and need few or no repairs, so that money is well invested in them; and I regard as a good investment the money afterwards laid out in a hay-house, a little boiling-house, a root-house, two fowl yards, and a commodious stone dwelling for the pig. My man's wages were raised by degrees; and they are now 14*s*. a week all the year round, with the cottage rent free. The wife has the use of my wash-house and its apparatus, and opportunities of earning a good deal by means of them. In case of my scheme not answering, there was a certainty that the cottage and other buildings would let at any moment, with the land; while their quality would not deteriorate with time, like that of brick or wooden buildings.

The other requisite preparations were tanks for manure, implements, and some additional fencing. Two tanks, well cemented within, and covered by heavy stone lids, receive the sewage and slops of every kind from the house, cottage, and cow stable; and a larger tank, among a clump of trees in a far corner of the field, receives the sweepings of stable and stye, and the bulk of the manure. The implements are spades, an elastic steel fork, hoes, rakes, a scythe, shears, and clippers, a heavy roller for the meadow, a chaff-cutter, a curry-comb and brushes for the cows' coats; troughs, milk-pails, and the apparatus of the boiling-house and dairy; to which were afterwards added a barrel on wheels to receive soap-suds and other slops at back doors for the liquid manure pit; a garden-engine of large powers, and a frame and hand-glasses for the kitchen-garden. About a third of these implements were necessary for the mere gardening which we attempted so unprofitably before we had a labourer on the premises.

I am not going to speak of our dairy affairs now; I will do so hereafter; but my present subject is the tillage of the soil: and I will therefore say no more here about cows than that we began with one, and finding that we could keep two for almost as little trouble as one—the stable and the man being provided—I rented another half acre adjoining my field, at 1*l*. 15*s*. a-year, and kept two cows, thus securing a supply of milk for the whole year. We produce food enough for about a cow and a half, besides vegetables and fruit for the household, and find it answer to buy the requisite addition to the winter food, as I will explain at another time.

Here, then, we were at the outset, with simply our cow-stable, pig-house, and tanks, and an acre and a quarter of ground on which to work, to produce food for a cow and pig, besides household vegetables; fettered also with the necessity, that, on account of the view from the windows, at least three-quarters of an acre must remain in grass, the most expensive of all conditions. We pared off the corners, and laid them into the arable part, in the first instance, so as to leave the grassy area just three-quarters of an acre. To finish with the pasture first, the treatment it requires is this: Before the winter rains, we give the grass a good dressing of guano every alternate year, or of bones broken, but not to powder, every third year. Early in winter the whole is strewn with manure from the tank, and a compost heap we have in a hidden corner of the new half-acre. At the end of February this is raked away, and the meadow is bush-harrowed. A month later it is well rolled and weeded, if any noxious weeds, such as oxeye daisies, or bishop's weed, are found rooted in it. If any moss appears after long rains it is treated with lime. This care is well repaid by the beauty of the surface and the value of the grass. The little spot is conspicuous for its greenness when all the rest of the valley is of a uniform hay colour; and there is no hay in the neighbourhood to compare with ours. The cows eat off the first growth in April. It is then shut up for six weeks or so for hay, and is mown towards the end of June, when it yields nearly three tons to the acre. We do not exhaust the ground by mowing it twice, but allow the cows to feed it pretty close till November. After two winters we found that the anxiety of keeping such hay stacked in a rainy climate was more than the thing was worth; and I therefore built a hay-house, and was only sorry that I had put it off so long. Knowing what the plague of rats is in such buildings, I adopted the only perfect security—that of using such materials as no vermin can penetrate. The floor was flagged as carefully as a kitchen-floor, and slate stones went deep into the ground below the flags. A few years later, when a winter inundation penetrated every place in the levels of the valley, and wetted our hay, I granted a raised wooden floor to the entreaties of our farm-man: and there our hay and straw keep perfectly well in all kinds of winters.

Hay, however, is an extravagant kind of food for cows; and ours have it only for variety, and as a resource when other things fail, and when they calve, or happen to be ill. Our main dependence is on roots and vegetables, straw and condiments. As this was nearly a new idea in the neighbourhood, we were prodigiously ridiculed, till our success induced first respect and then imitation. It was a current maxim, that it takes three acres of land to feed a cow; and this may be very true in the hill pastures, which are mossy and untended. Our milk would cost us sixpence a quart, it was said—we were starving our poor cow—we were petting our cow, so that she was like a spoiled child—such were the remarks till events silenced them, and people came to see how we arranged our ground, so as to get such crops out of it. We constantly gave in explanation the current rule: "the more manure, the more green crops; the more green crops, the more stock; the more stock, the more manure." And by degrees the true principle of stall-feeding and spade-tillage became clear to all inquirers.

Our soil is light,—not very deep (lying above slaty-stone) sufficiently fertile, and easily treated, but so stony in parts as to dismay a labourer from a clay or sand district. The neighbours advised my man to cover up the stones, and think no more of them; but we concluded that it would be better to make use of some of them. We dug deep where the garden paths were to be, and filled in the stones, so as to make drains of all the garden walks. Others went to mend the occupation-road which runs along the field, and through the half-acre. On the south side, and in the half-acre, there is scarcely a stone, and the tillage is perfectly easy. Our way is to dig two spits deep, straight down, manure richly, and leave abundant space between both the plants and the rows. Hence our fine roots, and our weight of produce.

I need say nothing of our garden tillage, except that, with the exception of winter potatoes, we obtain an abundant supply of vegetables for a household of four persons, and their occasional guests. All common fruits become more plentiful every year. This being understood, we are here concerned only with the food for the cows and pig. In summer we sow cabbage-seed,—being careful about the kind, as the common cow-cabbage spoils the milk and butter. A kind between the Ham and Victoria cabbage is by the Norfolk people considered the best. The young plants are pricked out in early autumn, some hundreds per week for six weeks, to secure a succession next year. They should be eighteen inches apart, in rows a yard apart: and if they can be allowed to keep their places till they weigh ten or twelve pounds apiece, they of course afford a great bulk of food for the animals. Anywhere above four pounds is, however, worth the ground. The rows being placed so wide apart is to allow of the sowing of roots between them.

In April and May we sow turnips (Swedes especially), carrots (particularly Belgian), and mangold[64] in the centre of the spaces left; and, by the time the root crops have been thinned, and are past the danger of the fly, the cabbages are fit to be cut. The alternate ones are taken first, and light and air are thus let in freely. The cabbages begin to be very substantial about mowing time, and fill up all intervals till November; that is, while the grass is growing after hay-making, and between the first, second, and third gathering of the mangold leaves. It is the fashion now to discourage the thinning of the mangold: but we find the roots rather the better than the worse for the process. If they were not, we could still hardly spare the resource of those three leaf crops; but the fact is, no such mangold as ours is grown anywhere near; and strangers come to look at it, both in the ground and in the root-house. We now devote the arable part of our rented half-acre to this root, except when it is necessary to grow grain for a change, which happens every third or fourth year; and this last year we obtained about six tons of mangold from a quarter of an acre. It keeps admirably; and our cows were still enjoying it a month before Midsummer. There is an occupation-road through the half-acre which produces only grass; and the same is true of a strip running its whole length, under a row of noble ash trees, which of course prevent all tillage under their shade and within the circuit of their roots. The arable portion amounts, in fact, to hardly one-third of an acre.

We early obtained a small addition to our territory in a rather odd way. After we had suffered from two or three invasions of sheep through the great ugly hedge, I received an occasional hint that the neighbouring tenant wished I would take that hedge into my own hands. Seeing no reason why I should trouble myself with such a vexatious and unprofitable piece of property, I paid no attention to the hints: but my farm-man at length intimated that he could make a good thing of it, if I would let him demolish the hedge, which he would undertake, except felling the pollard-ashes, with his own hands. He was sure the contents of the hedge, and the ground we should get by it, would pay for a good new fence. It did indeed pay. We had firewood enough for more than one winter, and a good deal of soil; and we gained a strip of ground about three feet wide, the whole length of the field. Moreover, my neighbour obtained the same quantity, to the great augmentation of his friendship to us. The new fence cost 9*l*. It is a crosspole fence—the only kind which is found effectual here against the incursions of sheep. They leap upon a wall; they burst through a hedge; they thrust themselves through a post-and-rail fence; but they can get no footing on a crosspole fence; and only the youngest lambs can creep through the interstices. The material used is split larch-poles; and those who object that such a fence is not durable, must have omitted the precaution of tarring the ends which enter the ground. With that precaution it may last a lifetime; and it is easily mended if a pole here and there should go before the rest. It occupies the smallest portion of ground—is no hindrance to air and sunshine, and is remarkably pretty. When covered with roses, as mine is for the greater part, it is a luxury to look upon, reminding travellers of the rose-covered trellises of hot countries,—as in Louisiana, Damascus, and Egypt.[65] We were so delighted with it that I carried it along the bottom of the field, where also I was not chargeable with the care of the fence. I see strangers come in and examine it, and try to shake it, as if they thought it a flimsy affair for a farm, even on a miniature scale; but I believe it will outlast the present generation of inhabitants, human and quadruped.

It will be necessary to give some account of our live stock and its produce before we can form an estimate of profit or loss on the whole scheme of my little farm. Meantime, we may say this much:

Twelve years ago, we saw about our dwelling an acre and a quarter of grass, in unsightly condition, grazed by a sickly cow; a few beds of flowers and a few more of vegetables—the former not well kept, and the latter far from productive—and, for the rest, a drive and little plantations, and slopes rarely neat, and always craving more care than we could give. For the grass I obtained, as I said, 4*l*. 10*s*. a-year; and, to an occasional gardener, I paid from 6*l*. to 10*l*. a-year. In connection with these particulars, we must remember the housekeeping troubles—bad butter, blue milk, and thin cream; costly vegetables which had travelled in the sun; hams costing 1*l*. at least; eggs at 1*d*. each, and fowls scarce and skinny; and all this in a place where the supply of meat is precarious at the most important time of year.

The state of things now is wonderfully different. The whole place is in the neatest order conceivable; the slopes are mown, and the shrubs trimmed, and the paths clean; and the parterres[66] gay, almost all the year round. With only three-quarters of an acre of grass, we have about 12*l*. worth of hay; and part grazing for two cows for six months of the year. We have roots to the value of about 8*l*. a year, exclusive of the benefit of their green part, which affords several cwts. of food. Then, there are the cabbages for the cows, which, in favourable seasons, have afforded the staple of their food for three or four months. In southern and eastern counties they would be more ample and certain dependence than in the north. Then for the house, we have always had an over-supply of vegetables (except the winter store of potatoes), the surplus going, rather wastefully, to the pig. Beginning with cress, and radishes, lettuce, and early potatoes, and going through the whole series of peas and beans, turnips and carrots, spinach, onions and herbs, vegetable marrow and cucumbers, cabbages, cauliflowers, and broccoli, up to winter greens, we have abounded in that luxury of fresh-cut vegetables which townspeople can appreciate. All the common fruits follow of course. The comfort of having an active man on the premises, ready for every turn, is no small consideration in a household of women.

All these things have been created, we must observe—called out of the ground where they lay hid, as it were. This creation of subsistence and comfort is a good thing in itself; it remains to be seen whether it is justified by paying its own cost. This we shall learn when we have reviewed the history of our Dairy and Poultry-yard.

DAIRY AND BACON

"I SHOULD HAVE SAID you would be more humane," observed a London friend to me, "than to shut up your cows. I could not have believed you would be so cruel."

A few minutes' conversation made a wonderful difference in this benevolent lady's impressions. She was a thorough Londoner, and knew nothing of cow tastes and habits. With the ordinary human tendency to fetishism she regarded cow-life from her own point of view, and pitied my Meggie and Ailsie for not seeing the lovely landscape as they lay ruminating. The argument may be shortly given. Granting that the so-called "natural condition" of animals is the happiest, which may not be true in the quadruped any more than the human case, it is impossible at this time of day to put our domestic cattle under the conditions of the primitive life of their race. When they roamed our island wild they could shelter themselves from the noonday heat in the forest, and escape the flies by getting into the water; whereas, when once cows are domesticated, there is an end of forest shade, and of recourse to lakes and rivers; and the question is, whether something better is not given. Taking the winter into the question, there can be no doubt about the matter. Lean cows were slaughtered in autumn, and salted down for winter food, in old times, because there were no means of feeding them during the interval between the late and early grass; and, as for those which were spared from the slaughter, we know what their wildness from hunger was by the end of winter. The cows on a small farm (or on a large one either) cannot have open woods and waters to resort to; and, if sent out to feed, have a half-and-half sort of life, the superiority of which to stall-feeding may be questionable. They have neither the natural nor the artificial protection from heat and flies, and their condition is less equable than that of the stall-fed cow. In high summer they may be very fat and sleek,—too fat to be perfect milkers; but in early spring they are meagre, ragged, and half dry, when the stall-fed animals are nearly as sleek and prosperous as at any other season.

Every observer remarks on the good plight of my cows when those of the neighbouring farmers are turned out upon the fells in spring: and, during the summer, if Meggie and Ailsie happen to be out towards noon, they turn into their stable of their own accord to escape the flies and enjoy the coolness. The test is the health of the animals; and, by all I have been able to learn, stall-fed cows, properly managed, live longer, give more milk in the long run, have fewer illnesses, and are better tempered than those which are treated in the ordinary method of our old-fashioned farming. When Cow Life Insurance societies become as numerous as they ought to be, their tables will soon show whether stall-feeding is favourable to life and health, or the contrary. Meantime, the world is grievously in want of agricultural statistics in that department, as in every other.

I may remark here, that the ladies who tell us of their four-acre farm, and all other farmers, large and small, will be wise to insure their cows' lives, if any well-established society for the purpose exists within reach. At this season in 1858, when I lost a cow for the first time, I should have been very glad of such a resource. The few shillings per year for each cow are worth paying, if never wanted back again: for the peace of mind is a main feature in the bargain, as in the case of life and fire insurance. One of the finest and healthiest young cows I ever saw, which had calved prosperously a year before, calved in June, 1858, in the midst of the thundery weather which then prevailed. The storm burst just after; my poor cow sank down, and never got up again. This was a case of sheer accident: no management could have prevented it; and the appropriate consolation would have been receiving her value from an Insurance Society if I had had the opportunity.

Country residents who know how often the familiar petition comes round on behalf of the cottager or small farmer who has lost a cow or two, can bear witness to the policy of establishing such a society in every rural neighbourhood, and taking care of its being founded on a safe basis. The subscriptions now given on petition would be better bestowed on such a foundation. Good would be done, and ease of mind afforded, all round; and after ten years or so, the collective records would yield some very valuable knowledge as to the life and health of farm-stock.

The combined experience of a neighbourhood or district must surely lead to an improved medical treatment of animals. The greatest drawback on small farming is the helplessness of the proprietor when a cow or a pig is ill. It requires to be on the spot to believe the nonsense that is talked on such occasions in retired villages, and what passions are called into play. A few months after I began, I was told that my cow was ill. The local doctor was sent for, and he gave his verdict and instituted the treatment. But I could make nothing of the matter at all—neither what ailed the cow, nor whether it was serious, nor even whether she might die. By the bustle and solemnity, and my man being seen to brush away tears when my back was turned, I augured the worst; but I do not at this moment know how far she was in danger. The report was: "'Tis the worm in the tail, that go all along her back and up into her head, so that her teeth are loose, and she can't properly eat." She was bled in the tail, dosed with physic, fed with meal, and rubbed, and in a day or two she was quite well. Other alarms of the same kind have occurred since; and the sense of blank ignorance in one's self, and of the quackery of those who pretend to know more, while the suffering animal is sinking before one's eyes, is decidedly the most disagreeable experience of rural life in my case. And then, if one asks a question, or demurs to bleeding (from which a cow rarely recovers completely), or proposes any simple method, or fails to send for the local oracle, or, worst of all, sends for a real veterinary surgeon too, there is an astonishing outburst of passions. Doctor and farm-man quarrel: "The lady may cure her own cows"—"Nobody will set a foot on the premises if new notions are to be tried"—and so forth. Happy they who live within immediate reach of a qualified veterinary surgeon! In the absence of such a resource there is, I believe, no doubt whatever that the simple rules and facts of homœopathic practice are the greatest possible boon. The operation of that method of practice in the case of cattle and horses is too remarkable to leave room for question, I understand, among those most opposed to it in the human case.

I have said all the harm I have to say of my first cow. She was a rather large but very pretty short-horn, of the local kind. It does not do for small farmers to try many experiments with different kinds of cows: and it is generally safest to be content with the local sort. I live too far north for Alderneys, which ladies often incline to, to their cost in the long run; but I hoped much from a cheap, hardy little Kerry cow, such as I have known to be very profitable in the midland counties; but she did not answer. Meggie, however, my first experiment, served and pleased me well for six years. I gave 15*l.* for her at six years old, and she was valued at 7*l.* when I exchanged her at the end of six years. Thus, spreading her prime cost—viz., 8*l.*—over the six years, together with 4 per cent. interest on the 15*l.*, she cost me, as a purchase, 1*l.* 18*s.* a-year.

The cost of her maintenance cannot be given with equal precision, because her food was as various as we could make it, and it is impossible to estimate the value of every article we grew. But we can ascertain within a narrow margin how much Meggie cost, and how well it answered to keep her. The proper amount of food for a milch cow is not less than 70lb. per day—a fatting bullock requiring about 90lb. For stall-feeding we must reckon the winter as lasting five months, in our northern counties. Each cow, therefore, must have four tons of roots and one ton of hay, with a few extras, such as I will presently mention. Allowing for calving-times, exigencies, and indulgences, throughout the year, we purchase about a ton of hay for each cow, in addition to our own crop. I pay a pound or two here and there in the neighbourhood for grass and brewers' grains, and buy Thorley's cattle-food, an occasional load of straw, and a little meal at calving-times. In ordinary seasons, the bought food may be set down at about 10*l.* for each cow. Her share of the man's wages may be reckoned at one-third, or 11*l.*, and of the cost of tillage at 1*l.* 10*s.* The extra manure, beyond her own yield, is about 1*l.* 5*s.*, and her share of the cost of utensils and their repairs, 1*l.* 5*s.*, and the interest of the capital invested in her stable and all the accessories by which she benefits, 1*l.* 10*s.* I think this all that Meggie can have cost me.

As for her produce, there was the annual calf, which brought, if a bull-calf, only 5*s.*, and if a wye (cow-calf), a guinea at the end of a week. She gave us, on the average of the year, ten quarts of milk per day. After calving, she gave sixteen quarts or more for a time; to set against which there was the decline and dryness before calving; so that we reckon the average at ten quarts. Her manure is already set off against her food. We have not here the London prices, which so brighten the accounts of the Four-Acre farm. We must reckon the new milk at 2*d.* the quart, and butter as averaging 11*d.* per lb. Our lowest price is 8*d.*, and the highest 1*s.* 3*d.* Reckoning the produce as milk, it brings 30*l.* 8*s.* 4*d.* per cow, for the year. I might magnify it by reckoning a part as butter; but I wish to be on the safe side, and will, therefore, put our sales and gains at the lowest.

COST OF EACH COW.

	£	*s.*	*d.*
Food bought	10	0	0
Attendance	11	0	0
Tillage	1	10	0
Manure	1	5	0
Utensils and repairs	1	5	0
Interest on capital	1	10	0
Prime cost and interest...	1	18	0
	£28	8	0

PRODUCE OF EACH COW.

	£	s.	d.
Milk	30	8	4
Calf (average).	0	13	0
	£ 31	1	4
Cost	28	8	0
	£ 2	13	4

This small surplus may be set apart to meet accidents; and thus Meggie just paid her own expenses, leaving to me and my household the satisfaction of seeing man, wife, and animals maintained, the place rendered fertile, and ourselves supplied with rural luxuries which were not to be had for money.

Afraid of the responsibility of inducing any rash experiment, I have rather over-estimated than underrated the expenses, and made the very least of our gains; and it must be remembered that in the neighbourhood of London, or any other large town, the expense of food and wages would be the same, while the sale of produce would bring in about one-third more.

The mode of life of a stall-fed cow is very simple. By 6 A.M., at the latest, in summer, and 7 A.M., in winter, her stable should be cleaned out,—all liquids swept into the drain and tank, all solids barrowed to the large tank down the field, and powdered charcoal, or Dr. Smith's Disinfectant, deposited where most needed.[67] A plentiful supply of air has been provided during the night by the opening of some of the windows, of which there are three. A small window in the roof, opened by a cord, secures the escape of foul air. The stable, being close to the cottage, is well warmed in winter. We find the cows do better without litter than with any kind we have been able to try. Cocoa-nut fibre mats were presented to me for trial, when it appeared that fern, haulm,[68] and straw, tempted the cows to eat their litter; but the mats were too warm, and the animal's hoofs grew long and became brittle. A smooth surface of cement or asphalte appears to answer best, provided it is kept in thorough repair, and made sloping in the slightest possible degree, so as to allow liquid to run off, without fatiguing the cow by depriving her of a level standing-place.

The cleaning of the place being done, the next thing is the milking; and then the breakfast; and then the rubbing down of the animal. Her coat should be first curried, and then brushed every day, and her legs—particularly the hind legs—well rubbed. Her coat ought to be as glossy as that of a horse; and if she is not thoroughly freed from dirt, she will be restless in her eagerness to rub herself against wall or post on every side. Duly dressed, she lies down to ruminate in calm content.

In summer, when the hay is growing, she has cut grass, more or less every day. We get it from sundry patches on our own ground—from strips under the trees, from the slopes, the borders, and three-cornered bits in angles of the garden, and from the ditch, hedge, and road in the half-acre; and also from any neighbour who will let us have it for the cutting, or a trifle over. There is some every day, till the cows can turn out after the hay-making. Meantime, there are the last of the mangold roots, and there is chopped straw dressed with Thorley's cattle-food, which is a great comfort as a resource, when food is scanty or precarious. The tradition of our district, of the eagerness of the cattle of the monks of Furness after the ash and holly sprays on the mountains,[69] guides us to another resource. A cow will brave many obstacles to get at the young sprays of the ash; so we crop ours from the pollards. The same with nettles in their season. We must not suppose these things bad food, because *we* should not like them. Brewers' grains are another resource. Cows are very fond of them. When the roots are done, the cabbages are coming on; and then many helps arise; the thinnings of the growing turnips and mangold, and afterwards their crops of leaves. These things, with the ever-growing grass, carry us on to November, when the last cabbage is eaten, and the pasture must be manured. Then begins the winter routine. The cinders from the house, and a penny sack of shavings from the bobbin-mill light the boiler fire, which keeps the food warm for the day. The turnips are eaten first, because they do not keep so well as the mangold. A cwt. of turnips per day is rather more than cows want, if there are carrots for them, or cut straw, with Thorley's food. The roots are sliced and boiled with the straw. The secret of giving turnips without fatal damage to the cream and butter is to pour off all the water, and give the roots dry, with fresh water to drink, of course.

The hay is the dessert—given dry if the cows prefer it so. To keep their teeth in use, they may have a mangold root or two in the course of the day—"to amuse themselves with," as the man says. They have three regular meals in the day, and something more during the longest days. In winter, they settle well for the night after six o'clock.

Our dairy is in rather an odd place—under the library. It is the place of most equable temperature on the premises; the coolest in summer, and the warmest in winter—being a part of the cellar blasted out of the rock, and its windows nearly level with the garden ground outside. It is fitted up with slate-stone shelves, and leaded cisterns for the milk. We have tried various new devices—glass, earthenware, and wood; but we find that the cream rises better in the old cisterns, lined with lead, than under any other circumstances. Our butter rarely gives any trouble in the making; and, since we fairly learned the art, it has had an excellent reputation. We do not often obtain so much as a pound from one quart of cream; and we are satisfied that this quantity cannot be got on an average of seasons and of cows; but on occasion we obtain it. The pig has the buttermilk and what skim-milk we do not use for our bread and cakes, nor sell. The consumption of cream in the household is not small. We relish it with our fruit and otherwise. We like custards and trifle and fruit-creams and white soups; and, now it is understood to have the properties which make cod-liver oil so much the fashion for weakly people, we agree how far preferable the domestic article is to the imported, and indulge largely in the medicine, ill or well.

It should not be omitted that our keeping cows is a social benefit. The troop of children coming for milk, morning and evening, is a pretty sight. I have added to the advantage of the supply that of requiring ready money for it. In old-fashioned places, where money matters are irregular, and long credits cause perpetual mischief and frequent ruin, and where some of the gentry give away milk to people perfectly able to pay for it, it is a social service to insist on both paying and receiving ready money. My cook is therefore charged with the dairy concerns, and upheld by her employers in giving no credit. Before we learned the ways of the place, customers who could afford strong drink and fine clothes went into debt to us for milk up to nearly 1*l.*, and then went to another dairy. It was no better kindness to them than to ourselves to allow this: and, now that our rule is inflexible, as to paying and being paid, we have no difficulty, except when, at times, our cows are to calve at too short an interval, and the supply runs short, and the customers "are fit to tear us to pieces," as cook says, for what we have to sell.

There is not much to tell of the pig. We bespeak one of a good breed each spring and autumn, bringing him home at from six to ten weeks old—old enough to keep himself warm and comfortable. His cost is then from 15*s.* to 25*s.*, according to the state of the world in regard to pig-keeping. Before the potato-rot, one might get for 10*s.* such a pig as afterwards cost 20*s.* Our pig's house is a substantial stone edifice, cool in summer and warm in winter, with a paved yard for eating, exercise, and basking in the sun. The pavement should come up every few years, and the soil below should be removed for manure, and new laid. A liberal use of disinfectants will be repaid by the health of the pig and the content of the neighbours; and there is no more valuable manure than the disinfectants which have done their work of purification. The house and yard must be kept swept and clean, and the straw frequently renewed, and then the animal itself will have good habits. Pigs are not dirty when they have any encouragement to be clean. Ours is washed every week, in warm soap and water, and well scrubbed behind the ears and everywhere, to its great ease and comfort. A highly economical remark of my man about this part of his work was, that he scrubbed the pig on washing days, because the soapsuds did just as well for manure after the pig had done with them, "and that," said he, "makes the soap serve three times over."

Buttermilk, skim-milk, refuse vegetables, kitchen-stuff bought for sixpence per week, grains now and then, and any coarse food rendered nutritious and delectable by Thorley's food or malt dust being sprinkled over it, keep our pig in health and happiness till he has accomplished the first six or seven months of his life. Then he must be fattened for three weeks. The more he is induced to eat during that time, the more profitable will he be; and his food must be of the best kind. Opinions differ as to whether oatmeal or barley-meal answers best. Our belief is that a mixture is the true thing. The barley is cheaper, and requires a month to produce its effect: the oat is dearer, but requires less than three weeks. It is the better, however, for being qualified with the barley; and we use them half-and-half, till the pig has had sixteen stone, costing £1 4*s*. His weight when killed is, on the average, twelve stone, which has fetched, within my experience, from 5*s*. to 7*s*. 3*d*. per stone. Our money gain, after all expenses are deducted, may thus vary from £1 to nothing on the pig; but the privilege of well-educated bacon, and hams of high quality, is no contemptible one, as will be owned by doubting and scrupulous purchasers of pork in towns. We and our friends can enjoy our sausages, pork-pies, hams, and bacon without drawback; and the value of the two latter in the commissariat in a region where the very legs of mutton in the butcher's shop have to be divided between urgent petitioners in the season, cannot be described.

No party is better pleased than the man in charge,—unless it be his wife. He buys half the pig at wholesale price: has his bacon cheap; and can, if he chooses, sell the ham at a great profit in the season. We kill our pork in the first days of November and the last of March.

There remains the produce of the poultry-yard to make out our bill of fare. That story is too long for this place, and must be told in another chapter.

THE POULTRY-YARD

IN ORDER to make money by poultry, in any proportion to the attention given to them, the speculator should be either a capitalist who provides an extensive apparatus for the supply of fowls and eggs to a neighbouring community, or a cottager or small farmer who can rear fowls in a chance-medley way, on what they can pick up for themselves. As I am neither a professional breeder of poultry, nor a cottager, nor yet a small farmer in the ordinary use of the term, I cannot and do not expect to make money to any notable extent by our fowls and ducks. As I have already intimated, the object is security against famine, where a whole neighbourhood depends on the justice and mercy of one butcher. When I relate that at an inn not three miles off, forty-five couples of fowls have been killed in one day, from the beef and lamb falling short of the demand, it will be easily conceived that it is no small comfort to be supplied, at all events, with eggs and bacon, fowls and ham, within our own gates. The country people would like very much to see the Queen among our mountains. They would give her a dinner of eggs and ham, and set her on a pony, and show her everything. It is certain beforehand what her diet would be if she came *incog.* At the little country inns,—each the sole house of entertainment in its dale or waterhead,—you always know what you will have.

"Can we have dinner?"

"O, yes."

"What can you give us?"

"What you like."

After inquiring in vain for beef or mutton, we are told,—

"But there's ham, and there's eggs."

"Very well: and what else?"

"Why there's eggs; and there's ham, and bacon."

If the Queen came unawares to some dwellings which are not inns, there might, in the height of the season, be the same bill of fare, and no other. The value of the resource must be the measure of our gain, under such circumstances; and not the money we make.

It becomes an increasing wonder every year why the rural cottagers of the United Kingdom do not rear fowls, almost universally, seeing how little the cost would be, and how great is the demand. We import many millions of eggs annually. Why should we import any? It seems as strange as that Ireland should import all its cheese, while exporting butter largely. After spending the morning among dairy-farms in Kerry, you have at dinner cheese from London: and, in the same way, after passing dozens of cottages on commons or in lanes in England, where the children have nothing to do, and would be glad of pets, you meet a man with gold rings in his ears, who asks you in broken English to buy eggs from the continent. Wherever there is a cottage family, whether living on potatoes or better fare, and grass growing anywhere near, there it would be worth while to nail up a little pent-house, and make nests of clean straw, and go in for a speculation in eggs and chickens. Seeds, worms, and insects go a great way in feeding poultry in such places; and then there are the small and refuse potatoes from the heap, and the outside cabbage leaves, and the scraps of all sorts. Very small purchases of broken rice (which is extremely cheap), inferior grain, and mixed meal, would do all else that is necessary. There would probably be larger losses from "vermin" than in better guarded places; but these could be well afforded, as a mere deduction from considerable gains. It is understood that the keeping of poultry is largely on the increase in the country generally, and even among cottagers; but the prevailing idea is of competition as to races and specimens for the poultry-yard, rather than of meeting the demand for eggs and fowls for the table. The pursuit is an excellent one, and everybody rejoices at the growth of such an interest: but the labourer and his family are not benefited by it, as a steady resource, as they might be by a constant succession of commonplace eggs and chickens, to be sold in the next town. As for any farmer who grows grain and has a homefield and a barn, he must be badly off for wife or daughter if he cannot depend on his poultry for a respectable amount of annual profit. We remember the exultation of a German settler in a western state of America, in speaking of his rise in life, shown by his "fifty head of hen." Perhaps it is not necessary to go so far as the prairies to acquire a stock in trade,—not so large, indeed, but profitable in equal proportion.

The least advantageous way of rearing fowls is just that which is now under our notice—that of a lady's poultry-yard on a small bit of land in a populous neighbourhood. The fowls cannot have full liberty; they must not trespass on the neighbours; and they are grievously trespassed on by the neighbours' cats and dogs. Yet the experiment answers in our case soundly and thoroughly, through the care and interest invested in the enterprise by my companion. She has worked through many difficulties, and raised the project to paying point, and beyond it, to the comfort of the household, her own great amusement and that of her guests, and the edification and benefit of the servants.

Our average stock is twenty hens, two cocks, five ducks, and one drake. Our accommodation will not allow any large increase of our average. The ducks are uncommonly fine specimens of the Aylesbury breed. One cock is a Cochin-China: the other of some common sort which makes less impression on strangers. A visitor lately met the Cochin-China sultan in the drive, and was so prodigiously impressed as to take off his hat to his majesty, who is indeed too heavy to be often met out walking.

The ducks were a present, some years ago, and the silk stocking has become worsted, and perhaps silk again, in the interval, from the changes necessary to keep up the vigour of the stock. Besides substituting a new drake every three years or so, we exchange some brood-eggs every season with some neighbour who has the same breed. We have not conveniences for rearing any great number of young ducks, and prefer selling the eggs, of which we have above 600 per annum. We kill a few ducks for our own table, reckoning their value, not at the London rate, but at 2*s*. 6*d*. each. In London, 7*s*. a couple would be asked for ducks which would not have two-thirds of their substantial merit when brought to table. Our duck eggs are in great request for poaching, and puddings, and custards; and well they may be, for their cubic contents must be nearly double those of ordinary hens' eggs.

It might be difficult to say which is cause and which effect in regard to our having two cocks and two poultry-yards. The double arrangement is desirable in every way. There should always be opportunities for separation and seclusion, in that community as in every other. For instance, the favourite aversion of the drake is his own ducklings. He would destroy them every one if we did not separate them from their passionate parent. The whole feathered colony is, at times, so like the Irish quarter in a port town, with its brawls and faction fights, that imprisonment or banishment is occasionally necessary, on the one hand, and an accident-ward for the victims on the other. We have one roosting-chamber in the upper part of the coal-shed, and the other in the upper part of the pig-house, each opening into its own yard, and having its ladder without and its perches within. In the small enclosures, made of trellised wood and wire netting, are pent-houses for the nests, which should always be on the ground, for the sake not only of the convenience of the sitting hen, but of the vigour of the brood. The shallow troughs for food and pans for water make up the rest of the apparatus. The places should be swept out several times a week, and strewn with some disinfectant in hot weather; and there should always be soft soil enough for the hens to make dust-baths in, and gravel enough to afford them pebble diet, according to their needs. There must always be a little heap of lime in some dry corner, if the egg-shells are to be worthy of their contents.

So much for what may be called the retreats or refuges

of the fowls: but their lives cannot be passed there. So we found. They must have a further range. The best plan, where space can be afforded (which is not our case), is to lay out for the fowls a long strip of grass fenced with wire—a regular Rotten Row[70] for their daily trot, race, or stately walk. As the nearest approach we could make to this, we fenced in with galvanised wire netting the belt of plantation which adjoins the lower fowl-house. There they have room to run and make dust-baths, and strut in the sun or repose in the shade at pleasure. A deep trough is sunk there, and filled with water for the ducks when they must be kept at home, and for the ducklings, which are not allowed to range the meadows, because such liberty is almost invariably fatal to them. Whether it is any particular food, animal or vegetable (we suspect a particular slug), or other dangers—as entanglement in the grass and weeds, cramp, enemies, or what not—it is very rarely that ducklings survive an attempt at a roving life. After witnessing every accident now stated, we believe the deleterious food to be sufficient reason for keeping the broods at home till they are well grown. The drake and his hareem spend the day abroad for several months of the year, going forth into the meadows—where they make a serviceable clearance of slugs—in the morning, after laying, and coming home in the evening for their supper. While the grass is growing for hay, we are obliged to keep them at home; and it is necessary to watch them when young vegetables are coming up and fruit is ripening. Nobody would believe without seeing it how high they can reach with their bills when currants and gooseberries hang temptingly; and in their love of strawberries they vie with humanity. After being kept at home, the ducks relax in their laying, and their feeding is expensive; but they really seem to go on laying longer every year: so perhaps we may train them, in course of time, to be "equal to either fortune."

For the sake of the young chicks, we have yet one other enclosure at the service of the fowls. There is a pretty little quarry below the terrace and orchard, from whence the stone for the terrace-wall was taken. A little wire fence is now drawn across the entrance, and the young broods and their mothers have it to themselves.

Such is their mode of life. As for what they live on, we make their food as various as possible, as in the case of the cows and the pig. The most expensive of all food we find to be barley *au naturel*. Not only is a considerable proportion thrown about and wasted, but much that is swallowed is never digested. We, therefore, give it as a change and indulgence; and by no means as the staple of their food, Indian meal is the best staple, according to our experience. It is well scalded, that the swelling may be done before it is swallowed instead of after—thus avoiding various maladies and perils from over-eating. Broken rice well boiled is good to a certain extent. Malt dust is a valuable resource. The demand is becoming so great that it will probably soon cease to be a cheap food; but while it remains so, it is a real boon, both to the fowls and their owner. They will eat almost anything that is sprinkled with malt-dust; and a 6*s*. sack of it goes a long way. A certain proportion of green food, and also of animal food, is indispensable. Lettuce-leaves, turnip-tops, cabbage-leaves, celery, should be thrown to them. They should have access to grass, to pick seeds and insects; and it is well to put a fresh sod into the poultry-yard whenever such a valuable thing can be spared. All the worms and insects that come in the gardener's way should be presented to them; and, when insects are scarce, scraps of raw meat, minced as fine as pins' heads, should be given. Add finely chopped egg for infant chicks, and I think the bill of fare is complete. As for the pepper-corn, which old wives recommend as the first thing to be swallowed, we reprobate the notion as we should in the case of any other new-born creature. In fact, it irritates the crop very mischievously, if it gives out its savour: and if it does not dissolve, it is nothing.

We do not find it necessary to make distinctions of seasons in hatching broods, as some people do. We like beginning early; but we know what we may expect from frosts and storms in March, and are content with what we get. If we have not a pretty full school by June, we shake our heads: but some July broods have been as fine and complete as any others on our list. An autumn brood or two—even a late one—is valuable; for the chickens are short-legged, and make excellent sitters.

By careful management, my companion has succeeded in distributing the moulting over a considerable space of time, and therefore in obtaining eggs in early winter. We have them now throughout the year. We lay by a hundred or more in lime water in the most plentiful season, for puddings in the time of scarcity; and then our small supply of November and December eggs is disposable for invalids, or other neighbours anxious to secure the delicacy.

Under this mode of management, our fowl account has stood thus for the last two years.

In 1857, we paid for food 17*l.* 1*s.* 8*d.*; and for improvements in the hen-house, 1*l.* 15*s.*; that is, our expenses were 18*l.* 16*s.* 8*d.*; eggs and fowls used and sold were worth 18*l.* 4*s.* 2*d.*; ten chickens and one young cock in stock, 1*l.* 5*s.*; making 19*l.* 9*s.* 2*d.*; which shows our profit to have been 12*s.* 6*d.*; in 1858, the cost of food was 16*l.* 8*s.* 2*d.*; and of improvement of stock, 11*s.* 9*d.*; together making 16*l.* 19*s.* 11*d.*; while our sales and use yielded 17*l.* 10*s.* 6*d.*; our profit, therefore, being 10*s.* 7*d.* London prices would have enriched us mightily; for we had 3,039 eggs, and killed sixty-three fowls (including a few ducks). Within a dozen miles of the General Post-Office, our produce would have been worth above 30*l.*; but it must be remembered that, in regard to our domestic consumption, we have the benefit of the country prices. As it is, we have a balance on the right side, instead of on the wrong, after all accidents and misfortunes are allowed for.

Those accidents are not only vexatious but grievous. The finest young cock we had ever reared was found dead and stiff one morning. His crop, alas! was full of ivy-leaves, which he had reached and snatched from the wall of the house, by some vigorous climbing out of bounds. Chicks, and even hens, now and then are cramped by change of weather, or other mysterious causes. If observed in time, they may be recovered by warmth, friction, and apparently by the unaccountable influence of the human hand: but if they hide their trouble they will be found dead. A stray duckling may lose itself in tall grass as in a jungle. A chick may be found drowned in an inch or two of water in a pan. At one time a hawk haunted us, and we either missed a chicken occasionally, or found it dropped, with a hole in its breast. Rats are to be expected wherever a lake or a river is near; but they are easily disposed of by taking up a flag, and, when their runs are traced, putting down strychnine on bread and butter. Nowhere but under pavement should that poison be placed, because it may be swallowed by some other creature than a rat: but in a subterranean way it is very useful. We have never made war in that way, as some people do, against the sparrows and chaffinches, which really are a nuisance. Where a house is covered with ivy and climbing-plants, and sheltered by copses, and where fowls are fed in the open air, freebooting tribes of birds will be encroaching and audacious. We fear that a large portion of our good meal and grain goes to glut our enemies in the ivy and the trees. But what can we do? We make nets to cover our sprouting vegetables and ripening fruit; and that is all we can do. But about the accidents. The worst are from prowling cats. The ladies of the Four Acres lost eight chickens by cats in one night, and we have lost eight chickens by cats in one day. Such a thing as the destruction of poultry by the neighbours' cats ought never to happen when it is once known how easy prevention is. We educate our own cat, and that at the cottage; and if the neighbors would do the same, there would be an end everywhere to the loss and discontent and ill-will which arise from this cause. When a cat is seen to catch a chicken, tie it round her neck, and make her wear it for two or three days. Fasten it securely; for she will make incredible efforts to get rid of it. Be firm for that time, and the cat is cured. She will never again desire to touch a bird. This is what we do with our own cats, and what we recommend to our neighbours; and when they try the experiment, they and their pets are secure from reproach and danger henceforth. Wild, homeless, hungry, ragged, savage cats are more difficult to catch; but they are outlaws, and may be shot with the certainty that all neighbors will be thankful.

My entire poultry-yard, except a few of the old hens on the perches, was in danger of destruction by an accident one summer night, and was saved by what I cannot but consider a remarkable exercise of energy on the part of my companion, M——. Few persons in the north of England will ever forget the thunder-storm on the night of the 24th of July, 1857. At 11, P.M., the rain came down in one sheet, instantly flooding the level ground to the depth of more than a foot, and the continuous thunder seemed to crack on one's very skull, while the blue lightning never intermitted for two seconds for above an hour. The heat was almost intolerable. Our maids, however, who keep very early hours, were sleeping through it all, when M—— escorted me (very feeble from illness) up-stairs, settled me with my book in my easy-chair, and bade me Good-night.

Presently I drew up a window-blind, to see the lightning better from my seat. In the midst of its blue blazes there was, more than once, a yellow flicker on the window-frame which I could not understand. I went to look out, and saw a yellow light whisking about far below, sometimes in the quarry, and then mounting or descending the terrace steps. It was M——, saving the fowls. She would not allow the maids, who were stirring enough now, to go out straight from their beds into the storm; and she knew it was useless to call the man from the cottage, who was a mere encumbrance on critical occasions. In fact, he and his wife were at that moment entirely persuaded that the end of the world was come. It was no form of speech, but their real conviction; and it could not have been asked of them to care about ducks and chickens. The maids were lighting a fire in the back-kitchen, and strewing the floor with straw, while M—— was out in a dress which could not be spoiled, lantern, basket and apron. Some of the hens and chickens were too cramped to move, sitting in the water. Some were taking refuge in the shrubs. Two ducklings were dead, and two more died afterwards. M—— went again and again, and to both the poultry-yards, and brought up forty fowls,—all that were in danger, every one of which would have been dead before morning. Of course she had not a dry thread about her, nor a dry hair on her head; but the wetting was a trifle in comparison with the bewildering effect of the thunder and lightning in such a midnight. She did not suffer for it more or less, and our poultry-yard was saved. The poor fowls were dried and rubbed, and made comfortable on their straw. A few were delicate for a little while; but only five died in all. It was not the pecuniary loss which M—— dreaded, but the destruction of her whole school of dependents, and the total discouragement which must have followed such a catastrophe. If the deluge had destroyed the colony that night, we should have had no more to tell of our poultry-yard. As it is, we have contemplated the proceedings of our hens and broods ever since with a stronger interest than ever before.

When a neighbour here and there said, "*I* would have let all the fowls of the air perish before I would have gone out on such a night," we think these friends of ours have yet to learn the pleasure and true interest of a rural charge, like that of a poultry-yard.

This is an impression often renewed in regard, not only to the poultry-yard, but to all the interests involved in a genuine country life. The ladies of the Four Acre Farm tell us of a visitor of theirs who could not conceive that women who can make butter could care for books. She wondered at their subscribing to Mudie's.[71] This is, to be sure, the very worst piece of ignorance of country-life and its influences that I ever read of; but it is only an exaggeration of a sentiment very common in both town and country. Some country as well as town gentry may say to us miniature farmers, "What is the use of so much doing for so little profit? A few shillings, or a few pounds, or a certain degree of domestic comfort and luxury,—this is all; and is it worth while?"

"No, this is not all," we reply. When we say what more

there is, it will be for others to decide for themselves whether it is worth while to use small portions of land, or to leave them undeveloped. It is a grave and yet cheerful consideration that the maintenance of our man and his wife is absolutely created by our plan of living; and it is worth something that the same may be said of several animals which are called into existence by it. As for ourselves and our servants, our domestic luxuries are the smallest benefit we derive from our out-door engagements. We should under no circumstances be an idle household. We have abundance of social duties and literary pleasures, in parlour and kitchen; but these are promoted, and not hindered, by our out-door interests. The amount of knowledge gained by actual handling of the earth and its productions, and by personal interest in the economy of agriculture, even on the smallest scale, is greater than any inconsiderate person would suppose; and the exercise of a whole range of faculties on practical objects, which have no sordidness in them, is a valuable and most agreeable method of adult education.

Whoever grows anything feels a new interest in everything that grows; and, as to the mood of mind in which the occupation is pursued, it is, to town-bred women, singularly elevating and refining. To have been reared in a farm-house, remote from society and books, and ignorant of everything beyond the bounds of the parish, is one thing; and to pass from an indolent or a literary life in town to rural pursuits, adopted with purpose, is another. In the first case, the state of mind may be narrow, dull, and coarse; in the latter, it should naturally be expansive, cheery, and elevated. The genuine poetry of man and nature invests an intellectual and active life in the open universe of rural scenery. If listless young ladies from any town in England could witness the way in which hours slip by in tending the garden, and consulting abut the crops, and gathering fruit and flowers, they would think there must be something in it more than they understand. If they would but try their hand at making a batch of butter, or condescend to gather eggs, and court acquaintance with hens and their broods, or assume the charge of a single nest, from the hen taking her seat to the maturity of the brood, they would find that life has pleasures for them that they knew not of,—pleasures that have as much "romance" and "poetry" about them as any book in Mudie's library. "But the time!" say some. "How can you spare the time?" Well! what is it? People must have bodily exercise, in town or country, or they cannot live in health, if they can live at all. Why should country folk have nothing better than the constitutional walk which is the duty and pleasure of townsfolk? Sometimes there is not half-an-hour's occupation in the field or garden in the day; and then is the occasion for an extended ramble over the hills. On other days, two, three, four hours slip away, and the morning is gone unawares: and why not? The things done are useful; the exercise is healthful and exhilarating,—in every way at least as good as a walk for health's sake; and there is the rest of the day for books, pen, and needle. The fact is, the out-door amusements leave abundance of time, and ever-renewed energy for the life of books, the pen, and domestic and social offices of duty and love.

Let those ladies whose lot it is to live in the country consider whether they shall lead a town or a country life there. A town life in the country is perhaps the lowest of all. It is having eyes which see not,—ears which hear not,—and minds which do not understand. A lady who had lived from early childhood in a country-house politely looked into my poultry-yard when it was new, and ran after me with a warm compliment.

"*What* a beautiful hen you have there;—what beautiful long feathers in its tail!"

"Why, S——," said I, "that is the cock."

"O—oh—oh!" said she, "I did not know."

Mr. Howitt[72] tells us somewhere of a guest of his who, seeing a goose and her fourteen goslings on a common, thought it must be very exhausting to the bird to suckle so many young ones. To women who do not know a cock from a hen, or green crops from white, or fruit-trees from forest-tress, or how to produce herb, flower, root, or fruit from the soil, it would be new life to turn up the ground which lies about them. Miniature farming would, in that very common case, not only create the material subsistence of the servants employed, but develop the mind and heart of the employer. This, and not the money made, is the true consideration when the question arises,—What shall a woman do with two or four acres?

Fig. 9. Cottages for Workers in Ambleside, circa 1860

Chapter Five

The Cost of Cottages[73]

SOME OBSERVATIONS that I made on cottage-building, under the title "Home or Hospital," in the 21st number of *Once a Week*, have occasioned so many inquires and remarks, that I feel it right and expedient to adopt a suggestion of one of my correspondents, and relate such facts as I can furnish on the subject of the cost of cottage-building.[74] I cannot explain, nor understand, the statements of some of these applicants as to the cost of good dwellings for labourers; and the wide difference between their estimates and my own experience, and that of several persons who have built cottages in various parts of the country, seems to show that there may be great use, if no great beauty, in a matter-of-fact account of what has been done, and may be done any day.

I have built five Westmoreland cottages, the specifications of which, and the receipted bills for which, lie before me now.

The first was a dwelling for my farm-man and his wife[75]—without children. It was built in conjunction with a wash-house for my own house, and a cow-stable for two cows, with all appurtenances. The cottage consists of two good rooms on the ground-floor, with two large closets—one used as a pantry, and the other containing a bed on occasion. The wash-house has the usual fittings—boiler, pump, and sink, and all conveniences. The cow-stable has stalls for two cows, and a smaller one for a calf: two windows in the walls, and one in the roof: a gutter and drain, joining the one from the cottage, and leading to a manure-tank, which is flagged and cemented so as to be perfectly water-tight, and closed with a moveable stone lid: all the buildings are two feet thick in the walls, which are of the grey stone of the district—mortared in the outer and inner courses, and the cavity filled in with rubble. The cottage kitchen has a range, with an oven; and the bedroom has a fireplace. The cost of this group of buildings was 130*l*.

The other cottages are, however, more in the way of my inquiring correspondents. The four are built in pairs, on a terrace, with a space of a few feet between the two pairs, and a flight of broad steps leading up from below. There is a good piece of garden ground to each cottage.

The walls are two feet thick, and may stand for centuries. The foundations are on excavated rock. The roofs are of Coniston slate, and the corner-stones are from the Rydal quarry. The woodwork being properly seasoned, and duly painted, there is no call for repairs beyond the occasional painting and whitewashing, and replacing of a slate now and then in stormy weather. A more durable kind of property can hardly be. When once warmed through, these dwellings, if well built at first, are warm in winter and cool in summer; and they are perfectly dry, which is not always the case with houses built of stone in blocks—some kinds of stone absorbing moisture.

The kitchens and passages are flagged. One pair has a boarded floor in the sitting-room; the other is flagged. Boards are usually preferred. Each cottage has two out-houses behind—a coal-shed and privy (with a patent water-closet apparatus)—the passage between the house and out-houses roofed with a skylight. There is a cistern in each roof to afford a fall for the water-closet. Each dwelling has a pump and sink; each kitchen an oven and range; each house has two closets (for which the thickness of the walls affords convenience). There is a fire-place in every room; a fanlight over the kitchen door; a window (to open) on the stairs; a dresser in the kitchen, and shelves in the pantry. Each cottage has a porch, like most dwellings in this part of the country, where the protection of a porch to the house-door is needed in stormy weather.

Such is the character of my cottages. As for their contents—the ground-floor consists of a kitchen, a good-sized, light, cheerful sitting-room, and a pantry under the stairs. In one pair, the living-room is 12 feet 8 inches long by 11 feet 3 inches broad, and 7 feet high. In the other pair, the same room measures 15 feet in length by 12 in breadth. The respective kitchens are 10½ feet by 10, and 12 feet by 10. Up-stairs there are three bedrooms, one of which is convenient for a double-bedded room. The estimate in the contract was 110*l* per cottage; but some of the conveniences above mentioned were an after-thought, and cost 7*l.* per house. Thus, the total cost of each dwelling was 117*l.* The tenants pay no rates, but a rent of 7*l.*, including the garden ground. These dwellings are in great request, and therefore inhabited by a superior set of tenants, who have, for the most part, done justice to their healthy and cheerful abodes by keeping them clean. They pay their rent half-yearly; and this last Martinmas all had paid before the rent-day arrived.

The nearest cottage to these is one built by a friend of mine, containing a sitting-room with a kitchen-range, a back-kitchen and out-house; and two bedrooms above, each with a fire-place. Cost, 100*l.* Rent, 5*l.*, exclusive of 5*s.* for garden-ground.

Ambleside is noted for its building arts, insomuch that its workmen (called "wallers" and "slaters") are sent for from Manchester, Liverpool, and even, as I am told, London. The wages of the "wallers" or masons, are 4*s.* a-day; and of labourers, 15*s.* a-week. The builder of these cottages, Mr. Arthur Jackson,[76] turns out thorough good work. It was from him, as well as from another good builder, since dead,[77] that I learned that in this place a substantial cottage of four rooms can be built for 60*l.*—as I know it can elsewhere. I have now applied again to Mr. Jackson for estimates; and he says that he can undertake to build for 60*l.* a house of four comfortable rooms, with a pantry under the stairs, and a fire-place in each room.[78] For 100*l.* he would build one with five rooms, three above and two below, with a scullery. He has never built in brick, because no bricks are seen here, except the few imported for the backs of fire-places; but he is disposed to think he could build at the same cost in a brick country. Some evidence which I have just received confirms his opinion.

Here is an account of three superior brick cottages lately built in the neighbourhood of Manchester. Each contains the same amount of in-door accommodation as my cottages. The dimensions are:—

The "house-room"	15½	feet by	12 feet
The kitchen.	9	"	10 ft. 2 in
The pantry	9	"	5 feet
Chief bedroom over the "house-room."			
Two other bedrooms, each	9	feet by	7 ft. 7 in.

The cost is, in detail, as follows:

MATERIAL.	£	s.	*d.*
Bricks	37	0	0
Flags	17	0	0
Mantelpieces	6	10	0
Slates.	30	0	0
Laths, hair, and lime	16	0	0
Timber	40	0	0
Chimney-pots	1	10	0
Nails and ironwork	17	0	0
Total	165	0	0

LABOUR	£	*s.*	*d.*
Bricklayer	36	0	0
Slater	7	0	0
Blacksmith	7	0	0
Plumber	29	0	0
Painter	24	0	0
Joiner	32	0	0
Carting, &c.	27	0	0
	162	0	0
Material	165	0	0
Total	327	0	0

Or 109*l.* each. The proportions being preserved, it appears that in Manchester, as here, a good cottage of four rooms, without accessories, can be built for 60*l.*

Mr. Bracebridge published a notice, some two years since, of some labourers' cottages built for him twenty years before, which had stood well, and appeared advantageous enough to recommend afresh. A row of six dwellings, admitting of a common wash-house and other offices, can be built for 500*l.*—their quality being as follows:—

House-room, 13 feet by 12; a chief bed-room over it, of the same size. A second bed-room, smaller by the width of the stairs, is over the kitchen and pantry. By spending six guineas more, a room may be obtained in the roof, 12 feet by 8, and 8 feet high, lighted from the gable, or by a dormer window. The detailed account may be seen in the "Labourer's Friend" for November, 1857 (p. 180), and further particulars in a letter to the same publication, dated March 13th, 1858.

The fullest account that I know of, and on the largest scale, of the cost and rent of cottages, is contained in the *Report of the Poor-law Commissioners on the Sanitary Condition of the Labouring Classes, in* 1842.[79] The date is rather old; but such change as has taken place in the last seventeen years is in favour of cottage-building, as a speculation, as well as in the quality of the dwellings. The economy, as well as the sanitary condition, is better understood.

At p. 400 of that Report there are tabulated returns from the officers of twenty-four Unions in the manufacturing counties, in which we see (among other particulars) the cost of erection and the rent of three orders of cottages. I can here cite only the extremities of the scales. The lowest order of dwellings, yielding a rent of 3*l.* 5*s.* per annum, cost originally from 28*l.* (at Stockport) to 60*l.* (at Glossop).

The next order, yielding a rent of 5*l.* 15*s.*, cost from 40*l.* (at Uttoxeter) to 90*l.* (at Burslem and Burton-upon-Trent).

The best class, yielding a rent of 9*l.* 2*s.*, cost from 75*l.* (at Salford) to 155*l.* (at Derby).

At pp. 401 and 402 of the Report, there is a long list of the same particulars, with the cost of repairs, in regard to rural cottages in England and Scotland. The cost of four-roomed cottages varies astonishingly, being as low as 20*l.* and 25*l.* in Bedfordshire and Cheshire, and as high as 180*l.* in Suffolk. The greater number are set down as between 40*l.* and 100*l.*

Any reader who refers to these tables will certainly amuse himself with the whole portion of the Report which relates to the cottage-improvement at that time achieved. Nothing will strike him more than the account (at p. 265) of the labourers' cottages built by the Earl of Leicester at Holkham, in Norfolk, showing what a home the labouring man may have for the interest of 100*l*, with something additional for repairs; say a rent of 6*l*., though his kindly landlord asked less. In brief, the tenant has a—

House-room . . . . . . .17 feet by 12, and 7½ feet high.
Kitchen and Pantry . .13 " 9, "
Three bedrooms above.

In the rear, a wash-house, dirt-bin, privy, and pig-cot: and 20 rods of garden ground. The drainage excellent, and water abundant. For the rest, I must refer my readers to the Report, from p. 261 to p. 275, with engraved plans and illustrations.

More modern narratives and suggestions abound,—judging by booksellers' catalogues and advertisements. One of the most interesting notices of the subject that I have lately seen is in the October number of the "English Woman's Journal,"[80] and in letters, called forth by that article, at pp. 283 and 284 of the December number of the same Journal.[81] If these letters disclose a painful view of the ownership and condition of many cottages, they are also encouraging in regard to the eagerness of respectable labourers for respectable homes. To an account of tenements of four rooms each, with out-buildings and garden, costing from 75*l.* to 80*l.* each, the rent of which is 4*l.* 10*s.*, the remark is added: —

"The rents are paid up very regularly, so that this Michaelmas, out of twenty-six occupiers, there was not one defaulter."

This question of the cost of cottages is a very important one,—not only because it is bad for labourers to be charged anything but the genuine price for their abodes, but because there is no chance for the working-classes being well housed unless dwellings of a good quality can be made to pay. At present, unconscionable rents are, on the one hand, extorted for unwholesome and decayed dwellings; and, on the other, it is supposed that nobody but wealthy landowners can afford to build good cottages,—such cottages being regarded as an expensive charity. In my small way, I am satisfied with my investment: I know that other people are: and I believe that it is possible to lodge the working population of the kingdom well and comfortably, without depraving charity on the one hand, or pecuniary loss on the other.

In many—perhaps in most places—however, the first stage of the business is yet unaccomplished. Society is not convinced of the sin and shame of restricting the building of abodes for the working-classes, and of making them pay high rents for places unfit for human habitation. I fear there are many neighbourhoods in England too like, in this respect, to the one in which I live,—where many of the abodes of the humbler inhabitants are a disgrace to any civilised community. If ever there was a settlement favoured beyond others in regard to natural sanitary conditions, it is Ambleside: and if any one spot can be found superior even to Ambleside, it is Windermere (five miles off), where the railway ends, and whence the Lake tourist, on his arrival, overlooks from a height a glorious view of lake, wood, and mountain. In both places there is scarcely any level ground in the whole area. The facilities for drainage cannot be surpassed. There is rock for foundations; and the water-supply is unbounded—unbounded as to quantity, if it were regulated and distributed with any degree of care and good sense. Good soil, good air, great variety of level, and plenty of water,—what more could we ask in choosing a dwelling-place? Yet there is disease, vice and misery which would be accounted intolerable if they came in the shape of inevitable calamity. Instead of general declarations, I will offer a few facts,—omitting at present any notice of such abodes as are private property, in the hope that when reform begins with public property, the owners of cottages and small houses will be awakened to a sense of what they are doing in letting such tenements as many in Ambleside, either by the shame of contrast, or by losing their tenants. While mansions and villas are rising throughout the neighbourhood, one has to wait years to obtain a few yards of ground on which to build a cottage. All possible discountenance is shown to cottage-building: and I have myself been told, many times a year, for many years, that the people could not pay rent for good cottages, and would not take them if they were provided to-morrow. This must be altogether a mistake. There is, as I said, great anxiety to occupy my cottages; and rents of 4*l.* and 5*l.* are paid for dwellings of which the following is a true account. They were measured and reported upon a day or two ago.

These houses are endowment property, under the care of the trustees of the school. The trustees do not dispute the condition of the property, nor defend the exorbitant rents they are obliged to demand; but they declare that they find it impossible to obtain from the Charity Commissioners the necessary powers for its improvement. They have repeatedly made application; but the delays, the mislaying of papers, the fruitless trouble incurred, has discouraged them. Meantime, the state of three houses, as examined, is this.

Number One is inhabited by a family of six persons. There is no water-supply whatever. There is no out-door convenience which can be used by decent people. There is no opening in back or sides, and no ventilation at all in the sleeping-place but one small pane, which the mother broke the other day, to prevent the young people being stifled (a danger increased, by the way, by the boys smoking their pipes within doors, even in the mornings). The six sleep in two beds scarcely larger than sofas. The living-room is 10½ feet long by 10 broad, and 7 feet 2 inches high.

Number Two contains a family of eight persons. The conditions as to air, water, and convenience, are the same; the living-rom is 10½ feet by 9. The rent is 4*l.*

Number Three contains a family of six. Conditions

mainly the same. The living-room is 7 feet 2 inches in height; but only 8 feet 6 inches long by 7 feet 9 inches wide. The rent is 5*l.*, the same that is paid by my friend's tenant for an airy, cheerful, well-found dwelling of four rooms and outhouse, on the hill-side.—This is all I will at present say of labourers' dwellings at Ambleside.

At Windermere a new town has sprung up since the establishment of the railway-station, and the temporary residence of a clergyman of architectural propensities; so that we naturally supposed the new settlement to be peculiarly healthy,—all fresh and new, and set upon a platform, absolutely tempting for drainage. Some weeks ago we were startled by news of a terrible fever—typhoid fever—at Windermere, the schoolmaster being dead, and several other persons who could ill be spared. The mortality between that time and this has been fearful. A good man who lived there desired, a few years since, to carry his large family to Australia. He was too old to go by the aid of the Emigration Commissioners, and his friends lent him the means to go and establish himself, with the intention of sending afterwards for his wife and seven children. He slowly made his way in Australia, has paid his friends, and is now, no doubt, looking forward to the arrival of his family in no long time; but, alas! this fever has carried off four out of the seven children. This is the news which is on the way to the affectionate father!

When one inquires the precise cause of the epidemic, one medical man says there is no sufficient house-drainage at Windermere; another says the mischief is owing to the quantity of decomposed vegetable matter—to the swamps, in short, on the platform; while another declares that the main evil is the accumulation of filth. Whether it be any one or all of these, the mortality is chargeable on ignorance or carelessness, or worse.

While such things are happening here, there, or everywhere, every year, it is a matter of no small consequence to ascertain the conditions on which our labouring population may be well housed,—as a matter of business, and not of mere charity; that is, under the steady natural laws of society, and not the fluctuating influence of human sensibilities, which have always more calls upon them than they can meet. When it is ascertained that it answers to labourers to pay from 3*l.* to 6*l.* rent, rather than have sickness in the house, and that they may have for that rent good dwellings of from four to six rooms, or equivalent attachments, there will be a manifest decrease in the sickness and mortality of the country.

CHAPTER SIX

THE ENGLISH LAKE DISTRICT[82]

INTRODUCTION

IT IS A DESIRABLE THING for every country that it should have within its borders a mountainous district. Though some people regard such a district as little better than waste land, unless it happens to be rich in minerals, it has a value, however wild it may be, as real and as great as can be boasted of by the richest plain; and a value the greater, perhaps, in proportion to the wildness. The wilder the mountain-region of any country, the more certain it is to be the conservator of the antiquities of that country. When invaders come, the inhabitants retreat to the fastnesses where they cannot be pursued; and in places cut off from communication do ancient ideas and customs linger the longest. Every mountain-chain or cluster is a piece of the old world preserved in the midst of the new; and the value of this peculiarity far transcends that of any profitable quality which belongs to territory of another kind.

There is, also, a value belonging to a mountainous district which in our particular time can hardly be over-rated. It is the only kind of territory in which utility must necessarily be subordinated to beauty. However open-hearted and open-eyed we may be to the beauty of utility itself, and of all that is connected with it, we cannot but enjoy the privilege of access to a region where grandeur and grace reign supreme from age to age, and the subsistence and comfort of men occur only as an accident or an afterthought. It is well that we should be able and disposed to honour and admire the great inventions and arrangements of men,—the sublime railway, the wonderful factory, the cheerful stretch of corn-fields, the hopeful school-organization, and all glorious associations of men for mutual benefit: but it is well also that we should have access to a region where the winds and the waters, the mists and the stars, old forests and unapproachable precipices occupy the space, and man is seen only here and there, sheltering himself in some recess, or moving, a mere speck, on the mountain-side, or drawing his subsistence from the trout-stream, whose flow is scarcely heard among the echoes of the mighty hills. Elsewhere we have beauty in the midst of use. In a mountain-district we have a complete world of beauty which cannot be touched by the hand of Use. Man may come and live, if he likes and if he can; but it must be in some humble corner, by permission, as it were, and not through conflict with the genius of the place. Nature and beauty here rule and occupy: man and his desires are subordinate, and scarcely discernible.

Yet it does not follow that the hilly retreats of any country are bare of human interest. As I have said, they are conservative of races, and manners, and traditions; and they also offer a quiet field to science. The other day I was climbing among the ridges of the highest mountain-cluster of the Lake District, when I came upon a rain-gauge, set up in a desolate and misty spot,—sometimes below and often above the clouds. There are four more set up, and carefully secured against the force of the gales, on other heights, and an aged shepherd has them in charge: he visits them once a month, to record what they show. As I watched the tall old man with his staff passing out of sight of the vast mountain-slope, I thought that knowledge and wisdom are as appropriate and as beautiful here as anywhere else on the earth. This mountain solitude is no scene for the busy handiwork of men, in their toil for bread or convenience; but neither is it a tomb "where no knowledge or device is found."[83] Contemplative science may sit upon these heights, for ever vigilant and for ever gratified; for here without pause come all the necessary aids and means in long array,—the stars and the sunshine, the gales and the mists, the hail and the lightnings,—all conceivable displays of light, and Nature's whole orchestra of sounds. Here is the eye of science trained and charmed by all that is luminous, from the glittering dewdrop, past the spectral mist, and the rainbow under foot, to the furthest gleam of the western sea: and the ear is roused and instructed by all mournful melodies, from the hum of the gnat in the summer noon, to the iron note of the raven, and the dash of the torrent, or the growl of the thunder, echoing through cavern and ravine. Here then, while man is subordinated, he is not excluded. He cannot obtrude his noisy devices and his bustling handiworks upon this royal domain of nature: but if he is humble and devoutly studious, Nature will invite his industry to prosper in her valleys, and his science to keep watch upon her heights.

The conservative office belonging to all mountain-districts has never been more distinctly performed than in the case of these west moorlands, from which Westmoreland takes its name. A remnant of every race hard pressed by foes in the rest of England has found a refuge among the fastnesses of the north-west. The first people of whom we have any clear impression as living here are the Druids, as the upper class, probably, of the Britons who inhabited the valleys. There are still oaks worthy to be the haunt of these old priests; but there were many more in the days of the Druids. There is reason to believe that the mountains were once wooded up to a great height, with few breaks in the forest; and it is still said by old people living at the foot of Helvellyn, that a squirrel might have gone from their chapel of Wythburn to Keswick, about ten miles, on the tree tops, without touching the ground. The remaining coppice of hollies, firs, birch, ash, and oak, show something of the character of the woods of which they are the degenerate remnants. And when we look upon Rydal Forest, and the oak woods of some of the northern seats, we see how much at home the Druid race or caste might formerly be in the region.

Several of their stone circles are scattered about the district, calling up images of the shaven-headed, long-bearded, white-robed priests, gathered in a glade of the neighbouring forest, or assembling in some cleared space, to put fire to their heaped sacrifice of animals and doomed criminals. Such punishments of criminals, here and in those days, were little enough like the executions in our cities in the present age. Then, as the rude music of the wild Britons drowned the cries of the victims, and the flames of the wicker pile cast a glare fitfully on the forest trees, or darted up above the fir-tops, the red deer shrank further into the brake; the wild bull sent an answering roar from the slope of the mountain, the wolf prowled about for the chance of a prey, and the eagle stirred his wings upon his eyrie. The Druid and his barbaric Britons, the red deer, the wild bull, and the wolf, are all gone from the living scene, to group themselves again for us, as we see, in the ghost-land of tradition; and the eagle shows himself so seldom, that his presence is looked upon as a mere casual return.

It was a strange day for the region when the Roman soldiers came: and strange must have been the sight to the sentinel set by the Britons to watch what the foreign invader was about to do. The sentinel would climb the loftiest tree of the highest forest line, and tell what he saw to his comrades below. He would tell of the Roman standards peeping out from the pathways in the woods, and the armour that glittered when the sun shone out, and the halt in the meadows at the head of Windermere, and the formation of the camp, the pitching of the tents in long lines, and the throwing up of the breast-works. Then he would come down, and lead the way for his warrior brethren to attack the enemy. However desperate might be the onset of the wild Britons in their skin garments, with scythes and clubs in hand, they could not dislodge the foe; and when they were driven back, to hide themselves again in caves and ravines, the enemy immediately began to make pathways for the passage of their soldiery. The echoes might be the sentries then, telling of the shock of falling trees, one by one, till a broad highway was made for many miles. Then there was the cleaving of the rocks, and the breaking of the stones for paving the highway, and building the piers of the bridges. By what we see now, we know that these Roman roads not only crossed the valleys, and cut over the spurs of the hills, but followed the line of some of the highest ridges. When the Romans had gained the summit of High Street, for instance, what a day it must have been for the natives! The lines and clusters of the soldiery must have been seen against the sky,—some bringing the stones, and others paving the broad way, and others keeping watch, while signal trumpets were blown from time to time, scaring the birds from their rock-nests, and making the British mother press her infant to her bosom, lest its feeble cry should be heard from the depths of the wood below.

These Britons hid so well, that they remained in considerable numbers when the Romans were gone. But they never regained possession of the fertile valleys and meadows: the Saxons and Danes took possession of them as the Romans left them. The Britons were now, however, well armed. They had obtained some of the Roman arms, and they could so well oppose the Saxon battle-axe and hammer, that they never yielded up their mountain region, except in small portions here and there, during the whole six hundred years of the Saxon dominion in England. They held their villages and hamlets, as well as their ravines and forests: and, for any thing that appears, they were living in almost their primitive condition among the west moorlands when the Normans arrived, and scattered the Saxons abroad, to find life and shelter where they could.

To these west moorlands the Saxons came, not now as conquerors, and to possess the land, but as fugitives, who had no chance but to become outlaws. Many a man of rank and wealth came hither to escape slavery, or the ferocious punishments inflicted by the Normans on those who meddled with their game. When a Saxon noble had seen his lands taken from him and given to some Norman soldier, his daughter compelled to marry any one of the foe who chose to demand her, his servant deprived of eyes or hands for having shot a deer in his own woods,—when his blood boiled under these injuries, and he could do nothing in self-defence; he gave the sign to his followers, caught horses where he could, and rode away to the west moorlands, to be henceforth the head of an outlaw band among the Fells, descending upon Yorkshire and the southern levels of Lancashire, to plunder for subsistence, and destroy everything Norman, in gratification of his revenge. After this time we know no more of the Britons; and the

Romans are traceable only by the remains of a camp, road, or bridge, here and there.[84]

Almost everywhere else in England the Saxons and Normans mingled, and intermarried, and forgot their enmity within two or three generations: but it was not so among the Fells. The lands might be nominally given away to Norman chiefs; but they did not come to take possession of them. The wild hills and moors yielded nothing worth insisting upon and holding by force; and they were too near Scotland, where there was an enemy always on the watch against the new possessors of England. So, while Norman castles domineered over the fertile lands of all southern districts, the Saxons kept their race, language, and, as far as possible, their usages, untouched among the Fells. Accordingly, instead of the remains of feudal castles and feudal usages among the more retired parts of this district, we find only the changes which have been made by Nature, or by the hand of the shepherd, the miner, or the forester, for the needs of their free inhabitants.

The Normans, however, approached as near as they could. It may be observed here that in the Lake District, the ground rises gradually from the outskirts to the centre. From surrounding levels swell gentle slopes, with shallow valleys between; and within these are higher hills, with deeper intervals, till we find, as a nucleus, the peaks of Scawfell and the neighbouring summits, cleft with chasms and ravines. Certain Norman nobles and monks, to whom lands had been granted, came and sat down in the levels, and spread their flocks and tributary husbandmen over the slopes and nearer valleys, though they appear never to have attempted an entrance upon the wilder parts. The abbey of Furness was established in A.D. 1127; its domains extending over the whole promontory of Furness, and to the north as far as the Shire Stones, on Wrynose; and being bounded on the east and west by Windermere and the Duddon. The mountain-land included here is not much: only the Coniston mountains and Wetherlam being of considerable elevation.

The Abbot of Furness was a sort of king in his place. His monastery was richly endowed by King Stephen,[85] and maintained in wealth by the gifts of neighbouring proprietors, who were glad to avail themselves, not only of its religious privileges, but of its military powers for the defence of their estates against Border foes and the outlaws of the mountains.

In the low grounds between the Scawfell Peaks and the sea, Calder Abbey was next placed. It dates from A.D. 1134; seven years after the establishment of Furness Abbey, of which it was a dependent. The small religious house of St. Bees was restored by a Norman about the same time. It was very ancient, and had been destroyed by the Danes; but it now became a Norman monkish settlement. Round to the north-east, and lying under the Picts' Wall, we find the Augustine Priory of Lanercost, founded in 1169 by the Norman lord of Gilsland. Several castles were scattered around the skirts of the mountain cluster: and as the serfs on the estates rose to the condition of tenants, facilities were continually offering for the new owners to penetrate more and more into the retired parts of the district.

The process appears to have been this, in the case of Furness Abbey:—The lord's land was divided into tenements. Each tenement was to furnish, besides proper rent, an armed man, to be always ready for battle on the Borders or elsewhere. The tenement was divided into four portions,—woodland, pasture, and arable land being taken as they came; and each portion was given to an emancipated serf. The four who were thus placed on each complete tenement took care of the whole of it;—one of their number always holding himself in readiness to go armed to the wars. Thus spread over the land, and secure of being permitted to attend to their business in all ordinary times, the tenants would presently feel themselves, and be regarded by the mountaineer, husbandmen on their own ground rather than retainers of the hostile lord; and their approach towards the fastnesses would be watched with less and less suspicion. As for the shepherds, they were more free still in their rovings with their flocks: and when, by permission of the abbots, they inclosed crofts about their hillside huts, for the sake of browsing their charge on the sprouts of the ash and the holly, and protecting them from the wolves[86] in the thickets, they might find themselves in a position for many friendly dealings with the dwellers in the hills. The inclosures for the protection of the flocks certainly spread up the mountain sides to a height where they would hardly be seen now if ancient custom had not drawn the lines which are still preserved: and it appears from historical testimony that these fences existed before the fertile valleys were portioned out among many holders. Higher and higher ran these stone inclosures,—threading the woods, and joining on upon the rocks. Now, the woods are for the most part gone; and the walls offend and perplex the stranger's eye and mind by their ugliness and apparent uselessness: but, their origin once known, we would not willingly part with them,—reminding us as they do of the times when the tenants of the abbots or military noble formed a link between the new race of inhabitants and the Saxon remnant of the old.

The holders of these crofts were the original of the Dalesmen of the present day. Their name arises, we are told, not from the dales of the region,—these tenants being chiefly dwellers on the heights,—but from the word *deyler*, which means *to distribute*. In course of time, when the Border wars were ended, and armed retainers were no longer needed, the distribution of the inhabitants underwent a change, and several portions of land were held by one tenant. To this day, however, separate fines are often paid for each lot; this recognition of a feudal superior, on the part of purchasers who have otherwise a freehold tenure of their lands, being a curious relic of ancient manners. The purchaser of two or three acres, subject to no other liability, will enjoy paying his nine pence a year to the lord, in memory of the time when tenancy was a sort of servitude, of which there are now no remains but in this observance.

For many centuries, an extraordinary supply of armed men was required; for the Border wars, which raged almost without intermission from the reign of the Conqueror to that of Queen Anne,[87] were conducted with great ravage and cruelty. Besides the frequent slaughter, many hundreds of prisoners were carried away, on the one side or the other, after almost every battle. The aim of the Scots usually was to attack and pillage Carlisle, Penrith and Cockermouth, and the neighbouring country: but though the devastation and pillage were chiefly experienced there, the loss of men was felt throughout the whole mountain district. The enemy sometimes fell on the Border towns in fair-time, for the sake of the booty: and sometimes they came down when least expected. We read of them as laying waste the district of Furness; and again as ravaging the whole country on their way into Yorkshire. Wherever they might appear or be expected, there must the armed vassal repair on summons; and for retaliatory incursions he must also be prepared. The curse of the war thus spread into the most secluded valleys, where there was no road by which soldiery might arrive, or cattle be carried away. The young wife or aged parents need not there apprehend that their cottage would be fired over their heads, or their crops be trodden into the bloody swamp of a battlefield; but they must part with the husband and the son, to overwhelming chances of death, wounds, or captivity. Under the constant drain of able-bodied men for many centuries, the homes of the region must have been but little like what English homes, and especially mountain homes, are usually considered to be;—abodes where life goes on with extraordinary sameness from generation to generation.

After the Union,[88] the Lake District became again one

of the quietest on the face of the earth. Except some little excitement and disturbance when the Pretender and his force marched from Carlisle, by Penrith and Shap to Kendal, there seems to have been no inroad upon the tranquillity of the inhabitants to this day for nearly a century and a half. If there be any exception, it is owing to that Border distinction which made Gretna Green,[89] and the conclusion of a certain sort of treaty there, the aim of a certain order of fugitives, whose pursuers were pretty sure to follow on their track. But this kind of Border contention must have been merely amusing to the Cumbrians; and the encounter and capture which they sometimes witnessed involved no danger to life or limb.

The changes which have taken place since the extinction of the Border wars at the Union are of the same quiet, gradual, inevitable kind, which Nature has been carrying on from the time that the mountains were upreared. Nature is always at work, producing changes which do not show from day to day, but are very striking after a course of years. She disintegrates the rocks, and now and then sends down masses thundering along the ravines, to bridge over a chasm, or make a new islet in a pool: she sows her seeds in crevices, or on little projections, so that the bare face of the precipice becomes feathered with the rowan and the birch; and thus, ere long, motion is produced by the passing winds, in a scene where all once appeared rigid as a mine: she draws her carpet of verdure gradually up the bare slopes where she has deposited earth to sustain the vegetation: she is for ever covering with her exquisite mosses and ferns every spot which has been left unsightly, till nothing appears to offend the human eye, within a whole circle of hills. She even silently rebukes and repairs the false taste of uneducated man. If he makes his new dwelling of too glaring a white, she tempers it with weather stains: if he indolently leaves the stone walls and blue slates unrelieved by any neighbouring vegetation, she supplies the needful screen by bringing out tufts of delicate fern in the crevices, and springing coppice on the nearest slopes. She is perpetually working changes in the disposition of the waters of the region. The margins of the lakes never remain the same for half a century together. The streams bring down soft soil incessantly, which more effectually alters the currents than the slides of stones precipitated from the heights by an occasional storm. By this deposit of soil new promontories are formed, and the margin contracts, till many a reach of waters is converted into land, inviting tillage. The greenest levels of the smaller valleys may be seen to have been once lakes. And while she is thus closing up in one direction, she is opening in another. In some low-lying spot a tree falls, which acts as a dam when the next rains come. The detained waters sink, and penetrate, and loosen the roots of other trees; and the moisture which they formerly absorbed goes to swell the accumulation till the place becomes a swamp. The drowned vegetation decays and sinks, leaving more room, till the place becomes a pool, on whose bristling margin the snipe arrives to rock on the bulrush, and the heron wades in the water-lilies to feed on the fish which come there, no one knows how. As the waters spread, they encounter natural dams, behind which they grow clear and deepen, till we have a tarn among the hills, which attracts the browsing flock, and tempts the shepherd to build his hut near the brink. Then the wild swans see the glittering expanse in their flight, and drop down into it; and the waterfowl make their nests among the reeds. This brings the sportsman; and a path is trodden over the hills; and the spot becomes a place of human resort. While Nature is thus working transformations in her deeper retreats, the generations of men are more obviously busy elsewhere. They build their houses and plant their orchards on the slopes which connect the mountains with the levels of the valleys: they encroach upon the swamps below them, and plough among the stones on the hill-sides,—here fencing in new grounds, there throwing several plots into one: they open slate quarries, and make broad roads for the carriage of the produce: they cherish the young hollies and ash, whose sprouts feed their flocks, thus providing a compensation in the future for the past destruction of the woods. Thus, while the general primitive aspect of the region remains, and its intensely rural character is little impaired, there is perhaps scarcely a valley in the district which looks the same from one half century to another.

The changes among the people proceed faster: and some of these changes are less agreeable to contemplate, however well aware we may be that they are to issue in good. Formerly, every household had nearly all that it wanted within itself. The people thought so little of wheaten bread, that wheat was hardly to be bought in the towns. Within the time of the existing generation, an old man of eighty-five was fond of telling how, when a boy, he wanted to spend his penny on wheaten bread; and he searched through Carlisle from morning to evening before he could find a penny roll. The cultivator among the hills divided his field into plots, where he grew barley, oats, flax, and other produce, to meet the needs of his household. His pigs, fed partly on acorns or beech mast, yielded good bacon and hams; and his sheep furnished wool for clothing. Of course he kept cows. The women spun and wove the wool and flax; and the lads made the wooden utensils, baskets, fishing-tackle, &c. Whatever else was needed was obtained from the pedlars, who came their rounds two or three times a year, dropping in among the little farms from over the hills. The first great change was from the opening of carriage-roads. There was a temptation then to carry stock and grain to fairs and markets. More grain was grown than the household needed, and offered for sale. In a little while, the mountain farmers were sure to fail in competition in the markets with dwellers in agricultural districts. The mountaineers had no agricultural science, and little skill; and the decline of the fortunes of the statesmen (estatesmen), as they are locally called, has been regular, and mournful to witness. They haunt the fairs and markets, losing in proportion to the advance of improvement elsewhere. On their first losses, they began to mortgage their lands. After bearing the burden of these mortgages till they could bear it no longer, their children have sold the lands; and among the shop-boys, domestic servants, and labourers of the towns, we find the old names of the former yeomanry of the district, who have parted with their lands to strangers. Much misery intervened during this process of transition. The farmer was tempted to lose the remembrance of his losses in drink, when he attended the fairs and markets. The domestic manufactures he carried with him,—the linen and woollen webs woven by his wife and daughters,—would not sell, except at a loss, in the presence of the Yorkshire and Lancashire woollens and cottons made by machinery. He became unable to keep his children at home, and they went off to the manufacturing towns, leaving home yet more cheerless—with fewer busy hands and cheerful faces—less social spirit in the dales—greater certainty of continued loss, and more temptation to drink. Such is the process still going on. Having reached this pass, it is clearly best that it should go on till the primitive population, having lost its safety of isolation and independence, and kept its ignorance and grossness, shall have given place to a new set of inhabitants, better skilled in agriculture and in every way more up to the times. It is mournful enough to a resident to meet everywhere the remnants of the old families in a reduced and discouraged condition; but if they can no longer fill the valleys with grain, and cover the hill-sides with flocks, it is right that those who can should enter upon their lands, and that knowledge, industry, and temperance, should find their fair field and due reward.

There has been much lamentation made about the

approach of railways to the district; and strenuous efforts were employed in vain to prevent their penetrating the mountain region. The thing is done now, and it can never be undone. One railway runs from Kendal to Carlisle, by Shap Fell; another skirts the mountain region to the northwest, passing from Carlisle to Maryport; another penetrates to Windermere from Kendal. It might be enough to say that, as the thing is done, and cannot be undone, there is nothing for it but to acquiesce, and make the best of it. But there is a more cheerful and grateful way of regarding the matter,—more cheerful, while not less serious. We can fully sympathize with the resident gentry, who, having either inherited the secluded abodes of their fathers, or come hither to live in the midst of quietness and beauty, dread the invasion of the quietness, and the impairing of some of the beauty. But, if they reckoned on having, for their own exclusive possession, any of the repose and beauty of the wide open earth, they reckoned on what they have no right to. They have hitherto enjoyed a rare privilege, a pure gift in their lot, temporary in its very nature; and when its term has arrived, they have no right to complain, as of any personal grievance. In the fulness of our sympathy for this class, we may even see with pleasure that the new state of things may yield them moral blessings of far greater value than anything they can lose. "The trail of the serpent" is in every earthly paradise, whether the dwellers heed it or not. Here it is evident enough to those who are not too familiar with the place to note its peculiarities. The life of refined enjoyment led by those who live in a beautiful seclusion, has a strong tendency to make them exclusive, fastidious, and too often insolent towards the world without. The danger of the growth of this temper is great to the most watchful and guarded; and it is certain that some who think the liberality of their tempers of more consequence than the seclusion of their valley, are personally thankful for the little shock which has roused them to a consideration of the claims of all fellow-heirs of the earth, and of the tenure on which they hold their local enjoyments.

We have full sympathy also with those who imagine that there will arrive by these railways an influx of moral and economical evil to the fixed population of the district. We do not agree with them as to the fact, but we respect the objection. Such persons fear that there will be a rush to the district; that starved artizans will come in crowds to displace the present occupants, or to divide their work: and that over-population, reduced wages, and pauperism, will be the consequence. But almost all the occupations of the region are so peculiar, so remarkably local, that it must be very long before strangers can compete with the old residents. Even the agriculture is modified by the locality: and if it were not, it is for the interest of all that the land should be in good hands; and the qualifications of those who can purchase and undertake to till lands are surely more promising than those of the parties who cannot hold the farms which have come to them as an hereditary possession. As for the other occupations of the region, it is difficult to see how the builders of Ambleside,—so noted in their craft as to be sent for from Liverpool, Manchester, and even London,—can be displaced and thrown out of work by hungry operatives from Manchester or Paisley. The same may be said of the copper and lead miners of Coniston and Borrowdale; the slate and stone quarrymen of Honister Crag, Rydal, and Langdale and many others. If more labour is wanted and can be maintained, it will gradually flow in, and be trained to its work: and this will be a good for all parties. But there can be no reasonable fear that trained and skilled local workmen can be excluded or depressed by untrained and unskilled strangers from the manufacturing towns.

As for the fear that the innocent rural population will be morally corrupted by intercourse with people from the towns, we have no apprehension of this, but are disposed to hope rather than fear certain consequences from the increased intercourse of the mountaineers with the people of large towns. We doubt at once the innocence of the one party and the specific corruption of the other. Scarcely anything can be conceived more lifeless, unvaried, and unideal, than the existence of the Dalesmen and their families; and where the intellect is left so idle and unimproved as among them, the sensual vices are sure to prevail. These vices rage in the villages and small towns; and probably no clergyman or Justice of the Peace will be ever heard speaking of the rural innocence of the region,—which is indeed to be found only in works of the imagination. The people have their virtues, many and great: they are kind as neighbours, and hospitable to strangers: their probity in money transactions is very remarkable: they are thrifty and prudent, as far as their knowledge goes, while liberal and genial in their dealings: they are independent in their ways and notions; sometimes shy in manners, but in temper easy and free. Now, while this is the case, and while they dwell among their free mountains, in the birthplace of their country customs, scattered or gathered together where every man of them is wanted, and of value, and where there is room for a good many more, it appears most improbable that they should learn from strangers a trickery, servility,—a mendicant habit of mind, which is altogether inappropriate to their condition of mind and life. It seems improbable, too, that the mendicant class of townsmen—or those who carry within them the mendicant mind—should come hither by railway to reside. If, by the apprehended corruption, a spirit of accumulation and worldliness is meant, it is here already, in a greater degree than in the towns. The clergy declare that their duties are so far different from those of their brethren in cities, that they have to preach against worldliness, instead of having to inculcate foresight and thrift. We speak here in a very general way, as we must when describing a general population anywhere. We may, no doubt, find spendthrift villagers, and intellectual Dalesmen in the region; but we understand the prevalent character of the people to be as we have said.

Thus we have no fear of either moral or economical mischief to the region from the opening of railroads into it. On the contrary, we hope for much good. To begin with the lowest consideration,—we hope for a fuller and cheaper supply of fuel; a matter of no small importance in a region of mists and snows, where rheumatism and consumption are the curse of old and young in mountain dwellings. We hope for the introduction of arts and conveniences which are elsewhere already at the command of men of the same quality as the residents here. We hope for a quickening of intellect and education of taste, which cannot be more wanted anywhere than they are here. In some of the vales, the inhabitants appear really scarcely able to speak. Their seclusion, and the deadness of their lives, reduce some few of them, though not poor, to the intellectual condition of the lowest specimen of coal-pit or factory training which has been adduced to rouse the sympathies of society. The men have some little stimulus and friction of mind by going to markets, and meeting neighbours when out at work: but the women, who stay at home, seeing scarcely a face for months together, except at an occasional fair, seem hardly able to express themselves by speech. If they have any thoughts, they cannot bring them out. Such as these live in the most retired parts: but even in the villages and little towns, there is among the labouring classes a slowness of mind, and difficulty of utterance, truly surprising to any one conversant with people of the same standing in cities, and certainly not, in his eyes, any token of a condition too good to be improved.

With the rousing of the intellect generally we may hope to see the improvement of taste in particular. The girls dress in a style which is quite gone out elsewhere—

at least in the retired parts. In towns, we are disposed to welcome among the poor an ambition to be well dressed, as some little safeguard against squalidness or recklessness. Here, where such safeguards are not wanted, there is something painful, if not ludicrous, in the passion for fine clothes, unregulated by any degree of taste. We were approaching a primitive little country church one morning lately, while its rusty outside bell was clanging to collect the worshippers. Among these was a group of country women, one of whom, a fair girl, was talking very loudly about ball-dresses, slackening her steps as she approached the porch, to finish telling her companions her conjectures as to whether Charles —— admired her most in her diamonds or her emeralds. In a humble dwelling, in a retired corner of the district, we saw a curious article hung up at the foot of the bed—a clear muslin frock, which would fit a child of four years old, trimmed with lace and satin ribbons, and stuck over, in the waist and sleeves, with atrocious artificial flowers, red and blue, with a morsel of tinsel in the middle of each bunch. The same want of taste is seen in the household ornaments, as far as their idea of art is concerned, though, when they are not thinking of art, their taste is good enough. One may see in the fire-places in summertime beautiful bunches of holly, or other green, refreshing the eye, while on the mantel-shelf are scarlet and blue earthenware castles, or the 'Children in the Wood,' lying in ball-dresses, with a lilac and green robin, very like a pelican in shape, covering them with cabbage leaves. Round the walls are pictures of the

'Resurrection,' or the 'Virgin and Child,' so shocking as to make one look away; or Queen Victoria, on a prancing yellow horse, in a scarlet riding habit, with a fierce plume of blue feathers in her hat. It will be strange if, in a short time, the railway does not bring into the district those specimens of art, in the shape of cheap casts and prints, which have of late years been a blessing diffused over every other part of the island. Meantime, we cannot believe that any inhabitant of the valleys would, if seriously asked, say that his happiness has been impaired by the sight of the parties who arrive by steamboat or railway, carrying their provisions, and sitting down in the churchyard, or under the trees of some knoll, to have their minds opened and their hearts softened by a spectacle of beauty which gives them for a time a new existence. The annoyance to residents is not from these; but from those self-called gentry who travelled hither before the railways were opened, and who came for other purposes than to enjoy the natural beauty laid open to all; people who prowl about the residences of the celebrated persons who live here for the sake of quietness, knocking at the door to ask for autographs, staring in at the windows, taking possession of the gardens, thrusting themselves into the houses with complimentary speeches, and then sending to the newspapers an account of all they saw and heard, and much that they merely imagined. If we were to tell what we have seen of the intrusions upon the domestic quiet of the aged poet[90] whose presence is the crowning honour of the district, it would be seen that before railway and steamer were heard of in the neighbourhood of Windermere, all chance of quiet was destroyed for three months of the year, for those whose leisure and whose homes should, in common gratitude, be better respected. The new facilities for access have not as yet increased this evil; for the new class of visitors have better manners than those who could afford to come by other means. Of this new class we would say—let them come; and the more the better! that the more refreshment of spirit may be shed from the fountains of beauty here into the dusty ways of common life in the towns.

In order to give a detailed account of the principal objects of interest in the Lake District in the most intelligible and practical form, we will divide the whole into four portions, which will be treated separately.

It has been observed that, from the sea-coast and level lands which surround the region, the whole rises towards the centre, where the loftiest mountain peaks are found: that is, the ridges on the whole rise, and the valleys deepen, and the summits become more imposing, till, near the centre, Scawfell, Bowfell, Gable, and the Langdale Pikes, tower over all. We propose to divide the region lying round these mountains into four: and the first that we will take shall be that which is bounded by the Duddon, the sea, and Ennerdale. And, as we have not space to review every possible way of traversing the ground, we will suppose the observer to proceed in the best way of all,—on foot, for the most part, with the relief of a country car or a horse on the high-roads in the outskirts.

I.

PERHAPS the best way of approaching the Duddon is to descend upon it from Walna Scar, from Coniston. When the traveller has left the bright and prosperous environs of Coniston behind him, and entered upon the moor, he begins to feel at once the exhilaration of the mountaineer. Behind him lies a wide extent of hilly country, subsiding into the low blue ridges of Lancashire. Below him, he sees when he turns, here and there a reach of the Lake of Coniston,—gray, if his walk be, as it should be, in the morning:

Fig. 10. Coniston Old Man

gray, and reflecting the dark promontories in a perfect mirror. To the right, as he proceeds, towers the Coniston mountain,—the Old Man; (Figure 10;) and the only traces of human existence that he can perceive are the tracks which wind along and up its slopes,—the paths to the copper-mine,—and a solitary house, looking very desolate among its bare fields and fences. Soon, however, when he has crossed one or two of the grassy undulations of the moor, be comes upon a party of peat-cutters, with their crate, and their white horse, which looks absolutely glittering in the sunlight, amidst the brownness of the ground. The next trace of man that he meets is in a little stone bridge spanning the rushing brown stream, the outlet of the tarn called Goat's Water, which has always water enough to make foam among the stones in its channel, and in winter is a torrent. Before him is a pretty steep ascent, with a well-marked track: and as soon as he begins to pant, and to complain of the heat, a breath of cool air comes to him over the ridge, warning him to turn and bid farewell to the scene behind him before a new one is disclosed.

What a disclosure it is, when he has gone a few steps further! To the right, (the north,) rise the highest summits of the district, Scawfell and Bowfell, with the lower Hardknot interposed between them and the eye. A little further round to the front, (the west,) are the sweeping Screes, behind which Wastwater is hidden. Over the ridges before him lies, with a high horizon line, the sea, blue in the morning light: and his eye discerns, faint and far, the hilly outline of the Isle of Man. All around him are fells, sloping down to the Duddon, and completely enclosing the little circular vale of Seathwaite, into which he is now to descend. These fells are, some of them, and especially the one on which he stands, green and smooth: others are brown with heather; or half-covered with wood; or broken up by gray rocks. Below him he sees,—not the Duddon, for it is hidden in a deep rocky channel,—but the vale so well known through Wordsworth's description of it in his notes to his Duddon Sonnets.[91] Down he goes into it, first by the green track across the fell, and then by a steep stony road, which lands him at last among the farmsteads of the vale, and the gray stone cottages, each overshadowed by its massive sycamores or light birch, and surrounded by its field plots.

Of course, his first inquiry is for the church, and Robert Walker's tomb: and he is told to follow the road above the beck (brook) till be comes to Newfield. The brook is so like a river that he takes it for the Duddon: but the Duddon, though close at hand, is not yet visible; there being still a ridge between its deep channel and the brook. A sweeter walk than this,—the two miles from the ridge of Walna Scar to Seathwaite church,—can scarcely be found, nor a more complete contrast than between the wildness of the moor and the rich broken ground of the vale, with its wooded and rocky knolls, its full stream, prosperous homesteads, and fertile fields. When the traveller reaches the church, he finds it little loftier or larger than the houses near. But for the bell, he would hardly have noticed it for a church on approaching: but when he has reached it, there is the porch, and the little graveyard, with a few tombs, and the spreading yew, encircled by the seat of stones and turf, where the early comers sit and rest till the bell calls them in. A little dial, on a whitened post in the middle of the enclosure, tells the time to the neighbours who have no clocks. Just outside the wall is a white cottage, so humble that the stranger thinks it cannot be the parsonage: yet the climbing roses and glittering evergreens, and clear lattices, and pure, uncracked walls, look as if it might be. He walks slowly past the porch, and sees a kind-looking elderly woman, who tells him that it is indeed Robert Walker's dwelling, and invites him in to see the scene of those wondrous charities of sixty-six years. Here it was that the distant parishioners were fed on Sundays with broth, for which the whole week's supply of meat was freely bestowed. Hither it was that, in winter, he sent the benumbed children in companies from the school in the church, to warm themselves at the single household fire, while he sat by the altar during all the school-hours, keeping warmth in him by the exercise of the spinning-wheel. But the story is too well known for any need to give its particulars here. The stranger sees that there is a school-house now, and admires the healthy looks of the children about the doors. If he stops to speak to them, or examines the gravestone of the pastor, he will probably be accosted by an elderly man, who will ask him his name, and tell him of his own relationship to Robert Walker,—that he is the grandson of Robert Walker's sister. He will tell of the alteration of the times, and how the Wesleyans have opened a chapel at Ulpha, which draws away some of the flock; and that others have ceased to come to church since the attempts to get copper from the neighbouring hills,—the miners drawing away the people to diversion on Sundays. The old stocks are gone, he says; and the new families are different. There used to be from seventy to ninety worshippers in the mornings; and from fifty to seventy in the evenings: and now there are seldom more than seventy.

The traveller will next take his choice whether to follow up the Duddon towards its source, through a tract of broken rocks; or down towards its mouth, through scenery growing more open and fertile, till the river spreads among sands, where it meets the sea; or he will cross it, and proceed over the next ridge into Eskdale.

If he follows the river downwards, he will probably choose to ascend Blackcomb, the solitary mountain which occupies the centre of the peninsula lying between the estuary of the Duddon and the sea. Of this mountain Wordsworth tells us,[92] that "its base covers a much greater extent of ground than any other mountain in those parts; and, from its situation, the summit commands a more extensive view than any other point in Britain." The old history of Nicolson and Burn[93] tells us, that "here ariseth gradually a very high mountain, called Blackcomb, which, standing near the sea, and having the two level counties of Lancashire and Cheshire on the south-east side thereof, may be plainly discovered on a clear day, from Talk-o'-the-Hill in Staffordshire, near one hundred miles distance. And from the top of Blackcomb one may see several mountains in North Wales, seven English counties, and as many in Scotland, together with the Isle of Man. This mountain, and the ridge of hills which run north-west from thence, are esteemed the best sheep heaths in the country." Here is great temptation to the traveller to ascend this solitary mountain; and we have further the assurance of Colonel Mudge, that when residing on Blackcomb for surveying purposes, he more than once saw Ireland before sunrise. But few visit the mountain, as it lies out of the track of ordinary travel through the district.

The traveller may follow the Duddon a few miles down its channel, and then cross it by the bridge near Ulpha, and proceed past Ulpha into Eskdale; or he may take a shorter and wilder route over the Fell from Seathwaite, dropping down into Eskdale at its most beautiful part. If he takes a guide, or, going alone, is careful to carry a pocket-compass, and not brave a fog, this way is undoubtedly the most desirable. He will cross the Duddon on the Stepping Stones, made memorable by two Sonnets of Wordsworth's,[94] and note well the features of the pass above, which is the finest part of the course of the river; and then, ascending the opposite ravine by the guidance of the brook within it, he will emerge on the hill-side near the farm of Grassgarth. Holding on awhile north-west, over the Fell, now swampy, and now slippery with drought, he will see Eskdale opening before him, and descend to it beside another brook, through hazel copses and fields, to the bridge over the Esk, which he has long seen from above. From Coniston to Seathwaite church he had walked about six miles; and now four or five more to this bridge; and about five lie between this bridge and the great waterfall, which is the finest object in Eskdale,—Stanley Ghyll, often called, but erroneously, Birker Force by the country people.

If he is tired, he can have a bed at the Woolpack, a wayside house, a mile from the bridge; or he may go on another mile to Bout, a hamlet where he may rest in comfort in the clean humble inn, and enjoy a series of exquisite pictures in the little ravine and on the uplands behind and above the mill. The view of Eskdale here is lovely, and the sea again bounds the view, the little town of Ravenglass lying visible in the bay where the Irt, the Mite, and the Esk flow into the sea. Perhaps the traveller may be able to engage a shandry here, to spare him some of the fatigue of the next day; or he may be fortunate enough to get a cast in the miller's cart, and lose nothing by having to stop to drop a sack of flour here and there. He may thus see something of the ways and appearance of the farm-houses, and hear the characteristic talk of the residents when exchanging news with the miller. In this case, however, he will appoint his meeting with the cart at the farm-house of Dalegarth, after seeing Stanley Ghyll, which he must on no account omit. This fall has, in itself, much of the character of Ara Force, the celebrated fall on Ulleswater; and the immediate surroundings may perhaps be rivalled by other waterfalls in the district. But the ravine itself is indisputably the finest in the region; and it is scarcely possible to say too much of the view from the Moss-house on the steep, which should certainly be the first point of view. From hence the eye commands the whole ravine, whose sides are feathered with wood from base to ridge. The fall is between two crags,—the one bare, the other crowned with pines; and if the spectator is there in the early morning, there may be a gush of sunlight coming in obliquely, which will give the last finish of beauty to that ultimate point of the view. Throughout the ravine, the young larches, the most modern feature, are so intermingled with the well-grown beech, oak, birch, and hollies, as to gratify the eye, instead of offending it, as they too often do. There is a bridge below, just seen from this height, which will tempt the stranger to find his way down; and there he will meet with two more, by means of which he will reach the fall. Here, among a wilderness of ferns and wild-flowers, he may sit in the cool damp abyss, watching the fall of waters into their clear rock-basin, till his ear is satisfied with their clash and flow, and his eye with the everlasting quiver of the ash-sprays, and swaying of the young birches which hang over from the ledges of the precipice. A path then leads him under the rocks, now on this side of the stream, and now on that, till he emerges from the ravine, and winds his way through the hazel copse to the gate, where the miller's cart may be in waiting.

Then he jogs along a tolerably level road, past home-steads, each overshadowed by its sycamore clump,—that luxury, introduced, we are told, within two hundred years, but now so common as to make one wonder what was in their stead before,—past wayside cisterns, where the waters from the hills are flowing in and out again the whole year round; past fields which expand and brighten as Eskdale opens out towards the sea; past Santon Bridge, where the Irt runs to the bay under an ivy-mantled bridge, through meadows and scattered woods; past Gosforth, a stirring and rising little town, where new dwellings, built of the red stone of the neighbourhood, are rising on every hand; up the hill whence there is a wide view of coast and sea, with the Isle of Man lying afar, so clear at times, when the wind is east, as that the shadows are seen filling the hollows of its hills; and then down between an avenue of beech, ash, and other trees, to Calder Bridge.

Here the miller's horse naturally turns its head,—for no one better understands its master's business,—to trot back again to Bout; and the traveller is left to order dinner, to be ready for his return from the Abbey. If he wishes for shade and quietness, to prepare mind and body for what he is next to see, he will go down through the inn garden, to the bridge, and perhaps waste an hour in watching the gush of the Calder past the curve of the red rock, and into the brown shadow of the low bridge, beneath which the vivid green ferns wave without ceasing. It is but a mile to the Abbey. Having gone through the village, and past the bare new red Church, he enters upon a scene so quiet, that a monkish feeling steals over him before he catches a sight of the Abbey. Nothing is heard as he passes along the shady road but the stroke of the woodman's axe, or the shock of a falling tree, or the whirr of the bustling magpie, or the pipe of the thrush, unsubdued by the noonday heat. The squirrel, perhaps, hies across the road; and where the sunshine streams in under the tent of a spreading beech, a pair of white butterflies may chase each other with a dancing flight round its trunk up into the lucent green shadow; but no rude sounds or sights mar the repose sacred in his mind to the old Cistercians who trod these ways in peace while all the world besides was at war.

At the end of a mile he looks about for the ruins,—on his right hand. He sees a tempting avenue, and thinks he will try it; so he ventures upon opening the gate, and advances under the chestnuts, limes, and beeches, till he perceives somewhat under their sweeping branches which shows him that he is right. The greensward at the outlet is so bright as to have the effect of a gleam of mild sunshine, even on a shady day or after sunset; and, springing clear from this sward, rise to the left the lofty pointed arches of the old ruin, in noble proportions, disclosing beyond a long perspective of grassy lawn and sombre woods. The Abbey is built of the red sandstone of the neighbourhood, now sobered down by time (it was founded in A.D. 1134) into the richest and softest tint that the eye could desire. But little is known of it beyond its date and the name of its founder, Ranulph, son of the first Ranulph de Meschines, a Norman noble.[95] The Church was small, as the scanty remains show; and the Monastery, which now looks like a continuation of the same building, could not have contained a numerous company. From the fragments of effigies preserved, it appears that some eminent persons were buried here; but who these knights and nobles were, there is no record available to tell, carefully as these memorials were wrought to secure the immortality of earth.

The eye is first fixed by the remains of the tower, from whose roofless summit dangles the tufted ivy, and whose base is embossed by the small lilac blossoms of the antirrhinum; but at last the great charm is found in the aisle of clustered pillars. Almost the whole aisle is standing, still connected by the cornice and wall which supported the roof. Luxuriant honeysuckle and ivy load these remains with verdure and luscious bloom, climbing up till they grow down again on the other side. The traveller will wander in and out among these pillars, and into the sombre corner where the tall ash grows over towards the old tower wall, making a sort of tent in the recess; he will look into every niche and damp cell in the conventual apartments, and go down to the red and tufted and broken river-banks, and watch its stream leaping and rushing along in its deep channel, under the over-arching trees, and he will say to himself, how well the old monks knew how to choose their dwelling-places, and what it must have been to the earnest and pious among these Cistercians to pace their river-bank, hidden in the shade, and to attune their thoughts to the unceasing music of the Calder flowing by. After all, it is a pity not to contemplate this place in the evening. It is a fine thing to see the shadows flung upon the sward, sharp in the broad sunshine, and to have the eye caught by the burnish of the ivy, and the sense soothed by the shade of the avenue: but the scene is sweeter when there is just glow enough in the west to bring out vividly the projections and recesses of the ruins; and when the golden moon hangs over the eastern mass of tree-tops, ready to give her light as the glow dissolves; and when the rooks are winging their way to settle for the night in the nearest wood.

Calder Abbey is on the estate of Captain Irwin, whose house, a plain substantial dwelling, stands rather too near the ruins. As he did not build it, this is no fault of his; and he does what he can in carefully preserving the Abbey, and permitting the freest access to it.

From Calder Bridge the traveller should take a car to Ennerdale Bridge, or the Boat-house, a public-house at the foot of Ennerdale Water, where he may usually find accommodation for the night. Few visitors come to this lake, because it is not easily accessible, except to pedestrians, from any quarter but the west. It is, however, well worth a visit from the independent walker, who can find his way out again over the eastern fells.

Let the proudest and most independent traveller, however, not be too proud and independent to take a guide in wild and unknown places. When he studies his map, and sees a track marked straight from one point to another, he cannot conceive of any danger; and he throws on his knapsack, takes his stick, and, with a compass in his pocket, does not doubt that he may defy all the misleading powers of heaven and earth. But, once out of reach of human help, he may find his case not so plain as he thought. Instead of one path, as marked on his map, he may find three, and perhaps the one on his map may have disappeared in a swamp, or under recent accidents. He finds himself on the edge of a precipice, and does not know how far to go back. He finds the bog deepen, and thinks he can scarcely be in the right road. He finds a land-slip, which compels him to make a wide circuit; and meantime it is growing dusk. Worst of all, a fog may come on at any moment; and there is an end of all security to one who does not know the little wayside marks which guide the shepherd in such a case. In every part of the region, tales are current of the loss of life, under such circumstances, even of natives. Besides the accidents by snow, there are records of some in almost every dale, of death by fog, wet, fatigue, or fall, where the lost were much fitter for mountain expeditions than any stranger can be.

In every direction from the foot of Ennerdale Water, except the roads behind him, the traveller will have to cross mountain or moor,—either immediately, or when the road becomes a mere track beyond the head of the lake; and he should inquire for a guide at once, or learn the probability of his obtaining one at his point of entrance upon the Fell. We could hardly give a better warning on this head than by telling what befel us in this very neighbourhood. We proposed, a party of three, to cross Blake Fell to Scale Hill, by a track distinctly marked in the map, and which, according to it and the Guide-book, would be more difficult to miss than to find. But meeting with uniform answers from all of whom we inquired along the previous road, as to the difficulty to strangers of finding the path over the Fell, if any adverse circumstances should occur, we stopped at the Boat House to inquire for a guide. It was long doubtful whether we could procure one; and while the search was making, we lay on the shingle on the margin of the lake, rather perplexed as to our course if no guide could be had. The waters grew grayer and rougher while we waited: but we thought no more of this than that the wind would be refreshing during the ascent; and the heat that day was intense. Soon, the messenger returned with the news that a guide would await us at the distance of a few fields; and when we met him, we found that the walk was not more than six miles;—a mere trifle on an afternoon of tolerable coolness: so we considered our affairs comfortably settled, and set off up the Fell, all in good spirits and security. The heat was still very great; so we took our time, and lagged behind the guide, though he carried our knapsacks. He was a quiet-looking, elderly mountaineer, who appeared to walk very slowly; but his progress was great compared with ours, from the uniformity and continuity of his pace. In the worst part of our transit, I tried the effect of following close behind him, and putting my feet into his footsteps, and I was surprised to find with what ease and rapidity I got on.

At first, we stopped frequently, to sit down and drink from the streams that crossed the track, or flowed beside it: and during these halts we observed that the blackness which had for some time been appearing in the west, now completely shrouded the sea. Next, we remarked that while the wind still blew in our faces,—that is, from the north-east,—the mass of western clouds was evidently climbing the sky. The guide quietly observed that there would be rain by-and-by. Next, when we were in the middle of the wide Fell, and we saw how puzzled we should have been to find a path while winding among the swampy places, even in the calmest weather, we pointed out to one another how the light fleeces of cloud below the black mass swept round in a circle, following each other like straws in an eddy. Soon, the dark mass came driving up at such a rate that it was clear we should not achieve our transit in good weather. The dense mist was presently upon us. On looking behind, to watch its rate of advance, I saw a few flashes of lightning burst from it. The thunder had for some time been growling afar, almost incessantly. The moment before the explosion of the storm was more like a dream than perhaps any actual experience I ever had. We were walking on wild ground, now ascending, now descending, a deep Tarn (Floutern Tarn) on our right hand, our feet treading on slippery rushes, or still more slippery grass: the air was dark as during an eclipse; and heavy mists drove past from behind, just at the level of our heads, and sinking every moment; while before us, and far, far below us—down as in a different world—lay Buttermere, and the neighbouring vales, sleeping in the calmest sunshine. The contrast of that warm picture, with its yellow lights and soft blue shadows, with the turbulence, and chill, and gloom of the station from which we viewed it, made me feel this the newest scene I had witnessed for many a year. I had but a moment to look at it; for not only did the clouds close down before my eyes, but the wind scudded round to the opposite point of the compass, throwing me flat as it passed. Within a few minutes, I had several falls, from the force of the wind and the treachery of the ground,—now, in a trice, a medley of small streams. It was impossible to stop the guide, much as I wanted to ask him to look back now and then, to see to the safety of my companions in the rear. In the roar of the blast, and the crash of the thunder, and the pelt of the hail, I might as well hope to make the elements hear. So it was necessary to keep up my pace, that he might not stride away from us entirely; my companions making a similar effort to keep up with me. Through stumblings and slidings innumerable, they did this,—the lightning playing about our faces the while, like a will-o'-the-wisp on the face of a bog. The hail and rain had drenched us to the skin in three minutes. The first hailstones penetrated to the skin. They were driven in at every opening of our clothes; they cut our necks behind, and filled our shoes. Our hats were immediately soaked through, and our hair wringing wet. The thunder seemed to roll on our very skulls. In this weather we went plunging on for four miles, through spongy bogs, turbid streams, whose bridges of stones were covered by the rushing waters, or by narrow pathways, each one of which was converted by the storm into an impetuous brook. When we had descended into a region where we could hear ourselves speak, we congratulated one another on our prudence in having engaged a guide. Without him, how should we have known the path from the brook, or have guessed where we might ford the streams, whose bridges were out of sight? Two horses, we afterwards heard, were killed on the Fell in that storm: and we should never have come down, we were persuaded, if we had been left to wander by ourselves. Even in the clearest and safest weather, it is well worth one's five shillings to be free from the responsibility of finding the way,—free of one's knapsack,—free to deliver up one's attention to the enjoyment of the distant scenery, and of the characteristic communications of the guide.

Not far from hence, an inexperienced tourist passed a day rather curiously, in the autumn of 1842, from starting without a guide from Wastdale Head over the Fell to Buttermere. "After wandering about for some time, he missed the road, and, instead of getting into Buttermere by the pass of Scarf Gap, he took the deep ravine between Kirkfell and the Gable, and arrived (without finding out his mistake) at the precise point from which he had started, having made a circuit of many miles."[96] That is, he spent his energies in walking completely round the same mountain.

The chief danger in such adventures on the Fells is from the bodily exhaustion caused by conflict with the elements in such exposed places. I have encountered a wind at the top of a pass which blew so continuously, as well as vehemently, that I am persuaded I could not have lived half an hour, if exposed without shelter, or possibility of retreat. One is astonished at the effect, after the first minute, of a continuous wind too strong to stand in: and, after the second, exhaustion begins; and a minute or two more brings a feeling of some alarm. Floods of rain are rather exhilarating in warm weather, at mid-day; but the number of victims to heavy rain in this district shows what it must be to encounter it in cold weather, and after too much fatigue. Three men, residents of Kentmere and Staveley, were lost in places quite familiar to them, a few seasons ago. A stout woodman and his son, and a tailor of their acquaintance, went up towards High Street to fish, in late autumn: they were so worn out and drenched with heavy rain on their return, that they died in the descent. From the situation of the bodies the relatives were persuaded that the strong woodman might have escaped, but that he would not leave his boy and less hardy comrade. It is a fearful mistake in pedestrian tourists to underrate the force of storms upon the Fells.

A little beyond Calder Bridge, the road to Ennerdale turns up to the right from the main road to Egremont and Whitehaven. It passes over bare fells, where the heat is excessive on a sultry day: but the views are fine, of the coast and sea as far as the headland of St. Bees. Below lies the little town of Egremont, of Norman name (the Mount of Sorrow), and distinguished by Norman traditions. It was at the gateway of Egremont Castle that the horn was hung, in crusading days, which was twice blown by the gallant Sir Eustace de Lucy.[97] As the Cumberlanders tell, Sir Eustace and his brother Hubert rode forth together to the Holy Wars; and Sir Eustace blew the horn, saying to his brother, "If I fall in Palestine, do thou return and blow this horn, and take possession; that Egremont may not be without a

Lucy for its lord." In Palestine, ambition of this lordship so took possession of Hubert, that he hired ruffians to drown his brother in the Jordan: and the ruffians assured him that the deed was done. He returned home, and stole into the castle by night, not daring to sound the horn. But he soon plucked up spirit, and drowned his remorse in revels. In the midst of a banquet, one day, the horn was heard, sounding such a blast that the echoes came back from the fells, after startling the red deer from his covert, and the wild boar from his drinking at the tarn. Hubert knew that none but Eustace could or would so sound the horn: and he fled by a postern while Sir Eustace entered by the gate. Long after the wretched Hubert came to ask forgiveness from his brother; and, having obtained it, retired to a convent, where he practised penance till he died. The ruins of this castle stand on an eminence to the west of the town, which, with its fifteen thousand inhabitants, is now commonplace enough.

The road passes under the hill Revelin (another Norman name) and approaches Ennerdale Water at its finest end. (Figure 11.) The lake is two miles and a half long; and at this lower end the mountains come down abruptly to the water. The traveller must take the road along its northern shore, as there is no room for a path on the southern; and pursue his way to the head of the lake, having the fine summits of the Pillar and Kirkfell before him as he goes. When he has left the lake behind him, he follows still the northern bank of the little river Liza, which flows into it, for a mile and a half, till he comes to

Fig. 11. Ennerdale Water

the farmhouse in Gillerthwaite, where he is to inquire for a guide. The guide will lead him on beside the stream, not crossing it till near its source, when they will turn to the right, up Blacksail, in search of the brook, which will show them the way down to Wastdale Head. The distinguishing features of this walk are the two great mountains, the isolated Pillar on the right, rising to the height of 2893 feet, and its craggy and precipitous sides forbidding the thought of ascent; and Kirkfell, round whose base the "inexperienced tourist" took his long day's walk. The ascent of this pass is steep and rocky; and its ridge is so narrow, that from it may be seen, by only turning the head, the vale from which the traveller has mounted, and that into which he is about to descend; that is, behind him, Gillerthwaite, with its circular green level, dropped over with wood, its farm-house, and stream, and lake outlet; and, before him, Mosedale, the wild valley which winds away between Kirkfell and Yewbarrow, and discloses in front the great central summits of Scawfell and Bowfell—the rallying point of our winding exposition. Even here, with these landmarks in sight, travellers have missed the way to Wastdale Head. Some years ago, three young ladies, coming from Buttermere, dismissed their guide at this point, having taken his directions how to proceed. They had five or six hours of daylight before them; but they wondered about till daylight again before they saw a house. They got to the left of a beck instead of the right, became bewildered, and did not reach the valley till three in the morning.

Wastdale Head is better known, year by year; and every one who has visited it will send others to enjoy its glorious beauty. It is one of those perfect levels, shut in by lake and mountains, which give a different impression from any other kind of scenery in the world. The mountain passes themselves are so high as to leave no appearance of outlet except by the lake; and of these passes there are but two—the one we are describing, and that over Sty Head, which, seen from any point, looks prodigiously steep, as indeed it is, though we have seen the impressions of horse-shoes upon it. The green and perfect level, to which the mountains come down with a sheer sweep, is partly divided off into fields, the stone fences of which are provided with that primitive sort of stile—stones projecting in oblique order. A few farm-houses are set down among these fields, here and there, on the bends of the rushing and gurgling stream. In its own separate enclosure is the chapel,—the humblest of chapels,—with its three windows, one at each side, and one at the east end, and its skylight over the pulpit, and its eight pews. There is now a school. A chapel and a school, and no public-house or inn! Long may it be so! A lady who lived some time in this nook took an interest in the children; and, finding that twenty might be mustered, she offered a guinea a year towards a school. Two gentlemen, who made this their headquarters for nine nights, while exploring the mountains, left a little money for the same purpose. The inhabitants entertain a schoolmaster on "whittle gate"[98] terms—*i. e.,* he boards at the farm-houses in turn; and an old man told us the other day that the plan prospers. "He gets them on very well," says the old man; "and particularly in the spelling. He thinks that if they can spell, they can do all the rest." We certainly wished, here and elsewhere—indeed, almost throughout the region—that good spelling would ensure personal cleanliness. The children certainly do not get on in that, however they may prosper with their spelling. The schoolmaster may think that this is not included in his province; but perhaps, if he and the clergyman were to insist, patiently and seriously, that "cleanliness is next to godliness," they might work a reform in the next generation. The dwellings are, in some respects, a pattern of neatness in the rural districts. The beds are perfectly luxurious in this respect. You might eat your dinner off the slate floor or the deal table; and pots and pans make a shining array; but it is best for one's own comfort, in certain of the dales, not to look at the children's hair, or the babies' faces, or anybody's skin or teeth. This must be from ignorance; for these same people are living in the midst of plenty. There are places where they employ a dancing-master for several weeks of the year, and dress gaudily in the dancing season. They attend fairs in good style, and support a schoolmaster, and fee the clergyman. Is it not possible to educate them up to a decent point of personal cleanliness? If parents fail to train their children to it, and the example of good habits here and there does not spread, is it not the business of the pastor and the teacher to take the matter in hand? It is time it was done.

As we have said, there is no inn at Wastdale Head. Within the memory of the existing generation a stranger was a very rare sight. The Tysons, who dwelt in the dale head half a century ago, used to open their doors to any one who dropped down from the passes, as a mere matter of necessity, as any one would house a traveller coming in from among the snows. At any hour of the day or night, Tyson would welcome such a wanderer to the family accommodations, and then guide him on his way out. But such chance wayfarers told of the beauty of the nook; and others came. Of late years there have been so many that Ritson the younger and his wife, who now occupy the dwelling-house, have increased its accommodations; so that they can lodge and board, in homely comfort, several guests. And very comfortable the place is, with its nice beds, good bread, eggs, potatoes, cheese, bacon and tea, and the kindness and goodwill of host and hostess.

Is there any traveller who needs a warning to be careful not to get any hospitable mountaineer into trouble about Excise matters? It is painful to think—but necessary to tell—how the generous hospitality of the dalesmen has occasionally been abused for the advantage of Excise informers. In a farm-house in Langdale the owner has been three times fined for furnishing a draught of beer to a thirsty traveller, who pressed for it, and afterwards laid down money, including the beer in the payment for the bread and cheese, thus bringing the case within the reach of the law; so that the farmer now, fearing the kind feelings of his own family in his absence, keeps no beer for his own drinking. Here and there, a resident who, living in comfort, has yet but little to do with money, has been heavily and long oppressed by the imposition of a fine and costs, for permitting a stranger to hire his horse and cart. The simple-minded people were long in learning the ways of the law, in its interference with their hospitality to wayfarers: and even those who understand the case, and are on their guard, have sometimes been cruelly used, as an adventure of the John Ritsons may show.

One evening, in a time of bad weather, when both father and son were absent, a party arrived from one of the passes, apparently much exhausted, and asked hospitality of John Ritson's wife. She did her best to make them comfortable; but, cautioned by her husband, she declined to supply any but the most indubitable articles of refreshment: and this, though she never makes any charge, but takes what her guests think proper to give. The fellow who came to entrap her—no traveller, but an informer by trade—complained movingly of fatigue and exhaustion, and implored her to let him have a little whiskey. She long refused, saying that she did not supply it; but he so appealed to her compassion, that at last she told him there was some in the cupboard, and he might help himself. When going away, he asked what there was to pay. She answered—"Nothing for the whiskey; for the rest, what he pleased." He made out that it would be, without the whiskey, so much: and he should lay down so much more, would that do? She replied, "If he pleased;" and set them forth on their way. Such was the transaction which the wretch went straight to report, and which he so reported as that John Ritson was fined twenty pounds, and charged with the costs—a heavy sum to a dalesman, who lives almost entirely on the produce of his farm, and is far out of the way of towns and markets. One such case should be a sufficient warning to a traveller not to ask for any exciseable articles in private dwellings in these dales; lest one infringement of the law should tempt to a repetition of an act considered innocent and merely hospitable, and the informer find his way in at last.

If the traveller means to ascend Scawfell the next day, he should see Wastwater this evening, which he can very well do after his moderate walk from the Ennerdale Boat House. This is not the best way of seeing Wastwater, which should be approached from the other end: but he cannot have everything at the very best here, any more than in other passages of human life: and he may yet see Wastwater

Fig. 12. Scawfell over Wastdale

in the best way, if he will walk four miles from Ritson's without looking behind him (Figure 12). Then he will have the glory of the scene on his return; and there is quite enough for him to enjoy on his way down, in the spectacle of the Screes, with the still and gray lake lying at the base—quite up to the base—of their prodigious sweep. The Screes form the south-eastern shore of the lake, which is three miles and a half long. The line of this singular range is almost unbroken. The crest consists of crags, bare of vegetation, except where a mere tuft or drip of ferns sprouts out at long intervals. At about a third of the way down, these crags are hidden by a slope of *débris,* slanting into the lake. This expanse of rotten stone and red gravel, streaked with the colours found where iron is present, is so loose that it is believed not even a goat could climb it. No man ever attempts it: so there it lies from year to year, untouched but by the forces of Nature. The summer thunderstorm and the winter tempest sometimes shiver the loosely-compacted crags above: and then, when a mass comes thundering down, and splashes into the lake, the whole range feels the shock, and slides of stones rush into the waters, and clouds of dust rise into the air. The accessible side of the lake affords a charming walk—the road winds so easily among the promontories and bays.

At the end of his four miles, the traveller may turn his head; and then he will see reason for this being called the most sublime of the lakes. We have seen it in the sunny morning, and in the calm gray evening, when a pearly light lay upon the waters; and again when heavy black clouds gathered about the stern mountain summits; and we have found it truly imposing under every aspect.

As he returns, the traveller will see as noble a group of mountains closing in Wastdale, as he can look upon from any one spot of the district. Carrying his eyes along from the Screes opposite, he sees next them the great Scawfell summits, which he hopes to reach to-morrow. Great End peeps over the ridge of Lingmell: and Lingmell (the lower slope of Scawfell), projects boldly into the dale, at the head of the lake. Great Gable closes in the whole pass. Next to it Yewbarrow advances towards him on his own side; and nearer, Middlefell; and he is standing under Buckbarrow. All these giant hills seem to grow, and deepen and darken as he advances among them, till he arrives at the rich green levels of the dale, and rejoices that they now fill the area which was once evidently occupied by the waters of the still retreating lake.

If it be still daylight, he had better go to bed notwithstanding: for he cannot be too early astir in the morning. John Ritson will get him up Scawfell in time to see the sun rise, if he wishes it. When we made the attempt (in which we were baffled) we rose at two, when the summer dawn was near breaking; and the walk up the dale towards Pease Ghyll was delicious, with the clear light brightening over Great End, and the fragment of a moon hanging over Scawfell. After half an hour's walk, we began to climb; and were soon gratified by fine glimpses into the abyss of Pease Ghyll, which gaped below us on the right, a rocky chasm, into and through which rushed a stream from the heights. Here, however, it became evident to us how great was our misfortune in John Ritson's having been absent on our arrival. Our guide, a very old man, was uncertain and changeable about the way by which he should take us; and he appeared far from strong enough to attempt an ascent so formidable, among precipitous rocks, loose stones, and slippery turf: so we were compelled to change our plan. We made him lead us over the lower ridges to Esk Hause, on our way to Langdale, by Sty Head and Sprinkling Tarns—a glorious mountain walk enough to those whose heads are not full of ambition to look abroad from the Pikes.

The best way to begin the ascent, for those who do not think the sight of Pease Ghyll worth the additional toil, is up Lingmell, which may be reached either by boat up the lake, or from Ritson's house. The distance from the base of Lingmell to the summit of Scawfell is about three miles; and the most active order of climbers may achieve the ascent in an hour and a half. But it is better to pause on the ridge of Lingmell, to see the glorious view there. There is always sufficient uncertainty about the weather, to the last moment, in a climate like ours, to make it wise to obtain what can be had in the course of an ascent to a very elevated peak like that of Scawfell, where a rapid congregation of vapours may shut out every object from the longing eye, at the instant of its greatest expectation. From this ridge, a sweeping course, over slopes, now of stones, and now of that species of moss which is the food of the reindeer, leads the traveller to the summit, and places him on the loftiest point in England, at a height of 3160 feet above the sea. The lower Pike, long supposed to be the loftiest of the two, is 3100 feet above the sea, and stands about 250 yards south-east of its companion, being separated from it by the remarkable chasm called Mickledore (Great Door).

Of the view from the summit we have the best account that could be desired in a letter from a friend of Mr. Wordsworth's, which is found in Mr. W.'s Guide to the Lakes:[99] "On the summit of the Pike," says the writer, "which we gained after much toil, though without difficulty, there was not a breath of air to stir even the papers containing our refreshment, as they lay spread out upon a rock. The stillness seemed to be not of this world: we paused, and kept silence to listen, and no sound could be heard: the Scawfell cataracts were voiceless to us; and there was not an insect to hum in the air. The vales which we had seen from Esk Hause lay yet in view; and, side by side with Eskdale, we now saw the sister Vale of Donnerdale terminated by the Duddon sands. But the majesty of the mountains below, and close to us, is not to be conceived. We now beheld the whole mass of Great Gable from its base—the Den of Wastdale at our feet—a gulf immeasurable; Grassmoor, and the other mountains of Crummock; Ennerdale and its mountains; and the sea beyond! We sat down to our repast, and gladly would we have tempered our beverage (for there was no well or spring near us), with such a supply of delicious water as we might have procured, had we been on the rival summit of Great Gable; for on its highest point is a small triangular receptacle in the native rock, which, the shepherds say, is never dry. There we might have slaked our thirst plenteously with a pure and celestial liquid; for the cup or basin, it appears, has no other feeder than the dews of heaven, the showers, the vapours, the hoar frost, and the spotless snow. While we were gazing around, 'Look,' I exclaimed, 'at yon ship upon the glittering sea!' 'Is it a ship?' replied our shepherd guide. 'It can be nothing else,' interposed my companion. 'I cannot be mistaken; I am so accustomed to the appearance of ships at sea.' The guide dropped the argument; but, before a minute was gone, he quietly said, 'Now look at your ship—it is changed into a horse!' So it was; a horse with a gallant neck and head. We laughed heartily; and I hope, when again inclined to be positive, I may remember the ship and the horse upon the glittering sea; and the calm confidence, yet submissiveness, of our wise man of the mountains, who certainly had more knowledge of the clouds than we, whatever might be our knowledge of ships.

"I know not how long we might have remained on the summit of the Pike, without a thought of moving, had not our guide warned us that we must not linger; for a storm was coming. We looked in vain to espy the signs of it. Mountains, vales, and sea were touched with the clear light of the sun. 'It is there,' said he pointing to the sea beyond Whitehaven; and there we perceived a light vapour, unnoticeable but by a shepherd accustomed to watch all mountain bodings. We gazed around again, and yet again, unwilling to lose the remembrance of what lay before us in that mountain solitude; and then prepared to depart. Meanwhile the air changed to cold, and we saw that tiny vapour swelled into mighty masses of cloud, which came boiling over the mountains. Great Gable, Helvellyn, and Skiddaw were wrapped in storm; yet Langdale, and the mountains in that quarter, remained all bright in sunshine. Soon the storm reached us; we sheltered under a crag; and, almost as rapidly as it had come, it passed away, and left us free to observe the struggles of gloom and sunshine in other quarters. Langdale now had its share, and the Pikes of Langdale were decorated by two splendid rainbows. Skiddaw, also, had his own rainbows. Before we again reached Esk Hause, every cloud had vanished from every summit. I ought to have mentioned, that round the top of Scawfell Pike not a blade of grass is to be seen. Cushions or tufts of moss, parched and brown, appear between the huge blocks and stones, that lie in heaps on all sides to a great distance, like skeletons or bones of the earth not needed at the creation, and there left to be covered with never-dying lichens, which the clouds and dews nourish; and adorned with colours of vivid and exquisite beauty. Flowers, the most brilliant feathers, and even gems, scarcely surpass in colouring some of those masses of stone which no human eye beholds, except the shepherd or traveller be led thither by curiosity; and how seldom must this happen! For the other eminence is the one visited by the adventurous stranger; and the shepherd has no inducement to ascend the Pike in quest of his sheep; no food being *there* to tempt them. We certainly were singularly favoured in the weather; for when we were seated on the summit, our conductor, turning his eyes thoughtfully round, said, 'I do not know that in my whole life, I was ever, at any season of the year, so high upon the mountains on so *calm* a day.' (It was the 7th of October.)"

From other visitors we learn that Ingleborough, in Yorkshire, and now and then the Welsh mountains, are visible from this summit.

Our traveller, about to conclude his circuit by descending upon the Duddon, must now make his way down first to Esk Hause, a central ridge, which commands, to singular advantage, a number of the leading valleys of the district, and sends down its first waters to the Esk. On the same morning, that 7th of October, the letter-writer above quoted saw it thus:—". . . Three distinct views. On one side, the continuous vale of Borrowdale, Keswick, and Bassenthwaite, with Skiddaw, Helvellyn, Saddleback, and numerous other mountains, and, in the distance, the Solway Frith, and the mountains of Scotland; on the other side, and below us, the Langdale Pikes, their own vale below *them*; Windermere; and far beyond Windermere, Ingleborough, in Yorkshire. But how shall I speak of the deliciousness of the third prospect! At this time, *that* was most favoured by sunshine and shade. The green vale of Esk, deep and green, with its glittering serpent-stream, lay below us; and on we looked to the mountains near the sea,—Blackcomb pre-eminent,—and still beyond, to the sea itself, in dazzling brightness. Turning round, we saw the mountains of Wastdale in tumult; to our right, Great Gable,—the loftiest; a distinct and huge form, though the middle of the mountain was, to our eyes, as its base." When we were on Esk Hause, the spectacle of these three lines of landscape was remarkable. Towards Keswick the atmosphere was thick, just to the degree that gave a visionary character to the long perspective. The lake of Derwent Water was hardly distinguishable from its shores, so that the wooded islands and the town of Keswick lay as if in air, still and unsubstantial. In the direction of Eskdale all was bright and glittering; while from Langdale and the head of Borrowdale the white mists came tumbling out towards us, as if to stifle us; and nothing could be seen except at intervals, when a whiff of wind disclosed long sweeps of the sides of the valleys, and stretches of the streams and fields below. It is these changes that give a singular charm to this mountain district. The residents of the valleys, in their occasional ascent to these heights, never see the scene twice alike; the great landmarks themselves being scarcely recognizable but by their forms.

From this ridge the traveller may descend upon the Esk and the Duddon, whose sources lie near each other; and thus is completed the traverse of the first of our four divisions.

II.

WE WILL BEGIN our second circuit by a descent from this mountain nucleus into the head of Borrowdale. The head of Borrowdale is forked, by the mountain Glaramara being set down in the midst. We will descend into the western vale, that of Seathwaite; and end our circuit by ascending the eastern, that of Stonethwaite.

Borrowdale was anciently called Boredale, "having its name probably from the wild boars which used in former times to haunt the woody part of Wastdale forest; the hill above it being called Styhead, where the swine were wont to feed in the summer, and fall down in autumn into this dale, where they fed upon nuts and acorns. Here are large flocks of sheep; and anciently were mines of lead and copper. Here also, in a very high and perpendicular rock called Eagle Crag, is every year an eyrie or nest of eagles." So says the old history.[100]

We have to pass down by Styhead; but we shall find no swine there, summer or winter. No creature now comes to drink at the tarn, the little clear rippling lake, where the mountaineer throws himself down to rest on the brink, when heated by the ascent from the vales. He has found everything sunny and dry, perhaps; but here he sees, by the minute diamond drops resting thick on the grass, that a cloud has lately stooped from its course, and refreshed the verdure in this retreat. It looks very tempting, this bright sheet of water; but no creature now comes to drink, unless a sheep may have strayed far from the flock, and in its terror may yet venture to stoop to the water, with many a start and interval of listening, till, at the faint sound of the distant sheep-dog, it bounds away. Some persons have laughed at the expression, in a grave poem, of the "solemn bleat" of

> "a lamb left somewhere to itself,
> The plaintive spirit of the solitude."[101]

But such persons cannot have met a stray sheep high on the mountains. Their associations are of market-day in a town, or of droves of cattle in a dusty road. If they had ever felt the profound stillness of the higher Fells, and heard it broken by a single bleat, repeated and not answered, they would be aware that there is as much solemnity as plaintiveness in the sound. It is a sport of ours in such places to answer the bleat, when we are going in such a direction as not to mislead the wanderer. Sometimes we have thus gained the confidence of a single lamb: sometimes we have gradually attracted a considerable number, beguiled them on for a space, and then left them wondering.

On proceeding down the pass, we see no prospect below of "nuts and acorns" enough to feed swine in their own dale. There are crags on every hand where eagles might build, and where they have built often enough to deprive us of the lark and other singing birds, which have thus been driven from the narrow vales which assuredly they would otherwise haunt. When the angler leaves his home in the dale, in the early morning, he may not hope to see the lark spring from the furrow, and soar above the shadows of the hills; nor will any other songster amuse his ear but such as lie deep within the covert of the wood: but when he is approaching the Tarn, high up on the mountain, and pauses to watch the herons at their fishing, and the wild ducks on the brink, before be frightens them away, he witnesses a sudden alarm, before there can possibly be any notice of his intentions; and then he knows where to look for the cause of all the scudding, and flapping, and screaming. He looks up, and sees no longer the sailing eagle, descending at every circuit, with a louder rush of wings, and casting a broader shadow, till it has swooped upon its victim, and is gone; but, now the eagle has departed, the meaner buzzard, pouncing from stone or tree, or heavily rising from its nest upon the moor: or the more active hawk, which scares away the water-fowl no less surely than the nobler bird, which is now rarely, if ever, seen. The shadow of the latter has, we know, fallen upon this Styhead tarn; for the eagles, disturbed on their own crag at the lower end of Borrowdale, established themselves first on a rock in Seathwaite, and afterwards flew over the ridge into Eskdale. The disturbance was, of course, from the shepherds, who lost so many lambs as to be driven desperate against the birds. There was no footing on the crag by which the nest could be reached, so a man was lowered by a rope sixty yards down the precipice: he carried his mountain-staff with him, its spiked end being the best weapon against the birds. He did not expect to kill the old ones; but, year after year, the eggs or the young were taken. If he brought away the young alive, he had the birds for his pains; if the eggs, every neighbouring shepherd gave five shillings for every egg. It is said that no more than two eggs were ever found at one time. The nest was made of twigs, and lined with a sort of grass from the clefts of the rock. When the fowler failed, and eaglets were reared, they were led away, as soon as strong enough, by the parent birds,—no doubt to settle in some other spot,—and the parents returned without them. One of this pair was shot at by the master of a sheep-dog which had been actually carried some way into the air by it, escaping only by its flesh giving way: the shot took effect, but the eagle disappeared for a time. About a week after, it was found lying on the grass on the uplands at Seatoller, nearly starved: its bill had been split by the shot, and the tongue was set fast in the cleft; it could not make much resistance, and was carried home captive. But when relieved and restored, it became so violent, that it was necessarily killed. Its mate brought a successor from a distance; a much smaller bird, and of a different species. They built, however, for fourteen more years in Borrowdale, before they flew over to Eskdale. They were not long left in peace there; and when the larger bird was at length shot, his mate disappeared entirely. Such devastation as was caused by these birds is not heard of now; but while there are crags aloft and lambs in the vales, there will be more or fewer, nobler or meaner, birds of prey. We are unable to ascertain positively, amidst conflicting testimony, whether any eagles at all remain in the region. It appears that one has certainly been seen within a few years; and almost every season there is a rumour of one having visited some point or another; but, on the whole, we find that the preponderance of belief is against there being any eagles' nest among the mountains of Westmoreland or Cumberland.

When the traveller has reached the stream, and crossed the bridge, he may begin to look for the Wad (black-lead) mine on the hill-side to his left. It is high up; but the heaps of rubbish still point it out to him plainly enough. In the clay-slate of this mountain is a bed of greenstone rock; and "nests" or "sops" or "bellies" of black-lead are found in the greenstone. The plumbago is the finest ever discovered; and from it the famous lead pencils are made which are used everywhere by sketchers. But there is great uncertainty about finding it: at one time a mass of it was discovered lying along like a mighty tree, the thicker part being of the finest quality, and the ramifications of a poorer, till, at the extremities, it was not worthy even to clean stoves. At other times, the searchers have been altogether at fault, for a long time together: and the works have occasionally been closed from this cause. There was a time when the value of this plumbago was so little known that the shepherds used it freely to mark their sheep: and next, the proprietors were obtaining from thirty to forty shillings a pound for the lead of one single "sop," which yielded upwards of twenty-eight tons. At that time houses were built at the entrance, where the workmen were obliged to change their clothes, under inspection, lest they should be tempted to carry away any of the precious stuff in their pockets. We believe the mine is at present in one of its turns of adversity; but, under the enterprising spirit of our times, probably some new "sop" will be hit upon before long, which will pay for the locking up of capital meanwhile.

Under the mine, and a little onward, amidst the copse-wood, are the dark tops of the Borrowdale yews to be seen, the "fraternal four," which, as Wordsworth tells us, form "one solemn and capacious grove."[102] The size attained by the yew in this district is astonishing. One which for many years lay prostrate at the other end of Borrowdale, measured nine yards in circumference, and contained 1460 feet of wood. The famous Lorton yew has about the same girth; and one of these four measures seven yards round, at four feet from the ground.

At Seatoller the road parts off right and left. We take the left, in order to quit Borrowdale for Buttermere; a magnificent walk, of a totally different character from any in our former circuit.

The road is very stony, and not a little steep: but the stream on the left hand, with its innumerable little falls, and the trees which sometimes overhang it, and the patches of grass and large smooth stones, tempting the traveller to many a halt, beguile him of heat and fatigue. And then, every time he turns, how exquisite are the glimpses into Borrowdale! Its cultivated levels contract, and the farm-steads disappear, one by one, as the projecting mountains overlap; till a mere triangular morsel remains—a hint of a peaceful valley lying among a billowy expanse of hills. It is always a pleasure to get out from between the fences upon the moor; and here the emancipation is soon obtained. The traveller mounts gradually by a horse-road,—a road practicable indeed for cars,—till be attains the summit of the turn under Honister Crag;—the dark, stupendous, almost perpendicular Honister Crag, where it almost takes one's breath away to see the quarrymen at work in the slate quarries above, looking like summer spiders hanging quivering from the eaves of a house. It was at the base of this crag that we once had the question forced upon us whether this was a car-road or not. A car, with four persons in it, had toiled slowly up from Borrowdale, without even the gentleman having once got out to relieve the horse. There were two young ladies also, who appeared capable of using their feet occasionally. The fourth was a stout lady: and all four were dressed as they might be for the flower-show at Chiswick. We were resting at the summit, with the crag opposite to us, when the car came up, and the driver civilly gave notice that the party had better alight, as the descent was so extremely rough and steep as to be unsafe for a loaded carriage. Instead of using their eyes to convince themselves that this was true, these gentry scolded the driver. The three juniors alighted, and set off arm-in-arm, slipping and suffering in their paper-soled shoes, and so engrossed with their hardships in having to walk down a stony hill, that they actually never once looked up at the Crag. They did not turn, to take a last look of Borrowdale; and now they actually passed under Honister Crag without seeing it! As for the lady, she loudly declared that she did not hire a car to be prevented riding in it; she should speak about it to the driver's employer, when she got home; and she should keep her seat: and so she did, scolding the driver, as well as the jolts would permit, as long as she remained within hearing. We imagined the amusement of the driver at this way of coming to see the country. He looked very civil and indifferent, not even objecting that it was not his wish that the pass should be so steep and stony. These are the strangers, and not those who come in third-class railway-carriages, and take their way on foot, who behave in a manner unworthy of the scenes around them: and even these may become softened and refined by what they see: and therefore they are welcome too.

The slate-quarrymen are a hardy race, capable of feats of strength which are now rarely heard of elsewhere. The most stalwart knight who ever came hither of old, with his full armour and battle-axe, to fight against the Scot, never carried a heavier weight, or did more wonders in a day, than these fine fellows. The best slate of Honister Crag is found near the top: and there, many hundred feet aloft, may be seen by good eyes the slate-built hovels of some of the quarrymen, while others ascend and descend many times between morning and night. Formerly, the slate was carried down on hurdles, on men's backs: and the practice is still continued in some remote quarries, where the expense of conveyance by carts would be too great, or the roads do not admit of it. Thirty years ago, a man named Joseph Clark made seventeen journeys, including seventeen miles of climbing and sharp descent, in one day, bringing down 10,880 lbs. of slate. In ascending, he carried the hurdle, weighing 80 lbs., and in descending he brought each time 640 lbs. of slate. At another time, he carried, in three successive journeys, 1,280 lbs. each time. His greatest day's work was bringing 11,776 lbs.; in how many journeys it is not remembered: but in fewer than seventeen. He lived at Stonethwaite, three miles from his place of work. His toils did not appear to injure him: and he declared that he suffered only from thirst. It was believed in his day that there was scarcely another man in the kingdom capable of sustaining such labour for a course of years.

In some places where the slate is closely compacted, and presents endways a perpendicular surface, the quarryman sets about his work as if he were going after eagles' eggs. His comrades let him down by a rope from the precipice, and he tries for a footing on some ledge, where he may drive in wedges. The difficulty of this, where much of his strength must be employed in keeping his footing, may be conceived: and a great length of time must be occupied in loosening masses large enough to bear the fall without being dashed into useless pieces. But, generally speaking, the methods are improved, and the quarries made accessible by roads admitting of the passage of strong carts. Still, the detaching of the slate, and the loading and conducting the carts, are laborious work enough to require and train a very athletic order of men. In various parts of the district, the scene is marked by mountains of *débris,* above or within which yawn black recesses in the mountain side, where the summer thunders echo, and the winter storms send down formidable slides into the vales below.

The stream in the valley beneath Honister Crag,—the beginning of the river Cocker,—must be crossed by stepping-stones or wading, according to the weather: for there is no bridge. At the end of this wild and stony valley, where sheep and their folds, and a quarryman's hut here and there, are the only signs of civilization, stands the farmhouse of Gatesgarth, with its clumps of sycamore and ash. The road thence to Buttermere, lying for the most part above the Lake of Buttermere, is bordered by the plantations which clothe the base of Great Robinson. This little lake is only a mile and a quarter long. At the head,—that is, the south-east,—it is apparently closed in by Honister Crag; and High Stile and Red Pike tower on the southwestern side. At its northern end, the lake has for its margin the green meadows which separate it from Crummock Water: and these meadows are dropped over with woods, hedges, and a few dwellings; so as to offer a tempting resting-place to the angler who comes to enjoy the plentiful sport yielded by the two lakes. On this level stands the little Buttermere inn: and on a rising ground by the roadside is the new Chapel, erected on the site of that which was celebrated for being the smallest in England,—being completely filled by half-a-dozen households.

Travellers who do not desire to make the longer circuit which we have to describe, turn off here among the mountains to the right, to pass through the Vale of Newlands to Keswick. We should desire nothing better than to go up the Vale for six miles or so, till we come in view of Derwent Water, and the rich plain which lies between it and Bassenthwaite, just for the sake of coming back again. The road is perfectly easy, winding up and along the green hills opposite Whiteless. The sweep of these bare green hills is fine; and the walk along their sides very exhilarating, from the airiness and freedom of the scene. The grand point of the journey is perhaps the turn into the second pass,—that of Newlands Haws,—where, at its head, Great Robinson sends down the first waters of one of the streams which go to make the Lake of Bassenthwaite. Above this pass it was that, according to tradition, there was once gold and silver found, enough to supply not only the kingdom but a considerable foreign market, till the works were destroyed, and the miners slain, in the civil wars. In modern times, however, more gold and silver have been sunk in the Newlands mine than raised from it. When the traveller has advanced far enough to obtain a good view of the plain, with Saddleback beyond, and to discover the blue mountains from which flow the Tyne and the Tees, he may rest and refresh himself, and reckon on new pleasures on his return. At the end of his walk, in his descent upon Buttermere, he will obtain charming glimpses of the two lakes, and be in face of a noble array of mountains, from Gable to Melbreak.

He must, of course, see Scale Force, on leaving Buttermere for the other end of Crummock Water. It is best, as far as the aspect of the fall is concerned, to go to it across the fields from the inn: but some of the low ground is so muddy, at all ordinary times, that the walk can be achieved in comfort only after very dry weather. If he goes in a boat, he is landed a mile from the Fall; and then his road is none of the easiest. Between stone-heap and swamp he must pick his way. But what a scene it is at last!—that deep chasm,—a hundred feet of fissure, with perpendicular or over-hanging walls, and a sheet of falling water one hundred and eighty feet high at the end! The relief of the verdure usually found under the spray of cataracts is not absent. The ash quivers from the crevice, and ferns wave on every ledge; and grass and mosses shine to the sense, like light in a dark place.

Crummock Water is less celebrated among the lakes than its peculiarities and beauties appear to deserve. From stations on its rocky and elevated shores the most striking views are obtained of the noble surrounding mountains, as far as the dark Honister Crag, which closes in the group; and the meadows between the two lakes afford a singular charm of contrast. (Figure 13.) From the lake, the heights

Fig. 13. Crummock Water, Buttermere, and Honister Crag

of Melbreak and its neighbour offer an aspect of colouring which is to be seen nowhere else in the district. Long sweeps of orange and gray soil and stones descend to the water; and above, there are large hollows, like craters, filled now with deep blue shadows, and now with tumbling white mists, above which yellow or purple peaks change their hues with every hour of the day, or variation of the sky. There is a good road along the whole of the eastern shore to the inn at Scale Hill; and of late years a delicious woodland path has been made from the landing-place to the inn—a distance of about a mile. The locality is a stormy one. We do not judge by our own experience, though that would lead us to think of Scale Hill as generally under a deluge of rain, while the dust lies thick on the nearest mail-road; but the features of the landscape indicate that the elements are boisterous here. The bare hot-looking *débris* on the Melbreak side, the chasms in the rocks, and the sudden swellings of the waters, tell of turbulence in all seasons. The most tremendous water-spout remembered in the region of the lakes descended the ravine between Grassmoor and Whiteside, in 1760; it swept the whole side of Grassmoor at midnight, and carried down everything that was lying loose all through the vale below, and over a piece of arable land at the entrance, where it actually peeled the whole surface, carrying away the soil and the trees, and leaving the rocky substratum completely bare. The soil was many feet deep, and the trees full-grown. Then it laid down what it brought, covering ten acres with the rubbish. By the channel left, it appears that the flood must have been five or six yards deep, and a hundred yards wide. Among other pranks, it rooted up a solid stone causeway, which was supported by an embankment apparently as strong as the neighbouring hills. The flood not only swept away the whole work, but scooped out the entire line for its own channel. The village of Brackenthwaite, which stood directly in its course, was saved by being built on a stone platform,—a circumstance unknown to the inhabitants till they now saw themselves left safe on a promontory, while the soft soil was swept away from beside their very doors, leaving a chasm where the flood had been turned aside by the resistance of their rock. The end of the matter was, that the flood poured into the Cocker, which rose so as to lay the whole north-western plain under water for a considerable time.

The pretty little lake of Lowes Water is easily reached from Scale Hill inn. It should be seen as the last of the chain, and as presenting some new aspects of the mountain group at this extremity. From Lowes Water the country sinks into the plain which lies between the mountains and the sea: the plain along whose margin are posted the towns of Whitehaven, Workington, and Cockermouth.

And by this time the traveller's eye is ready for the scenery of the plain. The dwellers in a flat country can hardly conceive the refreshment and pleasure given by a glimpse of a sunny champaign to one who has lived for a time shut in among mountains. A friend of ours, in delicate health, became nervous, and felt under a constant sense of oppression, after a three months' residence among the Westmoreland mountains; and cried heartily, from relief and joy, at the first issue upon a wide horizon, in descending into Lancashire. Some younger friends of ours, children who live in a small valley, amused us one day by their exclamations over a volume of Views of the Danube. Whenever they came to a scene almost blank,—a boundless German plain, with only a distant crocketted spire to relieve the uniformity,—they exclaimed in rapture, "Oh, how beautiful!" while they could see no charm in any very circumscribed scene. The traveller who has been long enough among the Fells to relish the sight of open country, could not find a better place for emerging than above the fertile vale of Lorton, on the way from Scale Hill to the mail-road to Keswick. The vale, shallow and wide, spreads out its expanse of fertile fields, endlessly intersected with fences, and dropped over with farms and hamlets, among which may be seen the dark speck of the great Lorton Yew. The view is bounded by the blue range of the Scotch mountains.

When the traveller turns away from this view, and proceeds towards his next lake, Bassenthwaite, he has Whinlatter on his left hand. If the season is sufficiently advanced, he finds it the gayest hill-side he ever saw,—positively gaudy with the blossom of the heather and the gorse. To reach Bassenthwaite Water, the traveller skirts Whinlatter, and passes through the village of Thornthwaite, the rich levels occupying the four miles between Derwent Water and Bassenthwaite being under his eye, and Skiddaw rising in front. The lake is narrow, averaging less than a mile in breadth. Its length is four miles; its scenery is rich, but tame in comparison with that of all the other lakes; its hills are the mere spurs of the interior clusters; and its charm is in opening out views from its foot, through radiating valleys, into the plain country which stretches to the sea and the Solway.

Skiddaw is 138 feet lower than the High Pike of Scawfell: and it may be ascended with ease; even horses being accustomed to reach the summit. Yet the tourist should not disdain this comparatively easy feat, for the views from Skiddaw are very unlike those from Scawfell: and to some persons they are far more interesting. Few of the lakes can be seen from the topmost station; even Derwent Water is hidden by intervening summits; but the crowd of mountain tops is glorious. We will not enumerate them, for it would be to name the whole list. But think of seeing Lancaster Castle in one direction, and the undulating surface of Wigton, Kirkcudbright, and Dumfries in another, with a peep at the Isle of Man between; and, if the day be particularly clear, and the hour favourable, a glimpse of Ireland! Lancaster Castle and Carlisle Cathedral in view at once! St. Bees Head, with the noiseless waves dashing up against the red rocks, almost within reach, as it were; and at the same moment, the Yorkshire summit of Ingleborough showing itself over the whole of Westmoreland which lies between!

Yet not a few persons prefer the ascent of Saddleback to that of Skiddaw. One attraction is the fine view of Derwent Water. "Derwent Water," says Southey, "as seen from the top of Saddleback, is one of the finest mountain scenes in the country."[103] Another attraction is Scales Tarn, a small lake, so situated at the foot of a vast precipice, and so buried among crags, as that the sun never reaches it except through a crevice in early morning; and the stars, it is avouched, are seen in it at noonday. Another attraction may be the comparative difficulty of exploring the solitudes of Old Blencathra, as Saddleback used to be called. One would go through much to see any Tarn of which it could be imagined, even erroneously, that the sun was never seen to touch it, or the stars to forsake it. What a singular feature is this incessant guardianship by the stars! What associations of vigilance and eternal contemplation it awakens! Who can wonder that men seek it,—over slippery Fells, and among rugged rocks, and treacherous bogs, through parching heat, and blinding mists and tempests! Here there are still other dangers, according to the testimony of explorers.

In 1793 a party went up by Scales Fell to see the Tarn. Their account is this:—"When we had ascended about a mile, one of our party, on looking round, was so astonished with the different appearance of objects in the valley so far beneath us, that he declined proceeding. We had not gone much farther, when another was taken ill, and wished to lose blood and return. I was almost ready to give up my project, which I should have done with great reluctance, as the day was remarkably favourable, and exhibited every scene to the greatest advantage. Mr. C. (the conductor) assured us if we proceeded a little way, we should find a resting-place, where the second defaulter might recover the effects of the journey. After labouring another half-hour, we gained the margin of an immense cavity in the side of the mountain, the bottom of which formed a wide basin, and was filled with water, that from our station looked black, though smooth as glass, covering the space of many acres. It is said to be so deep that the sun never shines upon it, and that the reflection of the stars may be seen therein at noonday; but this was a curiosity we did not enjoy." This was an ascent to the Tarn. We have an account of the still worse descent, accomplished by Mr. Green and Mr. Otley. "From Linthwaite Pike," says Mr. Green,[104] "on the above excursion, on a soft green turf, we descended steeply, first southward, and then in an easterly direction to the Tarn, a beautiful circular piece of transparent water, with a well-defined shore. Here we found ourselves engulfed in a basin of steeps, having Tarn Crag on the north, the rocks falling from Sharp Edge on the east, and on the west the soft turf on which we had made our downward progress. These side grounds, in pleasant grassy banks, verge to the stream issuing from the lake, whence there is a charming opening to the town of Penrith; and Cross Fell seen in extreme distance. Wishing to vary our line in returning to the place we had left, we crossed the stream, and commenced a steep ascent at the foot of Sharp Edge. We had not gone far before we were aware that our journey would be attended with perils; the passage gradually grew narrower, and the declivity on each hand awfully precipitous. From walking erect we were reduced to the necessity either of bestriding the ridge, or of moving on one of its sides, with our hands lying over the top, as a security against tumbling into the Tarn on the left, or into a frightful gully on the right,—both of immense depth. Sometimes we thought it prudent to return; but that seemed unmanly, and we proceeded; thinking, with

Shakspere, that 'Dangers retreat, when boldly they are confronted.' Mr. Otley was the leader; who, on gaining steady footing, looked back on the writer, whom he perceived, viewing at leisure from his saddle the remainder of his upward course. On better ground they had a retrospect on Sharp Edge,—which is the narrowest ridge on Saddleback, or any other north of England mountain: in places, its top is composed of loose stones and earth, and the stepping on the sides being as faithless as the top, the Sharp Edge expedition has less of safety to recommend it than singularity."

We hear elsewhere of these mountain pools reflecting the stars in the day time, when they are made into a sort of wells by the building up of the rocky walls around them. "Bowscale Tarn," says one reporter,[105] "is a lake, near a mile in circumference, three miles north-east of Scales Tarn, on the side of a high mountain, so strangely surrounded with a more eminently amphitheatrical ridge of rocks, that it excluded the benefit of the sun for at least four months in the middle of winter: but this is not its only singularity. Several of the most credible inhabitants thereabouts affirming that they frequently see stars in it at midday; but in order to discover that phenomenon, the firmament must be perfectly clear, the air stable, and the water unagitated. These circumstances not concurring at the time I was there, deprived me of the pleasure of that sight, and of recommending it to the naturalist upon my own ocular evidence. The spectator must be placed at least 200 yards above the lake, and as much below the summit of the semi-ambient ridge." It is in this Bowscale Tarn that, in the belief of the country people, there are two fish which cannot die. How long they are said to have lived we know not: but they are to continue to live for ever.

Keswick is usually made the head-quarters of tourists for some days,—and this is almost a necessary plan for those who travel only in carriages; but the more independent pedestrian will not find much to detain him in the town. Within reach are several little clean country inns, which will afford him opportunities for seeing, in the most varied manner, the world of beauties included in the Derwent Water district. Besides the inns in the plain, there is the 'King's Head,' at the entrance of the Vale of St. John's, five or six miles from Keswick; and the Lodore inn, near the head of Derwent Water; and further on, in Borrowdale, the little inn at Rosthwaite.

While at Keswick, the traveller will look with interest on Southey's residence, Greta Hall. He will probably visit the Museums; and he certainly ought not to omit seeing and studying Mr. Flintoft's Model of the Lake District,[106] which will teach him more in ten minutes of the structure and distribution of the country than he could learn from a hundred pages of description. On first entering the room, this model—under 13 feet by 10—looks a mere uneven, ugly bit of plaster: but a few moments are enough to engage the observer's attention so deeply, that he does not leave it till he has traced out almost every valley and pass in the district. He visits all the sixteen large lakes and the fifty-two small ones, and looks abroad from every summit in turn. This Model is held to be a work of extraordinary correctness; and a leisurely visit to it should be an object to every traveller who cares to know where he is, and where he is going. Every one will, of course, visit the Castle Head,—a walk of a mile from the inns; where, from an eminence, a fine view of the lake and environs is obtained. And it is worth while to ascend the long hill of Castlerigg, even if the traveller is not there in natural course on his way to Ambleside, to enjoy the magnificent view which some think unrivalled in the region; extending from the singular and solemn entrance of Borrowdale to the subsiding hills beyond the lake of Bassenthwaite. We have seen this view many times; and each time we have been more than ever taken by surprise by its wonderful range of beauty.

The celebrity of Derwent Water is out of all proportion to its size; for it is only three miles long, and never exceeds a mile and a half in breadth. (Figure 14.) Our own private opinion is, that the beauty of the lake itself does not answer to its reputation. The islands have no particular charm, and rather perplex the eye; and there is nothing striking in the immediate shores, along which a good road runs, nearly level, between fields and plantations. Walla Crag is fine, with its relief of foliage; and the cleft in it, which is called the Lady's Rake, is interesting from its tradition. It is said that the Countess of Derwentwater made her escape up this ravine, after the arrest of her husband. Lord's Island, the largest in the lake, belonged to the family—the Ratcliffes—and was a stronghold of theirs. It was confiscated, with their other possessions, after the Rebellion of 1715,

Fig. 14. Derwent Water and Skiddaw

and transferred to Greenwich Hospital. St. Herbert's Island contains the ruins of a hermitage, in relation to which a pretty story is told. St. Cuthbert and St. Herbert were very dear friends.[107] When St. Herbert came hither to repose from the cares of life, and end his days in prayer, he was far apart from his friend, as we all know: but he nightly prayed that they might be united in death, by being taken from the world at the same moment. The prayer was granted; and the scenes of the two deaths have been all the more sacred for the coincidence, in the popular mind, ever since.

Every one hears of the Floating Island, in connection with Derwent Water. The wise call it the Buoyant Island, after the hint given by Wordsworth in his 'Guide.'[108] It appears to be merely a loose mass of vegetation, which rises to the surface when swollen by the gases generated by the decay of its parts. When a boat-hook is struck into it, it puffs out carburetted hydrogen and azote.[109] Though this island is now no mystery, its appearance marks the year in which it happens; and the event is told in the newspapers from end to end of the kingdom. It happened last in 1842.

After all that has been said of the Fall of Lodore, it is certainly very fine, in any weather, and whatever quantity of water it may have to show. The main features—the mighty crags on either hand (Gowder on the left, and Shepherd's on the right,) and the ravine of piled blocks—are such as weather cannot impair; and we have not decided to this day whether we prefer visiting the Fall after rain and under a cloud canopy, or in a hot dry month of the year. The dash of the Fall is heard from the road; and it will guide the traveller through the little garden and orchard of the inn, and over the foot-bridge, and through the wood, to the stone bench in front of the Fall.

And now, what can any one say of the entrance upon Borrowdale, but—"Go and see it!" This is all we will say; for we might write a volume about the disposition of mountains and crags before one could even produce a state of mind which could conceive of what it is here—the tumbling together of steeps and slopes, precipices and promontories, woods, ravines, and isolated summits. Suffice it that the traveller will pass the village of Grange, and must remember that it was here that the old monks of Furness laid up their crops and other stores, when they were the owners of Borrowdale. (Figure 15.) He must just cast a

Fig. 15. Grange, Buttermere

glance up to the Bowder-stone, if he thinks, as we do, that there is nothing more to be seen which need move him to undertake the ascent to it. The block is said to weigh about 1771 tons, and stands 36 feet high. Its edge is embedded in the place where, to all appearance, it has fallen from above; and it looks like a ship lying on its keel. A mile beyond the Bowder Stone is the hamlet of Rosthwaite, where we always contrive to pass the night—in Sarah Simpson's well-tended house—when we give ourselves the treat of a visit to Borrowdale. A brother of Sarah Simpson, living at Rosthwaite, acts as guide over the neighbouring passes.

Notwithstanding what we have said of the entrance of Borrowdale, we yet prefer dropping into it above Rosthwaite, from Watendlath,—the extremely secluded valley which lies at the top of the Lodore Fall, and the rocks from which it tumbles. The way into Watendlath is easily found: it branches off to the left from the high road in coming from Keswick, and passes just behind Barrow House. The inhabitants of this valley are the most primitive we have met with in any part of the Lake District: and if the traveller wishes to see what men are—and yet more, women—

in point of intelligence, in a position which renders the human face a rare sight to them, he had better take his way to Upper Borrowdale through Watendlath. He must note the circular pool which supplies the waters of Lodore; and he should look through the chasm where the stream pours over, to see how gloriously the Lake and the Skiddaw range here combine. It is a perfect intoxication to traverse this valley when the heather is in bloom on its wild hill sides; and when summer breezes come over the ridge from Helvellyn to the east; and the great central summits of Scawfell and Bowfell show themselves in front over all the intervening heights. The descent upon Rosthwaite is the concluding treat. The way is easy,—a gentle slope over grass and elastic heather; and the whole surface of the slope is starred over with bright heath flowers. The head of the Dale, always awful, whether gloomy or bright, opens out, and seems to be spreading its levels for one's reception. The passes to Buttermere (by which we left the Dale at the outset), to Sty Head (by which we entered it), and to the Stake (by which we are about to leave it now), disclose themselves round the projecting Glaramara. The other way lie Grange and the Lake. Below us is Rosthwaite, with the brattling stream behind, which we must presently cross by stepping-stones to reach the inn.

And now the time is come for leaving Borrowdale. The top of the Stake Pass is five miles and a half from Rosthwaite. After the first mile, when the farm-house at Stonethwaite is passed, not another dwelling will be seen. The path follows, and at length crosses, the stream, which is the infant Derwent, finding its way down from Angle Tarn, lying high up in a recess of Bowfell. This valley of Langstreth is extremely wild; but there is no perplexity in it for the traveller who keeps the path in view. It is a pleasant path where it goes zigzag up the steep green slope, within hearing of the stream; and offers here an old oak, and there a waving birch within reach, where the traveller may sit and rest, while looking back upon the levels of Borrowdale. When he has reached the Top of the Stake, he is under the shadow of Bowfell, safely returned to his starting point, among the central summits of the region.

III.

THE TRAVELLER must not linger long on the heights, however; for there is no help there, in case of fatigue and hunger. He must come down into Langdale,—still by the same Stake Pass,—and repose himself at the farm-house at Millbeck, where he can obtain, not exciseable articles, but good plain food, and milk, and water. From the moment of his obtaining a view of Langdale from above, he will see this house, and meet with no kind of difficulty in reaching it, the path being distinctly marked all the way; a distance of above five miles from the Top of the Stake, according to the Guide-books.

The character of Langdale is distinctly marked, and pretty uniform from end to end. It has levels, here expanding and there contracting; and the stream winds among them throughout. There is no lake or pool: and the mountains send out spurs, alternating or meeting, so as to make the levels sometimes circular and sometimes winding. The dwellings, all, without exception, which lie below the head of the dale, are on the rising grounds which skirt the levels: and this, together with the paving of the roads in the levels, shows that the valley is subject to floods. The houses in Langdale,—of gray stone, each on its knoll, with a canopy of firs and sycamores above it, and ferns scattered all about it, and ewes and lambs nestling near it,—these dale-farms are cheerful and pleasant objects to look upon, whether from above or passing among them. Our traveller is, however, to pass only two or three, which lie between his descent and Millbeck.

From Millbeck, he will, of course, proceed to see Dungeon Ghyll Force. (Figure 16.) He must not, on hearing this name, let his imagination carry him to the foundations of some robber castle for its origin. In the language of the country people here a fissure or cavern in the rock is called a Dungeon. Ghyll means also a fissure: so Dungeon Ghyll is emphatically a fissure by name; and it certainly is so also by nature. The stranger must either take some one with him, to put him in the way (though the place is not more than half-a-mile off), or he must take care not to go up to the ghyll and stream behind the farm, which he will do as a matter of course unless warned to the contrary. What he wants is the next, to the left. When he reaches the spot where the dark chasm yawns, and the waters are loud, though he cannot see anything of the fall, let him not fear missing the sight. If there is a ladder, he must descend: if

Fig. 16. Dungeon Ghyll

not, or if it be broken, or rotten with continual wet, he can easily get down the rock. And there it is!—the fall in its cleft, tumbling and splashing, while the light ash, and all the vegetation besides, is everlastingly in motion from the stir of the air. Then let him look up, and see how a bridge is made aloft by the lodgment of a block in the chasm. He will be fortunate if he is there just at that hour of the summer afternoon when the sunlight gushes in obliquely,—a narrow, radiant, translucent screen, itself lighting up the gorge, but half concealing the projections and waving ferns behind it. The way in which it converts the spray into sparks and gems can be believed only by those who have seen it.

In order to get into Easedale, the traveller will take a guide from Millbeck, to conduct him to Stickle Tarn, and thence to Easedale Tarn. We could wish him no better treat than some hours' leisure for angling in Stickle Tarn, which is famous for its trout. This tarn is reached by a peat-road from Millbeck, and its circular basin, brimming with clear water, lies finely under the steep rocks of Pavey Ark. To us there is no object of this mountain scenery more interesting than its tarns. Their very use is one which gratifies one's sense of beauty. Their use is to cause such a distribution of the waters as may fertilize without inundating the lands below. After rains, if the waters all came pouring down at once, the vales would be flooded; as it is, the nearer brooks swell, and pour themselves out into the main stream, while the mountain brooks are busy in the same way above, emptying themselves into the tarns. By the time the streams in the valley are subsiding, the upper tarns are full, and begin to overflow; and now the overflow can be received in the valley without injury. We know of nothing in natural scenery which conveys such an impression of stillness as the tarns which lie under precipices. For hours together the deep shadows lie absolutely unmoved; and when movement occurs, it may be such as does not disturb the sense of repose: it is only the dimple made by a restless fish or fly, or the gentle flow of water in and out; or the wild drake may launch and lead his brood in the deep gray shadow opposite, paddling so quietly as not to break up the mirror, but merely to let in two converging lines of white light to illuminate the recess. We saw this happen on Easedale Tarn, and felt we could never lose the picture thus made for us in a moment.

And when the tempest takes its swoop upon the tarn, what a sight it is! While we are approaching the hollow where the tarn is known to lie, and some time before the waters are visible, little white clouds come whirling or puffing out, and drive against the mountain side. We expect, of course, to find a mist overhanging the tarn, and begin to wonder whether we shall see anything of it, after climbing so far on purpose: and lo! there it is, distinct enough, in a vast fury. What we saw was not mist, but spray, caught up by the wind, and whirled away. The four winds seem to have met in this hollow, and to be running the waters up towards the centre; or two are pursuing each other, and speeding over the surface in all sorts of rapid caprices. Such wild commotion, in a place so absolutely retired, produces an impression no less singular than that of the deepest stillness, when the solitary angler treads as softly, in changing his place, as if he feared to wake infant Nature from her noontide sleep.

If the traveller wishes to ascend Harrison Stickle, the loftiest of the Langdale Pikes, it will be from hence. The height of Harrison Stickle is 2409 feet above the level of the sea. If he does not ascend the Pike, he crosses the Fell to Easedale Tarn, and has before him a descent full of delights, from the dreary and lonely Fell down gradually into the beauty of Grasmere. From the Tarn, he follows the stream, past its many leaps, and rapids, and windings round obstructing rocks, till he finds himself standing above the Fall, called Sour Milk Ghyll Force. This name is said to be given to the Fall on account of the whiteness of its broken waters. It is a full and impetuous fall, visible from afar from the turbulence of its waters; yet we have seen it on a calm winter's day, suspended by frost; its recess, at all other times full of tumultuous noise, then as still as the tarn above from which it flows. Here, where the summer sunshine is apparently fought with and rejected, the mild wintry beams were silently received, and enshrined in crystal icicles.

The fine outline of Helm Crag, with its green sides and broken crest, now appears to the left; the fertile levels of Easedale lie below; and in front there is an opening to Grasmere, through which the church and village, the wooded knolls, the circular lake with its single green island clumped with pines, the rich sloping shores, and the green declivity of Loughrigg opposite, are disclosed to the eye, more and more fully, till the traveller arrives at Grasmere.

From the verdant and tranquil aspect. of the valley, it is usually and naturally supposed that Grasmere is named from its grassy slopes and shores; but its derivation is pointed out by its connexion with Grisedale, which opens laterally from it, under the shadow of Helvellyn. Gris is the old Saxon for wild swine; and the lake was once called Grismere,—the lake of the wild boar. A deep and still

Fig. 17. Grasmere, from Dunmail Raise

retreat this must have been in the days of wild boars! If the traveller has time, he should ascend the pass to Grisedale Tarn, from behind the Swan Inn—the tempting clean white house which catches the eye of everyone who visits Grasmere. Our business now is, however, to follow the high road over Dunmail Raise,—the pass which has Steel Fell on the west, and Seat Sandal on the east. At the highest point, this pass is only 720 feet above the sea; but, in a wind, the ascent is fatiguing enough, from the strength of the draught between the heights. (Figure 17.) The stream on the right divides the counties of Cumberland and Westmoreland. One object, so rude as not to attract attention unless pointed out, should not be missed: a pile of stones or cairn, which marks the spot of a critical fight in the olden time, when the Anglo-Saxon king, Edmund, defeated and slew Dumhnail, the British king, of Cumbria, and then put out the eyes of the two sons of the deceased king, and gave their inheritance to Malcolm, king of Scotland, to hold it in fee. This happened about A.D. 945.

A little inn, the 'Nag's Head,' stands by the roadside, about a mile and a quarter from the cairn. From thence the traveller should proceed to explore the Wythburn Water, or Leathes Water, now called Thirlmere. Too many visitors see this lake only from the mail-road, and then declare it the least interesting lake of the district: but they can form no estimate of its beauty without exploring its western bank,—a thing easily done, as there is a plain track the whole way. The track, admitting carts, leaves the mail-road not more than a mile from the Nag's Head, and winds between fields to a collection of houses, once called by the grand name of the City of Wythburn; and thence, past a farm or two, and between walls, till the traveller finds himself fairly on his way above the lake. As he looks round him he will wonder at the changes which have taken place since the days when the squirrel could go from Wythburn to Keswick without touching the ground. When the woods so covered the scene, this lake must have been gloomy indeed, overshadowed, as it always is, by Helvellyn, and shrouded besides, at that time, by an unbroken forest. Now light and colour are let in by the clearing of the ground; and the description of a recent observer shows how little like a forest scene it now is: "It was luxury to sit on a high grassy slope, between two bold promontories, and look down upon the black and solemn waters, the great Helvellyn rising steep and bare on the opposite shore. The scene was so sombre, even in the fine evening light of gay July, that a white horse in a cart moving slowly along the road under Helvellyn—a very minute object at such a distance—seemed to cast a light into the landscape! Then, in a few more steps, we emerged into a noble amphitheatre of rocks, retiring from the lake, and leaving a level meadow of the richest green for us to traverse. These rocks were feathered with wood to their summits, except where bold projections of gray or dun crags relieved the prevalent green with a most harmonious colouring. High up, almost at the very top, gushed out a foaming stream, from some unseen recess; and the waters leaped and tumbled in their long descent till they reached the meadow, through which they quietly slid into the lake. Our walk over the deep grass and heather must have been very noiseless; for I evidently gave as vivid a start as I received, when I came upon a little clear pool in the grass, with a reedy margin, whence a heron sprang up so close that I might almost have laid hold on its beautiful wings or long legs, as it hurried away, leaving the water dimpled and clouded in the spot where it had stood fishing when alarmed. Then our path lay along the margin of the lake, and then through a shady lane which opened into a farm-yard. We came now near the bridge, and were soon to be satisfied how a lake could be crossed by a bridge. In one spot, about halfway along the lake,—which is about two miles and a half in length, and from a quarter to half a mile in breadth,—the shores throw out promontories which leave no very wide space from point to point; and here there is a rising of the ground from below, so that the waters are shallow—even fordable at times for carts and horses. Piers of rough stone are built, and piles of them raised at intervals; and these intervals are crossed by planks with a hand-rail; so that it is a picturesque bridge enough."

Having reached the high road again, the next object is to cross over eastwards to Ulleswater. If the traveller means to make a short cut over the Fells, his guide will meet him at the King's Head,—a neat little inn, near the spot where he has entered upon the mail-road. If he prefers a longer journey by car, or on horseback, he must be met here, according to previous orders, and take the right hand road—that to Threlkeld, instead of the left hand road to Keswick. From the lovely vale of St. John's he will turn, after a time, over the somewhat dreary moor of Matterdale, whose religious name—sacred to the Virgin Mother—reminds us, as does Patterdale, of the monks who named them from their paternosters and Ave Marys, repeated as a tutelary charm as they travelled through these wilds.

From Matterdale the road drops down upon the western bank of Ulleswater, passing at length through Gowbarrow Park. There is perhaps nothing in the district finer than the interval between this entrance upon Gowbarrow Park and the head of the lake. The park is studded over with ancient trees; and the sides of its watercourses, and the depths of its ravines, are luxuriantly wooded. The gray walls of Lyulph's Tower rise on one of the finest points of view. This building is modern, being a hunting-seat erected by a late Duke of Norfolk: but it stands on the site of a former building named, as some think, from the same personage who gave its name to the lake—Ulf, or L'Ulf, the first baron of Greystoke. Others suppose it to signify simply Wolf's Tower. Some one from this house will show the way, over the open grass, and then through the wood, to Ara Force, a waterfall of remarkable beauty, buried deep in a wooded ravine.

As the traveller sits in the cool damp nook at the bottom of the chasm, where the echo of dashing and gurgling waters never dies, and the ferns, long grasses, and ash sprays wave and quiver everlastingly in the pulsing air; and as, looking up, he sees the slender line of bridge spanning the upper fall, he ought to know of the mournful legend which belongs to this place, and which Wordsworth has preserved.[110] In the olden time, a knight who loved a lady, and courted her in her father's tower here, at Greystoke, went forth to win glory. He won great glory; and at first his lady rejoiced fully in it: but he was so long in returning, and she heard so much of his deeds in behalf of distressed ladies, that doubts at length stole upon her heart as to whether he still loved her. These doubts disturbed her mind in sleep; and she began to walk in her dreams, directing her steps towards the waterfall where she and her lover used to meet. Under a holly tree beside the fall they had plighted their vows; and this was the limit of her dreaming walks. The knight at length returned to claim her. Arriving in the night, he went to the ravine, to rest under the holly until the morning should permit him to knock at the gate of the tower: but he saw a gliding white figure among the trees; and this figure reached the holly before him, and plucked twigs from the tree, and threw them into the stream. Was it the ghost of his lady love? or was it herself? She stood in a dangerous place: he put out his hand to uphold her: the touch awakened her. In her terror and confusion she fell from his grasp into the torrent, and was carried down the ravine. He followed and rescued her; but she died upon the bank—not, however, without having fully understood that her lover was true, and had come to claim her. The knight devoted the rest of his days to mourn her: he built himself a cell upon the spot, and became a hermit for her sake.

Place Fell is a fine mountain, coming out boldly into the lake on the opposite side: and Stybarrow Crag shoots up high overhead, as one follows the windings of the shore. (Figure 18.) One should not pass the next opening without going up to see the little hamlet which the children of the place have named 'Seldom Seen.' This is Glencoin—the Corner Glen, which is one of the sweetest nooks in the district.

The next stream which crosses the road is from Glenridding. Thick and dirty as its waters look, they come down from Kepple Cove Tarn and Red Tarn, high up on Helvellyn. It is from the lead-works that they take their defilement, in passing through Greenside. If the traveller

Fig. 18. Stybarrow Crag and Helvellyn, from Gowbarrow Park

had come over Helvellyn from Wythburn, or through Grisedale from Grasmere, he would have descended by the banks of this stream.

The inn at Patterdale—a luxurious family hotel—is four miles from Lyulph's Tower; and if the traveller has wisely walked from the entrance of Gowbarrow Park, he must still be fresh enough to ascend the glorious pass behind, to obtain a view of Brothers' Water, Hays Water, and Windermere from the top of the Kirkstone pass. If he likes, he can do the greater part of it on horseback or in a car. After three or four miles of winding road, among the rich levels of Patterdale, which is guarded by mountains jutting forwards, like promontories, he begins to ascend, passing Hartsop, and the pretty still sheet called Brothers' Water. Up and up he goes, between the sweep of Coldfell on his left, and the Scandale Screes on the right, no longer wondering at the tales current of the snowdrifts and murderous frosts which here attack the wayfarer in the winter season. Here there is no shelter or escape from the cutting wind, or the snows which cannot accumulate on the steep slopes, and must therefore drive in heaps into the pass. We have known enough of the biting of a north wind in April in this pass to feel that it must be a calm day indeed which would induce us to traverse it in winter. When the traveller has reached the toll-house, which is declared by an inscription of the Ordnance Surveyors to be the highest inhabited house in England, he obtains a noble view over Ambleside and its valleys at the Head of Windermere, the Coniston Mountains, and the whole of the district which lies between him and the sea; the sea itself being seen glittering, with perhaps a steamer upon it, in a clear and favourable light.

Returning down the pass, he first observes the fallen rock, ridged like a roof, whose form (that of a small church) has given the name to the pass: and next, is struck with the first sight of Brothers' Water from above: and all the way as he descends to it, the openings on the Scandale side, the left, charm his eye,—with their fissures, precipices, green slopes or levels, and knolls in the midst, crowned with firs. He will not now pass Hartsop, as before, but turn up the road to the right, among the farms, and reach and follow the Beck to its source at Hays Water. It is a lively stream to follow up; and, at a distance of a mile and a half from the main road, lies Hays Water, the large Tarn which is the

Fig. 19. Patterdale

delight of the angler, because the trout have abundantly delighted in it before him. It is overhung by High Street, so that perhaps the Roman eagles, as well as the native birds of the rocks, have cast their shadows upon its surface. Not far off lies Angle Tarn, on the southern end of Place Fell. Both these tarns send their brooks down, to swell the stream from Brothers' Water, which is itself supplied from the busy, noisy beck which descends the Kirkstone Pass. The whole forms a clear brown stream, winding through Patterdale, and quietly emptying itself into Ullswater, among the green meadows about its head. (Figure 19.)

It now remains to see the Ullswater mountains from the lake; and for this purpose the traveller must take a boat from Patterdale to Pooley Bridge. The lake, somewhat shorter than Windermere, has three reaches,—its form being that of the letter Z; and the diversity of view thus afforded is very striking. (Figure 20.) Place Fell, with its noble steeps, is the principal object at the upper part of the lake; and next, Helvellyn, which seems to rise in proportion as the distance is increased. The shores subside towards the foot of the lake, and a new country is entered on landing. Penrith, six miles distant from Pooley Bridge, is a

Fig. 20. Ulleswater

neat little town, busy, from being the great thoroughfare of the district, but not particularly interesting, except from some Druidical remains in its neighbourhood, and its vicinity to Brougham Castle. To the stranger, just arriving in the district, there is indeed the interest of seeing for the first time some of the peculiarities of the people,—their wooden shoes and slated floors, their fine old carved presses and chairs (the envy of curiosity seekers), and their air of homely prosperity. But it has not the charm of the little towns which are set down on the levels between two lakes, or which nestle in the skirts of a mountain, or spread themselves round the curve of a bay. As it is more modern,—or rather, as the notions and habits of its inhabitants are more modern than those of more primitive places,—we may hope it is less afflicted than other towns of the region with their curse and shame,—unhealthiness!

This unhealthiness is no less a shame than a curse: for the fault is in man, not in Nature. Nature has fully done her part in providing rock for foundations, the purest air, and amplest supplies of running water: yet the people of the towns live—as we are apt to pity the poor of the metropolis for living—in stench, huddled together in cabins, and almost without water. The wilfulness of this makes the fact almost incredible; but the fact is so. There are several causes for this; all of which are remediable. The great landed proprietors are, in too many cases, utterly careless about the ways of living of their humble neighbours; and those humble neighbors need enlightenment about sanitary matters. There are even instances known of landed proprietors, urging some feudal claim and authority, who absolutely forbid the erection of any new dwellings except on the site of former ones: and this in neighbourhoods where the population is rapidly increasing. There are some who interest themselves about the building of handsome houses for opulent persons, while they never raise a cottage, or leave the builders time or opportunity to erect cottages, or will dispose of their land for sites. It will be seen at a glance what a despotic and increasing power is thus held by these proprietors:—how absolutely dependant the labouring classes must be on the pleasure of their landlords, when any displeasing act, any unwelcome independence in religion, or politics, or pursuits, or habits, may subject them to warning to leave their cottages, while no others are to be had. The labouring class, therefore, though exempt from poverty, generally speaking,—indeed more prosperous as to gain than perhaps any other of their class in the kingdom,—are too often at the mercy of their rich neighbours, and suffer in health and morals as much as the poor of great towns. They are crowded together in dens and cabins, so that decency cannot be observed. They become profligate accordingly, to such a degree as is shocking and incredible to strangers who come hither with an expectation of finding "rural innocence" befitting the scene. Where the home is disgusting, men go to the public-house; and the staggering drunkards that one meets in the meadows, and the brawls that one overhears in the by-streets, and the domestic troubles which arise from licentiousness among people who are so crowded together that they cannot avoid each other, are a flagrant curse in this paradise of nature. In these little towns, where the fresh mountain winds are always passing hither and thither, and the purest streams are for ever heard gushing down from the heights, and the whole area is made up of slopes and natural channels, there are fever-nests, as in the dampest levels of low lying cities. The churchyards are so over-crowded in some places, that delicate persons cannot attend service without being ill; and some neighbouring houses are scarcely habitable. At Ambleside, where the small churchyard is inclosed by three roads, the sexton invariably faints when he opens a new grave. When there was a stir, a few years since, about a new church at Ambleside, the curate declared that the movement was made in order to obtain more room for the dead, rather than the living. As yet, nothing has been done. Fever, consumption, and scrofula, abound. And why is it so? Because few know of this state of things; and those who should care most about it care least; a large proportion of them, we fear, being too well satisfied with their possession of power to wish for any change. Nobody stirs;—neither land-owners, nor clergy, nor gentry, nor master-builders. Handsome houses rise in all directions, in the most beautiful valleys: new residents arrive, causing an increase in the number of the labouring class: and it is rare to see a new cottage in any corner, while one may observe three cottages thrown into one, to make a good house for one gentleman, whose occupancy throws three families out of health and hope. As to what can be done,—it is pretty clear. There is no occasion to wait for the enlightenment and regeneration of those who have shown how little they understand the duties of proprietorship. Let their eyes be opened, and their hearts be appealed to, by all means; for their own sakes as well as that of the oppressed: but there is no need to wait till they are wise. The general absence of poverty makes the way to amendment open and clear. The people are able and eager to pay good rents for decent and wholesome dwellings; and their probity about money matters is remarkable and unquestionable. There is, therefore, every inducement to capitalists at hand, and from a distance, to build in these neighbourhoods. There can hardly be a safer or more profitable investment than cottage-building here; and it is inconceivable that, if this were sufficiently known, the thing would not presently be done. But it is not known. The aggrieved class have no means of proclaiming their grievances; and they do not attempt it. They sicken and pine at home; they witness the corruption of some of their children, or, with a less sad heart, follow their coffins to the churchyard, while they hear that rich men round them are buying hundreds of acres, year by year, and leaving their vast estates to the management of stewards, who consider only their employer's taste, or his purse,—giving perhaps some of the contents of that purse in a corrupting bounty, while perpetuating a cruel oppression. If a single capitalist would begin the good work on one spot, with a clear purpose and the needful care, there is no saying what blessings might not spring from the act. It would be a very safe experiment; for a good dwelling is here as convertible a property as a bank-note. If the state of the case can only be fairly made known, we shall not long see the pallid faces of the townspeople contrast strangely with the ruddy health of the dalesmen; or a family of twelve people lodged in two rooms; or open cesspools and stagnant sinks in back streets; or women painfully carrying water up the hills,—so painfully as to be tempted to make the smallest possible quantity serve for household purposes. The railroads, which some have so much feared, will be no small blessing to the district if they bring strangers from a more enlightened region to abolish the town-evils, which harbour in the very heart of the mountains.

The parish of Brougham, Burg-ham, (meaning Castle-town), was the Brovacum of the Romans, where, as we learn from Nicolson and Burn, they had a company of Defensores, and left many tokens of their presence in antiquities which have come to light from time to time. The village of Brougham passed into the hands of the Veteriponts in the reign of John or Henry III. The Castle of Brougham has been held by the Veteriponts, Cliffords, and Tuftons; and is now the property of the Earl of Thanet. It is now in ruins: and fine ruins they are. They stand at the confluence of the Eamont and Lowther rivers, at the distance of a mile from Penrith.

Brougham Hall, the seat of Lord Brougham, is within a mile and a half of Penrith. The traveller should walk along the river-bank from the bridge at Brougham Hall to Askham, and then ascend the steep bank of red sandstone, overshadowed by trees, to the park of Lowther Castle.

The grounds here are fine; especially the terrace, which affords a noble walk. It is very elevated; broad, mossy, shady, breezy, and overlooking a considerable extent of country,—some of which is fertile plain, and some, a preparation for entrance upon the mountain district within. The most remarkable feature of this landscape is perhaps the hollow, within which lies Hawes Water. The park has some fine old trees; and the number and size of the yews in the grounds will strike the stranger. But great damage was caused in the woods by the extraordinary hurricane of 1839, which broke its way straight through, levelling everything in its path. On the road from Askham to Bampton, the high grounds of Lowther present on the left a nearly straight line of great elevation, along which runs the park wall, almost to the extremity of the promontory. From a distance, it looks the most enviable position for a park that can be imagined.

About five miles from Askham lies Hawes Water; a small lake, but of great beauty. It is little more than three miles long, and about half a mile broad. One side is richly wooded; the other nearly bare; and two bold promontories threaten to cut it in two, in one part, where the passage is only two or three hundred yards wide. Round the head of the lake cluster the great mountains of Harter Fell, High Street, Kidsey Pike, and others, leaving space among their skirts for the exquisite little valley of Mardale. Those who are able to obtain one of Lord Lonsdale's boats for the traverse of the lake may think themselves fortunate; for this is, of course, the most perfect way of seeing the surroundings of so small a sheet of water: and all other persons are deprived of the means of doing so. There are some good houses on the shores, and at the further end; but the occupants who live on the very brink are not allowed to keep any sort of boat. His lordship's boats are to be had for the asking, it is declared: but there is doubt, of course, about people being on the spot when the boat is wanted: and it must be bespoken at Askham: and all this is something different from the ordinary facility of obtaining a boat at once, wherever there are inhabitants. The walk, however, is easy and agreeable enough,—by a good road which runs along the western bank.

The crags which are heaped or sprinkled about the head of the lake are extremely fine. They jut out from the mountain side, or stand alone on the green slopes, or collect into miniature mountain clusters, which shelter tiny dells, whence the sheep send forth their bleat. There is a white house conspicuous at the head of the lake, which must not, under penalty of disappointment, be mistaken by the tired traveller for the Mardale Inn. The inn at Mardale Green is a full mile from the water; and sweet is the passage to it, if the walker be not too weary. The path winds through the levels, round the bases of the knolls, past the ruins of the old church, and among snug little farms, while, at one extremity of the dale is the lake, and the other is closed in by the pass to Kentmere and Sleddale, and the great Pikes tower on either hand. The stream which gushes here and pauses there, as it passes among rough stones or through a green meadow, comes down from Small Water, reinforced by a brook from Blea Water on High Street, which joins the other a little above Mardale.

The hostess at Mardale Green Inn will make her guests comfortable with homely food and a clean bed: and the host will, if necessary, act as guide up the passes.

The traveller may make his choice of three ways out by the Pass of Nanbield. He may take a turn to the left before reaching Small Water, and go down into Long Sleddale,— to which we know of no sufficient inducement, unless it be that the way is practicable for a horse, which the others are not: or he may ascend, by the pretty Blea Tarn, the slope of High Street on the right, see where the Roman road ran along its ridge, and descend into Troutbeck: or he may go forward past Small Water, leaving High Street unvisited on the right, and drop into Kentmere, study its character as he proceeds down its length, and then strike over the Fells to the right into Troutbeck. His choice will be much determined by weather, of course: and we wish him something more of a choice than was permitted to us lately by a wind which laid us flat on the summit of the pass, and made all thought of High Street quite out of the question.

There is no difficulty in the ascent from Mardale Green; but the traveller indulges in frequent rests, for the sake of looking back upon the singularly-secluded valley, with its winding stream, its faintly-marked track, and its little inn, recognised to the last by the sycamores and poplars which overshadow its roof and rustle before the door. Then he comes to the hollow where lies the Tarn,—Small Water. Here he will rest again, sitting among scattered or shelving rocks, and drinking from this pure mountain basin. Arrived at the top, he loses sight of Mardale and greets Kentmere almost at the same moment. The dale behind is wild as any recess in the district: while before him lies a valley whose grandeur is all at the upper end; and which spreads out, and becomes shallower with every mile of its recession from the mountain cluster which he is now about to leave.

When he has gone down a mile, he finds that he is travelling on one side of the Tongue of Kentmere,—the projection which, in this and some other valleys, splits the head of the dale into a fork. When he arrives at the chapel, he finds that there is a carriage-road which would lead him forth to Staveley and Kendal. But he is going over into Troutbeck: so he turns up to the right, and pursues the broad zigzag track which leads over the Fell, till Troutbeck opens beneath him on the other side. Before beginning the ascent, however, he will note Kentmere Hall,—the birthplace of Bernard Gilpin, in 1517.[111] If familiar with the old descriptions of the district, he will look for Kentmere Tarn, and wonder to see no trace of it. It is drained away; and fertile fields now occupy the place of the swamp, reeds, and shallow waters, which he might have seen but a few years ago. While this tarn existed, the mills at Kendal were very irregularly supplied with water. Now, when the streams are collected in a reservoir which the traveller sees in coming down from the Pass of Nanbield, and the intercepting tarn is done away with, the flow of water no longer fails.

He descends into Troutbeck by the road over Applethwaite Common, which brings him down upon the chapel and the bridge, in the very depth of the deep valley of Troutbeck. Or, if he likes to drop down at once, so as to alight in the dale at the extremity of Troutbeck Tongue, he will enjoy the walk along the whole length of this charming valley,—among its old-fashioned farmsteads, and primitive aspects of every kind. He must be careful to cross the beck, and proceed on the western side of the valley, if, as we must suppose, his object is to reach Lowwood Inn or Ambleside. If he means to make Bowness his resting-place, he may keep on the eastern side of the stream, and follow the road.

From the western road, there are exquisite views,—now of Troutbeck Tongue; next, of the deep levels through which winds the beck, peopled with trout, and therefore sought by the angler: next, of the chapel and bridge below; And then, when the road has wound some way over the boundary hills, of Windermere in almost its whole extent. The country people will tell him that "this is thought one of the handsomest views in these parts,—especially at the back-end of the year." It is always so "handsome," whether in the vivid green of spring, or the deep lustre and shadows of summer, or the radiant woodland hues of autumn, or the solemn lights of a wintry sunset, that we could make no choice among the four seasons. Has any one who wonders at this seen this view when there was a bar of red-hot snow on the ridge of Wansfell, and the islands lay purple in the crimson lake,—the Calgarth woods standing so still as that not a single twig let fall its burden of snow? If not, let him not wonder that the residents of the district hesitate between its winter and its summer charms.

The traveller cannot now miss his way down to the high-road from Kendal to Ambleside, which he will join at a short distance from Lowwood inn.

IV.[112]

WE MUST now set forth again from the central heights which have been our rallying-point throughout. Supposing the traveller once more on the Stake Pass at the head of Langdale, he must now neither turn up towards the Pikes as before, nor proceed down the dale, but go up the road to his right, which will lead him into the little valley chosen by Wordsworth for the retreat of the Solitary, in his

Fig. 21. Blea Tarn and Langdale Pikes

poem of the 'Excursion.'[113] There is a gray farm-house, which every eye will fix upon as the abode of the mourner; though it is now well sheltered with trees, which have grown up since the poem was written. Blea Tarn, with its rushy margin, lies at the bottom of the hollow; and all around rise the steep hills which the recluse was counselled to climb, for the medicinal influence of activity of body, promoting repose of mind. (Figure 21.) Thence the road conducts into Little Langdale—a scene of great wildness, with its heathery and rock-strewn steeps—its rushy springs and rude sheepfolds below, with a green and craggy hill rising in the midst of the wildness, like a bright island from a gloomy sea. In this dreary scene, a horse-road is observed sloping up the brown side of Wrynose, opposite. This track was once the only traffic-road from Kendal to Whitehaven; and it was traversed by pack-horses. Up that slope might be seen—not any sort of stage-coach, or wagon, or carrier's cart, but long trains of pack-horses, slowly trailing up the hills with their heavy loads, guided by the bell round the neck of the leader. A pack-horse is seldom or never seen there now; but a pack-man is a not infrequent sight. The travelling merchant has not yet disappeared; and it will probably be some time before he does; so completely are the dalespeople out of the way of shops and markets. We observe that these travelling merchants have lost much of their repute among residents, who are more up to the times than formerly. We were lately in a remote farmhouse,—the last in its dale—when a packman stalked in; a saucy fellow, something of an Autolicus,[114] with a dash of the bully, we thought, in his face and manner. Nobody would look at his wares; and when he was crossing the field, bending under his heavy load, the housewife observed that she never bought of those people; they put off such poor goods at such high prices. We did not at once impute all the blame to the pedlars, remembering that the good wife was probably comparing their prices with shop prices at Kendal or Ambleside, forgetting that the travelling merchant must pay himself for his time and toil in these long walks, and for the disadvantage of having a very limited stock: but the incident goes to show that the vocation of the pedlar is wearing out. There is, and will long be, however, some custom left. If servant-maids near towns can seldom resist the sight of bright shawls and gay ribbons hung over chair-backs, how seducing must such things be in the remote dales, where the women never see anything else from the world without, unless when attending some sale or fair within walking distance!

This pack-horse road, if pursued (which would not suit our purpose now), would soon lead near the Three Shire Stones, on Wrynose, which mark the meeting point of the counties of Lancaster, Westmoreland, and Cumberland, close by the sources of the Duddon. Instead of turning up this road, our traveller will hold right on, into Tilberthwaite, under the side of Wetherlam.

Here he is in the midst of magnificent slate quarries. Among their *débris,* and the confusion made by Nature, he passes, till, following the guidance of the fine brawling stream on his left, he reaches Shepherd's Bridge, and enters Yewdale. Yewdale is very glorious in all seasons; but perhaps most in autumn, when the heather-bloom is brightest, and before the leaves fall from the ash and birch, which spring and wave from the clefts of the high precipices and summits. The heather abounds in most of the dales hereabouts; but in Yewdale it spreads its purple expanse up to the base of the highest gray crags, and tufts and cushions the platforms of the very rock. How vivid is the contrast wherever a strip or patch of unmixed grass shows itself amidst the purple and the gray! and what a life is given to the scene by the sheep that find their way to these pasture-islands on the hill side! This is the place too for noting the intense green of the moss which grows on the shelves of the rock; and the silvery brightness of the mists which in an autumn morning curl and whirl about the bare summits, and come breathing out of the higher fissures. One of the crags here is called Raven Crag; and a pair of ravens is, at this time, dwelling in the neighbourhood. Long may it be before their iron note is listened for in vain by the wakeful echoes of the dale! But those echoes are too often disturbed by the shot of the ignorant and rash fowler, who takes aim at everything he sees. The miners about Coniston, and other workmen in the region, go out on holidays, to bring down everything they see on the wing; and the rarest birds have no more chance with them than so many crows. The eagle is gone; the buzzards are disappearing; and the raven has become very rare.

The traveller should see the copper-works at Coniston, (if he can obtain leave,) both for their own sake, and for the opportunity it gives him of observing the people engaged there, and because they lie in his way to the tarns on Coniston Old Man, and to the summit of the mountain itself. The Tarns are very interesting; Low Water, Goat's Water, Blind Tarn, and, some considerable way along the ridge, Lever's Water under Wetherlam. Some think the views from the top of the Old Man finer than from any mountain summit in the country, except Scawfell—not even excepting Helvellyn: and this may very well be, from the country being here open to the southern peninsulas and the sea, instead of bristling with mountain peaks all round. One of the productions of this neighbourhood is the celebrated potted char, known all over the country. There is char in Windermere, and several of the other lakes; but Coniston Lake produces by far the finest fish.

As the traveller is now about to enter upon a comparatively low country, well peopled, and with good roads, he will probably be disposed to give up his pedestrian mode of travelling, and proceed either on horseback or in a car. He can do this from Coniston, if he so pleases. He had better go down the lake on its eastern side, for various reasons; and chiefly, that he may obtain the best views of the exquisite head of the lake. Passing round Waterhead, he will presently ascend to a considerable height at the north-eastern end of the fine sheet of Coniston Water; and there he will assuredly pause, and hope that he may never forget what he now sees. He has probably never beheld a scene which conveyed a stronger impression of joyful charm; of fertility, prosperity, comfort, nestling in the bosom of the rarest beauty. It is too true that there is wrong and misery here, as elsewhere: but this does not lie open to the notice in a bird's-eye view. It is true that here, as elsewhere, there are responsible persons who are negligent; some of the working class who are ignorant and profligate; dwellings which are unwholesome; and lives which are embittered by sickness and mourning. But these things are not visible from point whence the traveller feasts his eyes with the scattered dwellings under their sheltering wood,—the cheerful town, the rich slopes, and the dark gorge and summits of Yewdale behind; while the broad water lies as still as heaven, between shore and shore. In these waters it was that Elizabeth Smith[115] used to dip her oar, on those summer days when she left her studies to show the beauty of Coniston to her mother's guests: and it was near the place where the traveller now stands that she died. Tent Lodge is erected on the spot where the tent was pitched in which she spent some of her feeblest and latest days.

It is sixteen miles from Coniston Water Head to the cheerful little town of Ulverston; from whence it is only seven miles to Furness Abbey.

This Abbey was first peopled from Normandy; a sufficient number of Benedictine monks coming over from the monastery of Savigny, to establish this house in honour of St. Marye of Furnesse. In a few years their profession changed,—they followed St. Bernard, and wore the white cassock, caul, and scapulary, instead of the dress of the gray monks. It is strange now to see the railway traversing those woods where these gray-robed foreigners used to pass hither and thither, on their saint's errands to the depressed and angry Saxons dwelling round about. The situation of the Abbey, as is usual with religious houses, is fine. It stands in the depth of a glen, with a stream flowing by; the sides of the glen being clothed with wood. A beacon once belonged to it; a watch-tower on an eminence accessible from the Abbey, whose signal-fire was visible all over Low Furness, when assistance was required, or foes were expected. The building is of the pale red stone of the district. It must formerly have almost filled the glen: and the ruins give an impression, to this day, of the establishment having been worthy of the zeal of its founder, King Stephen, and the extent of its endowments, which were princely. The boundary-wall of the precincts enclosed a space of sixty-five acres, over which are scattered remains which have, within our own time, been interpreted to be those of the mill, the granary, the fish-ponds, the ovens and kilns, and other offices. As for the architecture, the heavy shaft is here, as at Calder Abbey, found alternating with the clustered pillar, and the round Saxon with the pointed Gothic arch. The masonry is so good that the remains are even now firm and massive; and the winding staircases within the walls are still in good condition, in many places. The nobleness of the edifice consisted in its extent and proportions; for the stone would not bear the execution of any very elaborate ornament. The crowned heads of Stephen and his queen, Maude, are seen outside the window of the Abbey, and are among the most interesting of the remains. It is all very *triste* and silent now. The Chapter-house, where so many grave councils were held, is open to the babbling winds. Where the abbot and his train swept past in religious procession, over inscribed pavements echoing to the tread, the stranger now wades among tall ferns and knotted grasses, stumbling over stones fallen from their place of honour. No swelling anthems are heard there now, or penitential psalms; but only the voice of birds, winds, and waters. But this blank is what the stranger comes for. He has seen something of the territory over which the Abbots of Furness held a rule like that of royalty: and he now comes to take one more warning of how Time shatters thrones, dominations, and powers, and causes the glories of this world to pass away.

The stranger will vary his return by taking the road above Bardsea to Ulverston; and if he can, he should enjoy the glorious view from Birkrigg. From all the rising grounds, wide views over the Lancaster sands and the sea are obtained; and the traveller may find something cheering to the spirits in the open stretch of landscape, after his wanderings among the narrow dales.

Newby Bridge, at the foot of Windermere, is eight miles from Ulverston. The drive is pleasant, and the traveller may as well take that road to Hawkshead, instead of returning up the side of Coniston Water. There is not much to see at Hawkshead itself; but the views which it commands of the little lake of Esthwaite are pretty. Esthwaite Water is two miles long by half a mile wide. Its scenery is rather tame; but the valley has a cheerful and flourishing aspect, with its green slopes and farmsteads dotted about, here and there. From Hawkshead, the traveller will proceed to the ferry on Windermere, in order to close with this lake, and the valleys at its head, his exploration of the lake district. What he is to meet with in the remainder of his circuit, he has already been told in the paper on Windermere, which has obtained a prior place in this work.

What weather he has had—to put up with or enjoy—we have not declared or conjectured. Much depends on the season; but, as everybody knows, much rain is sure to fall where there are mountain tops to attract the clouds. The lake district does receive a high average of rain. Hence much of its rich and verdant beauty is derived; but hence also arises much discontent and complaint on the part of fastidious tourists. The residents are not heard to complain. They are not pressed for time in seeing the beauties of the region: and they know of no day in the year when they do not go out, and see such beauty as sends them home happy. Either they do not dislike getting wet, (which is one of the most exhilarating things in the world to those who deserve to enjoy it,) or they guard themselves against the weather by waterproof dress: and they see such beauty in the streams, and hear such chorusses of waterfalls, as those know nothing about who will go out only in sunshine. Again, if one part of the day is wet, another is dry: if it is rainy in one valley, the sun shines in the next; and the resident can use these opportunities at his pleasure. It must be understood that he is not liable to suffer in health. The climate is moist; but it is not damp. The soil is rock or gravel, and the air is fresh and free; and the average of health is high accordingly, where the laws of nature are not violated in the placing and construction of habitations.

For the guidance of the visitor, we may mention that, generally speaking, the worst months of the year in the Lake District are November and December, for storms; March, for spring gales; and July for summer rain. The driest season is usually for a month or more onward from the middle of May. September and October are often very fine months. Those who come but once, and take only a cursory view of the region, cannot be too careful in choosing the most favourable season for their trip. But to those who are thoroughly familiar with the characteristics of this paradise, there is no aspect or accident of earth and sky which has not its charm.

Chapter Seven

The Highest House in Wathendale A Tale[116]

I.

HIGH UP AMONG the mountains of Westmoreland, there is a valley which we shall call Wathendale. The lowest part of this valley is some hundreds of feet above the heads of the dwellers on the nearest mail road; and yet, as if such a place of abode was not near enough to the sky, there are houses as high up as they can well be put, in the hollows of the mountains which overlook the dale. One of these small farmsteads is as old-fashioned a place as can be seen; and well it may be so; for the last owners were fond of telling that the land had been in their family for five hundred years. A stranger might wonder what could carry anybody up to such a place five hundred years ago; but the wonder would only show that the stranger did not know what was doing in the district in those days. Those were the days when the tenants of the

Abbots of Furness used to hold land in the more fertile spots, in companies of four,—one of whom was always to be ready to go forth to fight in the Border wars.[117] And those were the days when the shepherds and herdsmen in the service of the Abbey used to lead their sheep and cattle as far up the mountains as they could find food,—to be the better out of the way of the marauders from the north. Besides the coarse grass of these uplands, there were the sprouts of the ash and holly, which were a good food for the beasts. To be sure, there were wolves, up in those lonely places; but they were kept out by rough stone walls, which were run up higher and higher on the mountain side, as the woods receded before the tillage of new settlers. The first of the Fells, who made their boast of a proprietorship of five hundred years, was probably a shepherd of the Abbots of Furness; who, having walled in some of the sprouting and sheltering wood on this upland, and built himself a hut of stones in the midst, became regarded as the tenant first, and then the proprietor, like many of the dwellers in the vales below. When the woods were decayed and gone, the croft came under tillage; and no tradition was told of the time when the Fells did not yearly crop, in one way or another, the three fields which were seen from below, like little patches of green beside the fissure which contained the beck (or brook) that helped to feed the tarn (or mountain pond) a quarter of a mile below.

There was grumbling in this mountain nest about the badness of our times in comparison with the old days;—grumbling in a different dialect from that which is heard in our cities; but in much the same spirit. In this house, people were said to be merrier formerly,—the girls spinning and weaving, and the lads finding plenty to do in all weathers; while the land produced almost everything that the family wanted,—with the help of the hill-side range for the cows and sheep. A man had not to go often to the market then; and very rarely was it necessary to buy anything for money, though a little bartering might go forward among the Dalesmen on occasion. Now——But we shall see how it was "now."

Mrs. Fell and her daughter Janet were making oaten bread one December day;—a work which requires the full attention of two persons. The cow-boy appeared at the door, with a look of excitement very unusual in him. He said somebody was coming; and the somebody was Backhouse, the travelling merchant. The women could not believe it,—so late in the year; but they left their baking to look out; and there, sure enough, was the pedlar, with his pack on his shoulders, toiling up the steep. They saw him sit down beside the barn, and wipe his brows, though it was December. They saw him shoulder his pack again; and then the women entered into consultation about something very particular that they had to say to him. As people who live in such places grow dull, and get to think and speak with extraordinary slowness, the plot was not complete when the pedlar appeared at the door. He explained himself quickly enough;—had thought he would make one more round, as the season was mild,—did not know how long the snow might lie when it did come,—believed people liked to wear something new at Christmas; so here he was. When would he take his next round? O! when the weather should allow of his bringing his stock of spring goods. He detected some purpose under the earnestness with which he was pressed to say when he would come. He would come when the Fells pleased, and bring what they pleased. He must come before the first of April, and must bring a bunch of orange flowers, and a white shawl, and—

"Two sets of orange flowers," said Janet.

"What! two brides!" exclaimed Backhouse. "Are they to be both married in one day?"

Mrs. Fell explained that there was to be a bride's maid, and that Janet wished that her friend should be dressed exactly like herself. Backhouse endeavoured to prove that only brides should wear orange flowers; but Janet was sure her friend would be best pleased to wear what she wore; and the pedlar remembered that nobody within call of the chapel bell would know any better; so he promised all that was desired. And next, he sold half the contents of his pack, supplying the women with plenty of needle-work for the winter evenings. Brides enjoy having a new wardrobe as much in the mountains as in towns—perhaps more.

Whenever the young carpenter, Raven, came up to see his betrothed, he found her sewing, and some pretty print, or muslin, or bit of gay silk lying about. It was all very pleasant. The whole winter went off pleasantly, except for some shadow of trouble now and then, which soon passed away. For instance, Raven was once absent longer than usual, by full three days; and when he did come, there were marks left that told that he had stayed away because he had been ashamed of two black eyes.

"He had been drinking, I dare say," said Mrs. Fell to Janet afterwards, with the air of indifference with which drunkenness is apt to be spoken of in the district. "I don't wonder he did not like to show himself."

"I don't think it is his way," observed Janet.

"No; it is not a habit with him; and they all do get too much now and then—two or three times a year—and it will be seldomer than that when be comes to live up here."

Raven was to be adopted as a son, on marrying the only child, and it was very right; for Fell was growing old; and he was more feeble than his years warranted. Rheumatism plagued him in the winter, and be was overworked in the summer. Raven would help to manage the little farm, and he would do all the carpentering work, and put the whole place in repair, outside and in. Everything was to go well after the wedding.

Sally, the bridesmaid, came in good time to put the orange flowers into her coarse Dunstable bonnet, which streamed with white ribbons. It was a fine April morning, when the party set off down the mountain for their walk of three miles to the chapel. The mother remained at home. When Fell returned, he told her it had gone off extremely well, and the clergyman had spoken very kindly; and that Fleming's cart was ready, as had been promised, to take the young people to the town where they were to be entertained at dinner. It was all right, and very pleasant.

And the old people sat down to dinner, dressed in their best, and saying, many times over, that it was all right with them, and very pleasant. The only thing was—if Raven's name had but been Fell! The Fells having lived here for five hundred years———

"The family, but not always the name," the wife observed. There was a Bell that lived here once; and the land would be in the family still, in the best way it could, as they had no children but Janet.

Well; that was true, Fell agreed; and it was all right, and very pleasant.

II.

THAT EVENING three ladies went up to the chapel to see the sunset from the churchyard, which commanded an exquisite view. It was a place in which, at such an hour, it was easy to forget, even with the graves before their eyes, that there was sin or sorrow in the world. The ladies sat on the steps till the last glow had faded from the clouds, and the mountains stood up, clear and solemn, against a green sky, from which every tinge of sunset had vanished; and then they came down, with thoughts as bright and calm as the stars which were beginning to come out overhead. When they entered on a long stretch of straight road, they saw before them an odd-looking group. In the dusk it seemed as if a man and woman were carrying something very heavy,—moving towards them at a pace hopelessly slow. A woman was some way in advance of them,—loitering and looking back. When they came up to her, it was a young woman, with orange flowers in her bonnet, and a smart white shawl on her shoulders. She was carrying a man's hat, new, but half covered with mud. It was now too clear that the heavy thing which the other two were trying to haul along was a man. Never did man look more like a brute. His face, when it could be seen, was odious; swollen, purple, without a trace of reason or feeling left in it; but his head hung so low, with his long black hair dipping on the ground, that it was not easy to see his face. His legs trailed behind him, and his new clothes were spattered with dirt.

"It looks like apoplexy," said the elder lady to her companions: and she asked the young woman who was carrying the hat, whether the man was in a fit.

"No, ma'am; he has only been overcome. It is his wedding. He was married this morning."

"Married this morning! And is that his wife?"

"Yes ma'am; and the other is bridegroom's man."

It would have touched any heart to see poor Janet, as the ladies passed,—her honest sun-burned face all framed in orange flowers grave and quiet, while she put forth her utmost strength (which was not small) to hold up her wretched husband from the dirt of the road. The other man was a comely youth, dressed in his best, with a new plaid fastened across his breast. The ladies looked back, and saw that it would never do. The elder lady returned, and laying her hand on the poor young woman's shoulder said,

"This is no work for you. It is too much for you. Let

him lie, while I speak to the people at this farm-house. I know them; and they will send a man to take him into the house."

Poor Janet spoke very calmly when she said they could take him a little farther; but her lips quivered slightly. The lady spoke to a man who was feeding calves in a stable; and asked him to help to dip the bridegroom's head in a cistern by the road side, and then take him into the house.

"How far is it from his home?" the lady inquired of Sally. "The High House in Wathendale! You will not get him there to-night at this rate."

The farm-house people promised a cart, if the party could wait till it came by.

"How could such a thing happen?" said the lady. "Is there no one to teach this man his duty better than this? Does he know the clergyman?"

"Yes, ma'am," said Sally,—adding, very simply, "but there would be no use in the clergyman speaking to him now, he would not understand."

"No, indeed," replied the lady. "But he will feel ill enough to-morrow, and then I hope somebody that he respects will speak to him in a way that he will remember."

"To think," she said to her companions, as they walked away past the cistern where the grovelling bridegroom was undergoing his ducking, "that that is the creature whom the poor girl bound herself this morning to love, cherish, and obey! What a beginning of the cherishing!"

Fell and his wife had not expected the young people home early; but it was much later than the latest time they had fixed, before they heard anything of them. When at last the party appeared, emerging from the night mist, all the three sober ones were dreadfully weary. The ascent had been terrible; for Raven had not yet begun to recover.

No fine sentiment was wasted upon the occasion; for the indifference which had rather shocked the ladies, was the real state of mind of people too much accustomed to the spectacle of intemperance. Mrs. Fell declared she was vexed by him—that she was; and then she put on her bed-gown, in order to sit up with her daughter, for Raven was now so sick that he must be waited on all night. Mrs. Fell said repeatedly, as so often before, that all men were apt to take too much now and then; and it would happen less often now he had come to live up here. Yet, her husband's words would run in her head, that it was all right, and very pleasant. When, in the dawn of the morning, her daughter made her go to bed, she dropped asleep with those words in her ears; while poor Janet, chilly, sick at heart, and worn out, was at length melting into tears.

When, the next afternoon, her husband sat nursing his aching head beside the fireplace, he was struck with some compunction at the sight of her red eyes. Of course, he declared, as drunkards always do, it should never happen again. Of course, he laid the blame, as drunkards always do, on other people. Of course, he said, as drunkards always do, that it was no habit of his; and that this was an accident—for once and away. Of course, his wife believed him, as young wives always do.

For some time it appeared all true, and everything went

on very cheerfully. On the fine days there was as much field-work as both men could do; and so many repairs were needed, of gates and posts, cart and cowhouse, dwelling-house and utensils, that all the rainy days for six months were too little for the carpentering Raven had upon his hands. He had not been tipsy above twice in all that time: once on a stormy day, when he had sat lazily scorching himself before the fire, with the labourer and cow-boy, who were driven in by stress of weather, and who yawned till they made the whole party weary. Raven disappeared for a couple of hours in the afternoon, and came out of the barn to supper in a state far from sober. The other time was when he had gone to market in October, to sell oats. At all other times he worked well, was kind to the old people, and very fond of Janet, and justified Fell's frequent declaration that it was all right now, and very pleasant.

The winter was the trying season. Sometimes the dwellers in the high house were snowed up, and many days were too stormy for work. The men grew tired of sitting round the fire all day, hearing the wind blow and the rain pelt; and the women were yet more tired of having them there. There were no books; and nobody seemed to think of reading. There were some caricatures of the Pope and of Buonaparte,[118] and a portrait of King George the Third, on the walls; and these were all the intellectual entertainment in the house, unless we except four lines of a hymn which Janet had marked on her sampler, when she was a child. Raven went more and more to the barn, sometimes on pretence of working; but his hammer and saw were less and less heard; and instead of coming in cheerfully to supper, he was apt to loiter in, in a slouching way, to hide the unsteadiness of his gait, and was quarrelsome with Fell, and cross to Janet. He never conducted himself better, however; never was more active, affectionate, helpful, and considerate, than at the time when old Fell sank and died,—during that month of early spring when Janet was confined. He was like son and daughter at once, Mrs. Fell declared—and doctor and nurse, too, for that matter: and his father-in-law died, blessing him, and desiring him to take care of the farm, and prosper on it, as it had been in the family for five hundred years.

When the old man was buried, and the seed all in the ground, and Janet about again, Raven not only relaxed in his industry, but seemed to think some compensation due to him for his late good behaviour. Certain repairs having been left too long untouched, and Mrs. Fell being rather urgent that they should not be further neglected, it came out that Raven had sold his tools. Sold his tools!—Yes; how could he help it? It was necessary, as they had all agreed, to change away the old cow for a spring calver; and what could he do but sell his tools to pay the difference? Janet knew, and so did her mother, though neither of them said so, that more money had gone down his throat, all alone in the barn, than would have paid for the exchange of cows.

The decline of their property began with this. When decline has begun with the "statesmen" of the Lake District, it is seldom or never known to stop; and there was nothing to stop it in this case. On a small farm, where the health and industry of the owner are necessary to enable him to contend with the new fashions and improvements of the low country, and where there is no money capital behind to fall back upon, any decline of activity is fatal; and in two or three years Raven's health had evidently given way. His industry had relaxed before. He lost his appetite; could not relish the unvaried and homely fare which his land supplied; craved for dainties which could not be had, except by purchase; lost his regular sleep, and was either feverish and restless, or slept for fifteen hours together, in a sort of stupor. His limbs lost their strength, and he became subject to rheumatism. Then he could not go out in all weathers to look after his stock. One of his best sheep was missing after a flood; and it was found jammed in between two rocks in the beck, feet uppermost,—drowned, of course. Another time, four more sheep were lost in a snow-drift, from not being looked after in time. Then came the borrowing a plough. It was true, many people borrowed a plough; nobody thought much of that—nobody but Mrs. Fell. She thought much of it; for her husband, and his father before him, had always used their own ploughs. Then came borrowing money upon the land, to buy seed and stock. It was true, many "statesmen" mortgaged their land; but then, sooner or later, it was always found too difficult to pay the interest, and the land went into the hands of strangers; and Mrs. Fell sighed when she said she hoped Raven would remember that the farm had been in one family for five hundred years. Raven answered that he was not likely to forget it for want of being told; and from that moment the fact was not mentioned again. Mrs. Fell kept it in her heart, and died in the hope that no new-fangled farmer, with a south-country name, would ever drive his plough through the old fields.

III.

AFTER HER MOTHER'S DEATH, Janet found her hands over-full of work, when her heart was, as she thought, over-full of care. She did not know how much more she could bear. There were two children now, and another coming. Fine children they were; and the eldest was her pride and comfort. He was beginning to prattle; and never was speech so pretty as his. His father loved to carry him about in his arms; and sometimes, when he was far from sober, this child seemed to set his wits straight, and soften his temper, in a sort of magical way. There was the drawback that Raven would sometimes insist on having the boy with him when he was by no means fit to have the charge of so young a child: but the mother tried to trust that all would be well; and that God would watch over an innocent little creature who was like an angel to his sinning parent. She had not considered (as too many do not consider), that "the promises" are given under conditions, and that it is impious to blame Providence for disasters when the conditions are not observed. The promises, as she had heard them at the chapel, dwelt on her mind, and gave her great comfort in dark seasons; and it would have been a dreary word to her if any one had reminded her that they might fail through man's neglect and sin. She had some severe lessons on this head, however. It was pleasant to hear that day and night, seed-time and harvest, should not cease; and when difficulties pressed, she looked on the dear old fields, and thought of this: but to say nothing of what day and night were often to her—the day as black to her spirits as night, and the night as sleepless as the day—seed-time was nothing, if her husband was too ill or too lazy to sow his land; and the harvest month was worse than nothing if there was no crop; and there was no true religion in trusting that her babes would be safe if she put them into the hands of a drunkard, who was as likely as not to do them a mischief. And so she too sadly learned. One day, Raven insisted on carrying the boy with him into the barn. He staggered, stumbled, dashed the child's head against the door-post, and let him fall. It was some minutes before the boy cried; and when he did, what a relief it was! But, O! that cry. It went on for days and nights, with an incessant prattle. When at last he slept, and the doctor hoped there would be no lasting mischief, the prattle went on in his sleep, till his mother prayed that he might become silent, and look like himself again. He became silent; but he never more looked like himself. After he seemed to be well, he dropped one pretty word after another,—very slowly,—week by week, for long months; but the end of it was that he grew up a dumb idiot.

His father had heart and conscience enough to be touched by this to the point of reformation. For some months, he never went down into the valley at all, except to church, for fear of being tempted to drink. He suffered cruelly, in body as well as mind, for a time; and Janet wished it had pleased God to take the child at once, as she feared her husband would never recover his spirits with that sad spectacle always before his eyes. Yet she did not venture to propose any change of scene or amusement, for fear of the consequences. She did her utmost to promote cheerfulness at home; but it was a great day to her when Backhouse, paying his spring visit, with his pack, produced, among the handbills, of which he was the hawker, one which announced a Temperance meeting in the next vale. The Temperance movement had reached these secluded vales at last, where it was only too much wanted; and so retired had been the life of the family of the High House, that they had not even heard of it. They heard much of it now; for Backhouse had sold a good many ribbons and gay shawls among members who were about to attend Temperance festivals. When he told of processions, and bands of music, and public tea-drinkings, and speeches, and clapping, with plenty of laughter, and here and there even dancing, or a pic-nic on a mountain, Janet thought it the gayest news she had ever heard. Here would be change, and society, and amusement for her husband—not only without danger, but with the very object of securing him from danger. Raven was so heartily willing, that the whole household made a grand day of it—labourer, cowboy, and all. The cows were milked early, and for once left for a few hours. The house was shut up, the children carried down by father and mother; and, after a merry afternoon, the whole party came home, pledged teetotallers.

This event made a great change in Raven's life. He could go down among his old acquaintances now, for he considered himself a safe man; and Janet could encourage his going, and be easy about his return; for she, too, considered all danger over. Both were deceived as to the kind and degree of safety caused by a vow.

The vow was good, in as far as it prevented the introduction of drink at home, and gave opportunity for the smell, and the habit, and the thought of drink to die out. It was good as a reason for refusing when a buyer or seller, down in the vale, to seal a bargain with a dram. It was good as keeping all knowledge of drinking from the next generation in the house. It was good as giving a man character in the eyes of his neighbours and his pastor. But, was it certainly and invariably good in every crisis of temptation? Would it act as a charm when a weak man—a man weak in health, weak in old associations, weak in self-respect—should find himself in a merry company of old comrades, with fumes of grog rising on every side, intoxicating his mind before a drop had passed his lips? Raven came to know, as many have learned before him, that self-restraint is too serious a thing to be attained at a skip, in a moment, by taking an oath; and that reform must have gone deeper, and risen higher, than any process of sudden conversion, before a man should venture upon a vow; and in such a case, a vow is not needed. And if a man is not strong enough for the work of moral restraint, his vow may become a snare, and plunge him into two sins instead of one. A Temperance pledge is an admirable convenience for the secure; but it must always be doubtful whether it will prove a safeguard or a snare to the infirm. If they trust wholly to it, it will, too probably, become a snare—and thus it was with poor Raven. When the Temperance lecturer was gone, and the festival was over, and the flags were put away, and the enthusiasm passed, while his descents among his old companions were continued, without fear or precaution, he was in circumstances too hard for a vow, the newness of which had faded. He hardly knew how it happened. He was, as the neighbours said, "overcome." His senses once opened to the old charm, the seven devils of drink rushed into the swept and garnished house, and the poor sinner was left in a worse state than ever before.

Far worse; for now his self-respect was utterly gone. There is no need to dwell on the next years,—the increase of the mortgage, the decrease of the stock,—the dilapidation of house, barn, and stable,—the ill-health and discomfort at home, and the growing moroseness of him who caused the misery.

No more festivals now! no talk to the children of future dances! and so few purchases of Backhouse, that he ceased to come, and the household were almost in rags. No more going to church, therefore, for anybody! When the wind was in the right quarter for bringing to the uplands the din-dinning of the chapel bell, Janet liked to hear it, though it was no summons to her to listen to the promises. The very sound revived the promises in her mind. But what could she make of them now? An incident, unspeakably fearful to her, suddenly showed her how she ought to view them. The eldest girl was nursing her idiot brother's head in her lap while the younger children were at play, when the poor fellow nestled close to her.

"Poor Dan!" said she. "You can't play about, and be merry, like the others: but I will always take care of you, poor Dan!"

Little Willy heard this, and stopped his play. In another moment his face flushed, his eyes flashed, he clenched his hands, he even stamped as he cried out,

"Mother, it's too bad! Why did God make Dan different from the rest?"

His panic-stricken mother clapped her hand over his mouth. But this was no answer to his question. She thought she must be a wicked mother, that a child of hers should ask such a question as that. It was not often that she wept; but she wept sorely now. It brought her back to the old lesson of the seed-time and harvest. The promise here, too, failed, because the conditions were not fulfilled. The hope had been broken by a collision with the great natural laws, under which alone all promise can be fulfilled. But how explain this to Willy? How teach him that the Heavenly Father had made Dan as noble a little fellow as ever was seen, and that it was his own father there that had made him an idiot?

When Raven came in, he could not but see her state; and he happened to be in so mild a mood, that she ventured to tell him what her terror and sorrow were about.

He was dumb for a time. Then he began to say that he was bitterly punished for what was no habit of his, but that he vowed——

"No, no—don't vow!" said his wife, more alarmed than ever. She put her arm round his neck and whispered into his ear,

"I dare not hear you vow any more. You know how often——You know you had better not. I dare not hear you promise any more."

He loosened her arm from his neck, and called Willy to him. He held the frightened boy between his knees, and looked him full in the face, while he said,

"Willy, you must not say that God made Dan an idiot. God is very good, and I am very bad. *I* made Dan an idiot.

The stare with which Willy heard this was too much for his mother. She rushed upstairs and threw herself upon the bed, where she was heard long afterwards sobbing as if her heart would break.

"Father," said Willy, timidly, but curiously, "did you make mother cry too?"

"Yes, Willy, I did. It is all my doing."

"Then I think you are very wicked."

"So I am—very wicked. Take care that you are not. Take care you are never wicked."

"That I will. I can't bear that mother should cry."

IV.

JANET DID all she could to arrest the ruin which all saw to be inevitable. Her great piece of success was the training she gave to her oldest daughter, little Sally. By the time she was twelve years old, she was the most efficient person in the house. Without her, they could hardly have kept their last remaining cow; and many a time she set her mother at liberty to attend upon her father and protect him, when otherwise the children must have engrossed her. There was no cowboy now; and her mother too often filled the place of the labourer, when the sowing or reaping season would otherwise have passed away unused. It was a thing unheard of in the district that a woman should work in the fields; but what else could be done? Raven's wasted and trembling limbs were unequal to the work alone; and, little as he could do at best, he could always do his best when his wife was helping him. So Sally took care of poor Dan and the four younger ones, and made the oaten bread with Willy's help, and boiled the potatoes, and milked and fed the cow, and knitted, at all spare minutes; for there was no prospect of stockings for anybody, in the bitter winter, but from the knitting done at home. The children had learned to be thankful now, when they could eat their oat bread and potatoes in peace. They seldom had anything else; and they wanted nothing else when they could eat that without terror. But their father was now sometimes mad. It was a particular kind of madness, which they had heard the doctor call by a long name (delirium tremens), and they thought it must be the most terrible kind of all, though it always went off, after a fit of it, which might last from a day to a week. The doctor had said that it would not always go off—that he would die in one of the attacks. The dread was lest he should kill somebody else before that day came; for he was as ungovernable as any man in Bedlam[119] at those times, and fearfully strong, though so weak before and after them.

When it was possible, the children went down into the valley, and sent up strong men to hold him; but if the weather was stormy or if their father was in the way, they could only go and hide themselves out of his sight, among the rocks in the beck, or up in the loft, or somewhere; and then they knew what their mother must be suffering with him. By degrees they had scarcely any furniture left whole but their heavy old-fashioned bedsteads. The last of their crockery was broken by his overturning the lame old table at which they had been dining. Then their mother said, with a sigh, that they must somehow manage to buy some things before winter. There really was nothing now for any of them to eat out of. She must get some wooden trenchers and tin mugs; for she would have no more crockery. But how to get the money! for the whole of the land was mortgaged now.

A little money was owing for oats when November arrived; and the purchaser had sent word that he should be at a certain sale in Langdale, at Martinmas; and that if Raven should be there, they could then settle accounts. Now, this money had been destined to go as far as it would towards the payment of interest due at Christmas. But if Raven went to the sale (the usual occasions for social meetings in the Lake district, in spring and autumn), he would only waste or lose the money. He had long ceased to bring home any money, unless his wife was with him; and then it was she that brought it, and, if possible, without his knowledge. She must go with him, and lay out the money immediately, in necessaries for the house and the children, before her husband could make away with it, in a worse way than if he threw it into the sea.

They went, at dawn, in a clear cold November day. Raven had taken care of himself for a day or two, aware of the importance of the occasion, and anxious not to disable himself for the first social meeting he had enjoyed for long, and thinking, in spite of himself, of the glasses of spirits which are, unhappily, handed round very often indeed at these country sales. As the walk was an arduous one for an infirm man, and the days were short, and the sale was to last two days, the children were to be left for one night. Oatmeal and potatoes enough were left out for two days, and peat, to dry within the house, for fuel. Willy engaged to nurse the baby, while Sally looked to the cow. Their mother promised the little ones some nice things for the winter, if they were good while she was gone; and their father kissed them all, and said he knew they would be good.

And so they were, all that first day; and a very good dinner they made, after playing about the whole morning: and they all went instantly to sleep at night, while Sally sat knitting for an hour longer by the dim red light of the peat fire. The next day was not so fine. The mountain ridges were clear; but the sky was full of very heavy grey clouds; and before dinner, at noon, there was some snow falling. It came on thicker and thicker; and the younger children began to grow cross, because they could not go out to play, and did not know what to do with themselves. Sally cheered them with talking about how soon mother would come home. Mother had not come, however, when the little things, worried and tired, went to bed. Nor had she come, hours after, when Sally herself wanted very much to be asleep. She had looked out at the door very often, and it was still snowing; and the last time, such a cloud of snow was driven against her face, that it was a settled matter in her mind at once that father and mother would not be home to-night. They would stay in the vale for daylight, and come up to breakfast. So she put on another peat, to keep in the fire, and went to bed.

In the morning, it seemed dark when baby cried to get up; and well it might; for the window was blocked up with snow, almost to the very top. When the door was opened, a mass of snow fell in, though what remained was up to Willy's shoulders. The first thing to be done was to get to the cow, to give her her breakfast, and bring baby's. So Sally laid on her last dry peat, and filled the kettle; and then she and Willy set to work to clear a way to the cow. They were obliged to leave baby to the little ones; and it took an hour to cross the yard. Willy was to have brought in some fuel; but the peat-stack was at the end of the house, and, as they could see, so completely buried in snow as to be hopelessly out of reach. Here was the milk, however, and there was a little of the oatmeal left, and some potatoes. Sally wished now they had brought in more from the barn; but who could have thought they would want any more? Father would get them presently, when he came.

But nobody came all that day. Late at night, all the children but Sally were asleep at last, though they had been too cold and too hungry to go to rest quietly, as usual. The fire had gone out since noon; and the last cold potatoes had been eaten in the afternoon. Sally was lying with the baby cuddled close to her for warmth: and, at last, she fell asleep too, though she was very unhappy. In the morning, she felt that their affairs were desperate. Willy must get down the mountain, be the snow what it might, and tell somebody what state they were in; for now, there was no more food for the cow within reach, and she gave very little milk this morning; and there was nothing else. It had not snowed for some hours; and Willy knew the way so well that he got down to the valley, being wet to the neck, and having had a good many falls by the way. At the first farm-house he got help directly. The good woman took one of the labourers with her, with food, and a basket of dry peat, and a promise to clear the way to the oat-straw and hay, for the relief of the cow. The farmer set off to consult the neighbours about where Raven and his wife could be; and the rest of the family dried the boy's clothes, and gave him a good bowl of porridge.

In a very short time, all the men in the valley and their

dogs, were out on the snow, their figures showing like moving specks on the white expanse. Two of them, who had been at the sale, knew that Raven and his wife had set out for home, long before dark on the second day. Raven was, as might be expected, the worse for liquor; but not so much so but that he could walk, with his wife to keep him in the path. They might possibly have turned back, but it was too probable that they were lost. Before night, it was ascertained that they had not been seen again in Langdale; and in two days more, during which the whole population was occupied in the search, or in taking care of the children, their fate was known. Raven's body was found, a little way from the track, looking like a man in a drunken sleep. Some hours after, the barking of a dog brought the searchers to where Janet was lying, at the foot of a precipice, about thirty feet deep. Her death must have been immediate. It seemed that her husband, overcome by the effect of the cold (which, however, had not been excessive) on his tipsy brain, had fallen down in sleep or a stupor; and that Janet, unable to rouse him, had attempted to find her way back; and, by going three or four yards aside from the path, in the uniformity of the snow, had stepped over the rock. There was a strange and ghastly correspondence between the last day of her married life and the first; and so thought her old friend and bridesmaid, Sally, who came over to the funeral, and who, in turning over the poor remnants of Janet's wardrobe, found the bunches of orange flowers carefully papered up and put away in the farthest corner of a drawer.

There was nothing left for the children, but the warning of their father's life, and the memory of their mother's trials. They were not allowed to go upon the parish—not even Dan. It was plain that he would not live very long; and neighbourly charity was sure to last as long as he. The others were dispersed among the farms in that and the nearest vales, and they have grown up as labourers. The land and buildings had been mortgaged beyond their value, and they went at once into the hands of strangers.

Chapter Eight

Lights of the English Lake District[120]

AT THE OPENING of the present century, the Lake District of Cumberland and Westmoreland was groaned over by some residents as fast losing its simplicity. The poet Gray[121] had been the first to describe its natural features in an express manner; and his account of the views above Keswick and Grasmere was quoted, sixty years since, as evidence of the spoiling process which had gone on since the introduction of civilization from the South. Gray remarked on the absence of red roofs, gentlemen's houses, and garden-walls, and on the uniform character of the humble farmsteads and gray cottages under their sycamores in the vales. Wordsworth[122] heard and spoke a good deal of the innovations which had modified the scene in the course of the thirty years which elapsed between Gray's visits (in 1767–69) and his own settlement in the Lake District; but he lived to say more, at the end of half a century, of the wider and deeper changes which time had wrought in the aspect of the country and the minds and manners of the people. According to his testimony, and that of Southey,[123] the barbarism was of a somewhat gross character at the end of the last century; the magistrates were careless of the condition of the society in which they bore authority; the clergy were idle or worse,—"marrying and burying machines," as Southey told Wilberforce;[124] and the morality of the people, such as it was, was ascribed by Wordsworth, in those his days of liberalism in politics, to the state of republican equality in which they lived. Excellent, fussy Mr. Wilberforce thought, when he came for some weeks into the District, that the Devil had had quite time enough for sowing tares while the clergy were asleep; so he set to work to sow a better seed; and we find in his diary that he went into house after house "to talk religion to the people." I do not know how he was received; but at this day the people are puzzled at that kind of domestic intervention, so unsuitable to their old-fashioned manners,—one old dame telling with wonder, some little time since, that a young lady had called and sung a hymn to her, but had given her nothing at the end for listening. The rough independence of the popular manners even now offends persons of a conventional habit of mind; and when poets and philosophers first came from southern parts to live here, the democratic tone of feeling and behavior was more striking than it is now or will ever be again.

Before the Lake poets began to give the public an interest in the District, some glimpses of it were opened by the well-known literary ladies of the last century who grouped themselves round their young favorite, Elizabeth

Smith.[125] I do not know whether her name and fame have reached America; but in my young days she was the English school-girls' subject of admiration and emulation. She had marvellous powers of acquisition, and she translated the Book of Job,[126] and a good deal from the German,—introducing Klopstock[127] to us at a time when we hardly knew the most conspicuous names in German literature. Elizabeth Smith was an accomplished girl in all ways. There is a damp, musty-looking house, with small windows and low ceilings, at Coniston, where she lived with her parents and sister, for some years before her death. We know, from Mrs. Elizabeth Hamilton's and the Bowdlers' letters, how Elizabeth and her sister lived in the beauty about them, rambling, sketching, and rowing their guests on the lake.[128] In one of her rambles, Elizabeth sat too long under a heavy dew. She felt a sharp pain in her chest, which never left her, and died in rapid decline. Towards the last she was carried out daily from the close and narrow rooms at home, and laid in a tent pitched in a field just across the road, whence she could overlook the lake, and the range of mountains about its head. On that spot now stands Tent Lodge, the residence of Tennyson and his bride after their marriage.[129] One of my neighbors, who first saw the Lake District in early childhood, has a solemn remembrance of the first impression. The tolling of the bell at Hawkeshead church was heard from afar; and it was tolling for the funeral of Elizabeth Smith. Her portrait is before me now,—the ingenuous, childlike face, with the large dark eyes which alone show that it is not the portrait of a child.

It was through her that a large proportion of the last generation of readers first had any definite associations with Coniston.

Wordsworth had, however, been in that church many a time, above twenty years before, when at Hawkeshead school. He used to tell that his mother had praised him for going into church, one week-day, to see a woman do penance in a white sheet. She considered it good for his morals. But when he declared himself disappointed that nobody had given him a penny for his attendance, as he had somehow expected, his mother told him he was served right for going to church from such an inducement. He spoke with gratitude of an usher at that school, who put him in the way of learning the Latin, which had been a sore trouble at his native Cockermouth, from unskilful teaching. Our interest in him at that school, however, is from his having there first conceived the idea of writing verse. His master set the boys, as a task, to write a poetical theme,—"The Summer Vacation"; and Master William chose to add to it "The Return to School." He was then fourteen; and he was to be double that age before he returned to the District and took up his abode there.

He had meantime gone through his college course, as described in his Memoirs,[130] and undergone strange conditions of opinion and feeling in Paris during the Revolution; had lived in Dorsetshire, with his faithful sister; had there first seen Coleridge,[131] and had been so impressed by the mind and discourse of that wonderful young philosopher as to remove to Somersetshire to be near him; had seen Klopstock in Germany, and lived there for a time; and had passed through other changes of residence and places, when we find him again among the Lakes in 1779, still with his sister[132] by his side, and their brother John, and Coleridge, who had never been in the District before.

As they stood on the margin of Grasmere, the scene was more like what Gray saw than what is seen at this day. The churchyard was bare of the yews which now distinguish it,—for Sir George Beaumont[133] had them planted at a later time; and where the group of kindred and friends—the Wordsworths and their relatives—now lie, the turf was level and untouched. The iron rails and indefensible monuments, which Wordsworth so reprobated half a century later, did not exist. The villas which stud the slopes, the great inns which bring a great public, were uncreated; and there was only the old Roman road where the Wishing-Gate is, or the short cut by the quarries to arrive by from the South, instead of the fine mail-road which now winds between the hills and the margin of the lake. John Wordsworth guided his brother and Coleridge through Grisedale, over a spur of Helvellyn, to see Ullswater; and Coleridge has left a characteristic testimony of the effect of the scenery upon him. It was "a day when light and darkness coexisted in contiguous masses, and the earth and sky were but one. Nature lived for us in all her wildest accidents." He tells how his eyes were dim with tears, and how imagination and reality blended their objects and impressions. Wordsworth's account of the same excursion is in as admirable contrast with Coleridge's as their whole mode of life and expression was, from first to last. With the carelessness of the popular mind in such cases, the British public had already almost confounded the two men and their works, as it soon after mixed up Southey with both; whereas they were all as unlike each other as any three poets could well be.

Coleridge and Wordsworth were both contemplative, it is true, while Southey was not: but the remarkable thing about Coleridge was the exclusiveness of his contemplative tendencies, by which one set of faculties ran riot in his mind and life, making havoc among his powers, and a dismal wreck of his existence. The charm and marvel of his discourse upset all judgments during his life, and for as long as his voice remained in the ear of his enchanted hearers; but, apart from the spell, it is clear to all sober and trained thinkers that Coleridge wandered away from truth and reality in the midst of his vaticinations, as the *clairvoyant* does in the midst of his previsions, so as to mislead and bewilder, while inspiring and intoxicating the hearer or reader. He recorded, in regard to himself, that "history and particular facts lost all interest" in his mind after his first launch into metaphysics; and he remained through life incapable of discerning reality from inborn images. Wordsworth took alarm at the first experience of such a tendency in himself, and relates that he used to catch at the trees and palings by the roadside to satisfy himself of existences out of himself; but Coleridge encouraged this subjective exclusiveness, to the destruction of the balance of his mind and the *morale* of his nature. He was himself a wild poem; and he discoursed wild poems to us,—musical romances from Dreamland; but the luxury to himself and us was bought by injury to others which was altogether irreparable, and pardonable only on the ground that the balance of his mind was destroyed by a fatal intellectual, in addition to physical intemperance. In him we see an extreme case of a life of contemplation uncontrolled by will and unchecked by action. His faculty of will perished, and his prerogative of action died out. His contemplations must necessarily be worth just so much the less to us as his mental structure was deformed,—extravagantly developed in one direction, and dwarfed in another.

The singularity in Wordsworth's case, on the other hand, is that his contemplative tendencies not only coexisted with, but were implicated with, the most precise and vivid apprehension of small realities. There was no proportion in his mind; and vaticination and twaddle rolled off his eloquent tongue as chance would have it. At one time he would discourse like a seer, on the slightest instigation, by the hour together; and next, he would hold forth with equal solemnity, on the pettiest matter of domestic economy. I have known him to take up some casual notice of a "beck" (brook) in the neighborhood, and discourse of brooks for two hours, till his hearers felt as if they were by the rivers of waters in heaven; and next, he would talk on and on, till stopped by some accident, on his doubt whether Mrs. Wordsworth gave a penny apiece or a halfpenny apiece for trapped mice to a little girl who had undertaken to clear the house of them. It has been common to regret that he held the office of Stamp-Distributor in the District; but it was probably a great benefit to his mind as well as his fortunes. It was something that it gave him security and ease as to the maintenance of his family; but that is less important than its necessitating a certain amount of absence from home, and intercourse with men on business. He was no reader in mature life; and the concentration of his mind on his own views, and his own genius, and the interests of his home and neighborhood, caused some foibles, as it was; and it might have been almost fatal, but for some office which allowed him to gratify his love of out-door life at the same time that it led him into intercourse with men in another capacity than as listeners to himself, or peasants engrossed in their own small concerns.

Southey was not contemplative or speculative, and it could only have been because he lived at the Lakes and was Coleridge's brother-in-law that he was implicated with the two speculative poets at all. It has been carelessly reported by Lake tourists that Southey was not beloved among his neighbors, while Wordsworth was; and that therefore the latter was the better man, in a social sense. It should be remembered that Southey was a working man, and that the other two were not; and, moreover, it should never be for a moment forgotten that Southey worked double-tides to make up for Coleridge's idleness. While Coleridge was dreaming and discoursing, Southey was toiling to maintain Coleridge's wife and children. He had no time and no attention to spare for wandering about and making himself at home with the neighbors. This practice came naturally to Wordsworth; and a kind and valued neighbor he was to all the peasants round. Many a time I have seen him in the road, in Scotch bonnet and green spectacles, with a dozen children at his heels and holding his cloak, while he cut ash-sticks for them from the hedge, hearing all they had to say or talking to them. Southey, on the other hand, took his constitutional walk at a fixed hour, often reading as he went. Two families depended on him; and his duty of daily labor was not only distinctive, but exclusive. He was always at work at home, while Coleridge was doing nothing but talking, and Wordsworth was aborad, without thinking whether he was at work or play. Seen from the stand-point of conscience and of moral generosity, Southey's was the noblest life of the three; and Coleridge's was, of course, nought. I own, however, that, considering the tendency of the time to make literature a trade, or at least a profession, I cannot help feeling Wordsworth's to have been the most privileged life of them all. He had not work enough to do; and his mode of life encouraged an excess of egoism: but he bore all the necessary retribution of this in his latter years; and the whole career leaves an impression of an airy freedom and a natural course of contemplation, combined with social interest and action, more healthy than the existence of either the delinquent or the exemplary comrade with whom he was associated in the public view.

I have left my neighbors waiting long on the margin of Grasmere. That was before I was born; but I could almost fancy I had seen them there.

I observed that Wordsworth's report of their trip was very unlike Coleridge's. When his sister had left them, he wrote to her, describing scenes by brief precise touches which draw the picture that Coleridge blurs with grand phrases. Moreover, Wordsworth tells sister Dorothy that John will give him forty pounds to buy a bit of land by the lake, where they may build a cottage to live in henceforth. He says, also, that there is a small house vacant near the spot.—They took that house; and thus the Wordsworths became "Lakers." They entered that well-known cottage at Grasmere on the shortest day (St. Thomas's) of 1799.[134] Many years afterwards, Dorothy wrote of the aspect of Grasmere on her arrival that winter evening,—the pale orange lights on the lake, and the reflection of the mountains and the island in the still waters. She had wandered about the world in an unsettled way; and now she had cast anchor for life,—not in that house, but within view of that valley.

All readers of Wordsworth, on either side the Atlantic, believe that they know that cottage, (described in the fifth book of the "Excursion,")[135] with its little orchard, and the moss house, and the tiny terrace behind, with its fine view of the lake and the basin of mountains. There the brother and sister lived for some years in a very humble way, making their feast of the beauty about them. Wordsworth was fond of telling how they had meat only two or three times a week; and he was eager to impress on new-comers—on me among others—the prudence of warning visitors that they must make up their minds to the scantiest fare. He was as emphatic about this, laying his finger on one's arm to enforce it, as about catching mice or educating the people. It was vain to say that one would rather not invite guests than fail to provide for them; he insisted that the expense would be awful, and assumed that his sister's and his own example settled the matter. I suppose they were poor in those days; but it was not for long. A devoted sister Dorothy was. Too late it appeared that she had sacrificed herself to aid and indulge her brother. When her mind was gone, and she was dying by inches, Mrs. Wordsworth offered me the serious warning that she gave whenever occasion allowed, against overwalking. She told me that Dorothy had, not occasionally only, but often, walked forty miles in a day to give her brother her presence. To repair the ravages thus caused she took opium; and the effect on her exhausted frame was to overthrow her mind. This was when she was elderly. For a long course of years, she was a rich household blessing to all connected with her. She shared her brother's peculiarity of investing trifles with solemnity, or rather, of treating all occasions alike (at least in writing) with pedantic elaboration; but she had the true poet's, combined with the true woman's nature; and the fortunate man had, in wife and sister, the two best friends of his life.

The Wordsworths were the originals of the Lake *coterie*, as we have seen. Born at Cockermouth, and a pupil at the Hawkeshead school, Wordsworth was looking homewards when he settled in the District. The others came in consequence. Coleridge brought his family to Greta Hall, near

Keswick; and with them came Mrs. Lovell, one of the three Misses Fricker, of whom Coleridge and Southey had married two.[136] Southey was invited to visit Greta Hall, the year after the Wordsworths settled at Grasmere; and thus they became acquainted. They had just met before, in the South; but they had yet to learn to know each other; and there was sufficient unlikeness between them to render this a work of some time and pains. It was not long before Southey, instead of Coleridge, was the lessee of Greta Hall; and soon after Coleridge took his departure, leaving his wife and children, and also the Lovells, a charge upon Southey, who had no more fortune than Coleridge, except in the inexhaustible wealth of a heart, a will, and a conscience. Wordsworth married in 1802; and then the two poets passed through their share of the experience of human life, a few miles apart, meeting occasionally on some mountain ridge or hidden dale, and in one another's houses, drawn closer by their common joys and sorrows, but never approximating in the quality of their genius, or in the stand-points from which they respectively looked out upon human affairs. They had children, loved them, and each lost some of them; and they felt tenderly for each other when each little grave was opened. Southey, the most amiable of men in domestic life, gentle, generous, serene, and playful, grew absolutely ferocious about politics, as his articles in the "Quarterly Review" showed all the world. Wordsworth, who had some of the irritability and pettishness, mildly described by himself as "gentle stirrings of the mind," which occasionally render great men ludicrously like children, and who was, moreover, highly conservative after his early democratic fever had passed off, grew more and more liberal with advancing years. I do not mean that he verged towards the Reformers,—but that he became more enlarged, tolerant, and generally sympathetic in his political views and temper. It thus happened that society at a distance took up a wholly wrong impression of the two men,—supposing Southey to be an ill-conditioned bigot, and Wordsworth a serene philosopher, far above being disturbed by troubles in daily life, or paying any attention to party-politics. He showed some of his ever-growing liberality, by the way, in speaking of this matter of temper. In old age, he said that the world certainly does get on in minor morals: that when he was young "everybody had a temper"; whereas now no such thing is allowed; amiability is the rule; and an imperfect temper is an offence and a misfortune of a distinctive character.

Among the letters which now and then arrived from strangers, in the early days of Wordsworth's fame, was one which might have come from Coleridge, if they had never met. It was full of admiration and sympathy, expressed as such feelings would be by a man whose analytical and speculative faculties predominated over all the rest. The writer was, indeed, in those days, marvelously like Coleridge,—subtile in analysis to excess, of gorgeous imagination, bewitching discourse, fine scholarship, with a magnificent power of promising and utter incapacity in performing, and with the same habit of intemperance in opium. By his own account, his "disease was to meditate too much and observe too little." I need hardly explain that this was De Quincey;[137] and when I have said that, I need hardly explain further that advancing time and closer acquaintance made the likeness to Coleridge bear a smaller and smaller proportion to the whole character of the man.

In return for his letter of admiration and sympathy, he received an invitation to the Grasmere valley. More than once he set forth to avail himself of it; but when within a few miles, the shyness under which in those days he suffered over-powered his purpose, and he turned back. After having achieved the meeting, however, he soon announced his intention of settling in the valley; and he did so, putting his wife and children eventually into the cottage which the Wordsworths had now outgrown and left. There was little in him to interest or attach a family of regular domestic habits, like the Wordsworths, given to active employment, sensible thrift, and neighborly sympathy. It was universally known that a great poem of Wordsworth's was reserved for posthumous publication, and kept under lock and key meantime. De Quincey had so remarkable a memory that he carried off by means of it the finest passage of the poem,—or that which the author considered so; and he published that passage in a magazine article, in which he gave a detailed account of the Wordsworths' household, connections, and friends, with an analysis of their characters and an exhibition of their faults. This was in 1838, a dozen years before the poet's death. The point of interest is,—How did the wronged family endure the wrong? They were quiet about it,—that is, sensible and dignified; but

Wordsworth was more. A friend of his and mine was talking with him over the fire, just when De Quincey's disclosures were making the most noise, and mentioned the subject. Wordsworth begged to be spared hearing anything about them, saying that the man had long passed away from the family life and mind, and he did not wish to disturb himself about what could not be remedied. My friend acquiesced, saying, "Well, I will tell you only one thing that he says, and then we will talk of something else. He says your wife is too good for you." The old man's dim eyes lighted up instantly, and he started from his seat, and flung himself against the mantel-piece, with his back to the fire, as he cried with loud enthusiasm, "And that's *true*! *There* he is right!"

It was by his written disclosures only that De Quincey could do much mischief; for it was scarcely possible to be prejudiced by anything he could say. The whole man was grotesque; and it must have been a singular image that his neighbors in the valley preserved in their memory. A frail-looking, diminutive man, with narrow chest and round shoulders and features like those of a dying patient, walking with his hands behind him, his hat on the back of his head, and his broad lower lip projected, as if he had something on his tongue that wanted listening to,—such was his aspect; and if one joined company with him, the strangeness grew from moment to moment. His voice and its modulations were a perfect treat. As for what he had to say, it was everything from odd comment on a passing trifle, eloquent enunciation of some truth, or pregnant remark on some lofty subject, down to petty gossip, so delivered as to authorize a doubt whether it might not possibly be an awkward effort at observing something outside of himself, or at getting a grasp of something that he supposed actual. That he should have so supposed was his weakness, and the retribution for the peculiar intemperance which depraved his nature and alienated from their proper use powers which should have made him one of the first philosophers of his age. His singular organization was fatally deranged in its action before it could show its best quality, and his is one of the cases in which we cannot be wrong in attributing moral disease directly to physical disturbance; and it would no doubt have been dropped out of notice, if he had been able to abstain from comment on the characters and lives of other people. Justice to them compels us to accept and use the exposures he offers us of himself.

About the time of De Quincey's settlement at Grasmere, Wilson, the future CHRISTOPHER NORTH,[138] bought the Elleray estate, on the banks of Windermere. He was then just of age,—supreme in all manly sports, physically a model man, and intellectually, brimming with philosophy and poetry. He came hither a rather spoiled child of fortune, perhaps; but he was soon sobered by a loss of property which sent him to his studies for the bar. Scott[139] was an excellent friend to him at that time; and so strong and prophetic was Wilson's admiration of his patron, that he publicly gave him the name of "The Great Magician" before the first "Waverley Novel" was published. Within ten years from his getting a foothold on Windermere banks, he had raised periodical literature to a height unknown before in our time, by his contributions to "Blackwood's Magazine"; and he seemed to step naturally into the Moral Philosophy Chair in Edinburgh in 1820. Christopher North has perhaps conveyed to foreign, and untravelled English, readers as true a conception of our Lake scenery and its influences in one way as Wordsworth in another. The very spirit of the moorland, lake, brook, tarn, ghyll, and ridge breathes from his prose poetry: and well it might. He wandered alone for a week together beside the trout-streams and among the highest tarns. He spent whole days in his boat, coasting the bays of the lake, or floating in the centre, or lying reading in the shade of the trees on the islands. He led with a glorious pride the famous regatta on Windermere, when Canning[140] was the guest of the Boltons[141] at Storrs, and when Scott, Wordsworth, and Southey were of the company; and he liked almost as well steering the packet-boat from Waterhead to Bowness, till the steamer drove out the old-fashioned conveyance. He sat at the stern, immovable, with his hand on the rudder, looking beyond the company of journeymen-carpenters, fish- and butter-women, and tourists, with a gaze on the water-and-sky-line which never shifted. Sometimes a learned professor or a brother sportsman was with him; but he spoke no word, and kept his mouth peremptorily shut under his beard. It was a sight worth taking the voyage for; and it was worth going a long round to see him standing on the shore,—"reminding one of the first man, Adam," (as was said of him,) in his best estate,—

the tall, broad frame, large head, marked features, and long hair; and the tread which shook the ground, and the voice which roused the echoes afar and made one's heart-strings vibrate within. These attributes made strangers turn to look at him on the road, and fixed all eyes on him in the ball-room at Ambleside, when any local object induced him to be a steward. Every old boatman and young angler, every hoary shepherd and primitive housewife in the uplands and dales, had an enthusiasm for him. He could enter into the solemnity of speculation with Wordsworth while floating at sunset on the lake; and not the less gamesomely could he collect a set of good fellows under the lamp at his supper-table, and take off Wordsworth's or Coleridge's monologues to the life. There was that between them which must always have precluded a close sympathy; and their faults were just what each could least allow for in another. Of Wilson's it is enough to say that Scott's injunction to him to "leave off sack, purge, and live cleanly," if he wished for the Moral Philosophy Chair, was precisely what was needed. It was still needed some time after, when, though a Professor of Moral Philosophy, he was seen, with poor Campbell,[142] leaving a tavern one morning, in Edinburgh, haggard and red-eyed, hoarse and exhausted,—not only the feeble Campbell, but the mighty Wilson,—they having sat together twenty-four hours, discussing poetry and wine with all their united energies. This sort of thing was not to the taste of Wordsworth or Southey, any more than their special complacencies were venerable to the humor of Christopher North. Yet they could cordially admire one another; and when sorrows came over them, in dreary impartiality, they could feel reverently and deeply for each other. When Southey lost his idolized boy, Herbert, and had to watch over his insane wife, always his dearest friend, and all the dearer for her helpless and patient suffering under an impenetrable gloom,—when Wordsworth was bereaved of the daughter who made the brightness of his life in his old age,—and when Wilson was shaken to the centre by the loss of his wife, and mourned alone in the damp shades of Elleray, where he would allow not a twig to be cut from the trees she loved,—the sorrow of each moved them all. Elleray was a gloomy place then, and Wilson never surmounted the melancholy which beset him there; and he wisely parted with it some years before his death. The later depression in his case was in proportion to the earlier exhilaration. His love of Nature and of genial human intercourse had been too exuberant; and he became incapable of enjoyment from either, in his last years. He never recovered from an attack of pressure on the brain, and died paralyzed in the spring of 1854. He had before gone from among us with his joy; and then we heard that he had dropped out of life with his griefs; and our beautiful region, and the region of life, were so much the darker in a thousand eyes.

While speaking of Elleray, we should pay a passing tribute of gratitude to an older worthy of that neighborhood,—the well-known Bishop of Llandaff, Richard Watson,[143] who did more for the beauty of Windermere than any other person. There is nothing to praise in the damp old mansion at Calgarth, set down in low ground, and actually with its back to the lake, and its front windows commanding no view; but the woods are the glory of Bishop Watson. He was not a happy prelate, believing himself undervalued and neglected, and fretting his heart over his want of promotion; but he must have had many a blessed hour while planting those woods for which many generations will be grateful to him. Let the traveller remember him, when looking abroad from Miller Brow, near Bowness. Below lies the whole length of Windermere, from the white houses of Clappersgate, nestling under Loughrigg at the head, to the Beacon at the foot. The whole range of both shores, with their bays and coves and promontories, can be traced; and the green islands are clustered in the centre; and the whole gradation of edifices is seen, from Wray Castle, on its rising ground, to the tiny boat-houses, each on its creek. All these features are enhanced in beauty by the Calgarth woods, which cover the undulations of hill and margin beneath and around, rising and falling, spreading and contracting, with green meadows interposed, down to the white pebbly strand. To my eye, this view is unsurpassed by any in the District.

Bishop Watson's two daughters were living in the neighborhood till two years ago,—antique spinsters, presenting us with a most vivid specimen of the literary female life of the last century. They were excellent women, differing from the rest of society chiefly in their notion that superior people should show their superiority in all the acts of their lives,—that literary people should talk literature, and scientific people science, and so on; and they felt affronted, as if set down among common people, when an author talked about common things in a common way. They did their best to treat their friends to wit and polite letters; and they expected to be ministered to in the same fashion. This was rather embarrassing to visitors to whom it had never occurred to talk for any other purpose than to say what presented itself at the moment; but it is a privilege to have known those faithful sisters, and to have seen in them a good specimen of the literary society of the last century.

There is another spot in that neighborhood which strangers look up to with interest from the lake itself,—Dovenest, the abode of Mrs. Hemans[144] for the short time of her residence at the Lakes. She saw it for the first time from the lake, as her published correspondence[145] tells, and fell in love with it; and as it was vacant at the time, she went into it at once. Many of my readers will remember her description of the garden and the view from it, the terrace, the circular grass-plot with its one tall white rose-tree. "You cannot imagine," she wrote, in 1830, "how I delight in that fair, solitary, neglected-looking tree." The tree is not neglected now. Dovenest is inhabited by Mrs. Hemans's then young friend, the Rev. R. P. Graves; and it has recovered from the wildness and desolation of thirty years ago, while looking as secluded as ever among the woods on the side of the Wansfell.

All this time, illustrious strangers were coming, year by

year, to visit residents, or to live among the mountains for a few weeks. There was Wilberforce, spending part of a summer at Rayrigg, on the lake shore. One of his boys asked him, "Why should you not buy a house here? and then we could come every year." The reply was characteristic:—that it would be very delightful; but that the world is lying, in a manner, under the curse of God; that we have something else to do than to enjoy fine prospects; and that, though it may be allowable to taste the pleasure now and then, we ought to wait till the other life to enjoy ourselves. Such was the strait-lacing in which the good man was forever trying to compress his genial, buoyant, and grateful nature.—Scott came again and again; and Wordsworth and Southey met to do him honor. The tourist must remember the Swan Inn,—the white house beyond Grasmere, under the skirts of Helvellyn. There Scott went daily for a glass of something good, while Wordsworth's guest, and treated with the homely fare of the Grasmere cottage. One morning, his host, himself, and Southey went up to the Swan, to start thence with ponies for the ascent of Helvellyn. The innkeeper saw them coming, and accosted Scott with "Eh, Sir! ye 're come early for your draught to-day!"—a disclosure which was not likely to embarrass his host at all. Wordsworth was probably the least-discomposed member of the party.—Charles Lamb and his sister[146] once popped in unannounced on Coleridge at Keswick, and spent three weeks in the neighborhood. We can all fancy the little man on the top of Skiddaw, with his mind full as usual of quips and pranks, and struggling with the emotions of mountain-land, so new and strange to a Cockney, such as he truly described himself. His loving readers do not forget his statement of the comparative charms of Skiddaw and Fleet Street; and on the spot we quote his exclamations about the peak, and the keen air there, and the look over into Scotland, and down upon a sea of mountains which made him giddy. We are glad he came and enjoyed a day, which, as he said, would stand out like a mountain in his life; but we feel that he could never have followed his friends hither,—Coleridge and Wordsworth,—and have made himself at home. The warmth of a city and the hum of human voices all day long were necessary to his spirits. As to his passage at arms with Southey,—everybody's sympathies are with Lamb; and he only vexes us by his humility and gratitude at being pardoned by the aggressor, whom he had in fact humiliated in all eyes but his own. It was one of Southey's spurts of insolent bigotry; and Lamb's plea for tolerance and fair play was so sound as to make it a poor affectation in Southey to assume a pardoning air; but, if Lamb's kindly and sensitive nature could not sustain him in so virtuous an opposition, it is well that the two men did not meet on the top of Skiddaw.—Canning's visit to Storrs, on Windermere, was a great event in its day; and Lockhart tells us, in his "Life of Scott,"[147] what the regatta was like, when Wilson played Admiral, and the group of local poets, and Scott, were in the train of the statesman. Since that day, it has been a common thing for illustrious persons to appear in our valleys. Statesmen, churchmen, university-men, princes, peers, bishops, authors, artists, flock hither; and during the latter years of Wordsworth's life, the average number of strangers who called at Rydal Mount in the course of the season was eight hundred.

During the growth of the District from its wildness to this thronged state, a minor light of the region was kindling, flickering, failing, gleaming, and at last going out,—anxiously watched and tended, but to little purpose. The life of Hartley Coleridge has been published by his family; and there can, therefore, be no scruple in speaking of him here. The remembrance of him haunts us all,—almost as his ghost haunts his kind landlady. Long after his death, she used to "hear him at night laughing in his room," as he used to do when he lived there. A peculiar laugh it was, which broke out when fancies crossed him, whether he was alone or in company. Travellers used to look after him on the road, and guides and drivers were always willing to tell about him; and still his old friends almost expect to see Hartley at any turn,—the little figure, with the round face, marked by the blackest eyebrows and eyelashes, and by a smile and expression of great eccentricity. As we passed, he would make a full stop in the road, face about, take off his black-and-white straw hat, and bow down to the ground. The first glance in return was always to see whether he was sober. The Hutchinsons must remember him. He was one of the audience, when they held their concert under the sycamores in Mr. Harrison's grounds at Ambleside; and he thereupon wrote a sonnet, doubtless well known in America.[148] When I wanted his leave to publish that sonnet, in an account of "Frolics with the Hutchinsons," it was necessary to hunt him up, from public-house to public-house, early in the morning. It is because these things are universally known,—because he was seen staggering in the road, and spoken of by drivers and lax artisans as an alehouse comrade, that I speak of him here, in order that I may testify how he was beloved and cherished by the best people in his neighborhood. I can hardly speak of him myself as a personal acquaintance; for I could not venture on inviting him to my house. I saw what it was to others to be subject to day-long visits from him, when he would ask for wine, and talk from morning to night,—and a woman, solitary and busy, could not undertake that sort of hospitality; but I saw how forbearing his friends were, and why,—and I could sympathize in their regrets when he died. I met him in company occasionally, and never saw him sober; but I have heard from several common friends of the charm of his conversation, and the beauty of his gentle and affectionate nature. He was brought into the District when four years old; and it does not appear that he ever had a chance allowed him of growing into a sane man. Wordsworth used to say that Hartley's life failure arose mainly from his having grown up "wild as the breeze,"—delivered over, without help or guardianship, to the vagaries of an imagination which overwhelmed all the rest of him. There was a strong constitutional likeness to his father, evident enough to all; but no pains seem to have been taken on any hand to guard him from the snare, or to invigorate his will, and aid him in self-discipline. The great catastrophe, the ruinous blow, which rendered him hopeless, is told in the Memoir; but there are particulars which help to account for it.[149] Hartley had spent his school-days under a master as eccentric as he himself ever became. The Rev. John Dawes of Ambleside was one of the oddities that may be found in the remote places of modern England. He had no idea of restraint, for himself or his pupils; and when they arrived, punctually or not, for morning school, they sometimes found the door shut, and chalked with "Gone a-hunting," or "Gone a-fishing," or gone away somewhere or other. Then Hartley would sit down under the bridge, or in the shadow of the wood, or lie on the grass on the hill-side, and tell tales to his schoolfellows for hours. His mind was developed by the conversation of his father and his father's friends; and he himself had a great friendship with Professor Wilson, who always stood by him with a pitying love. He had this kind of discursive education, but no discipline; and when he went to college, he was at the mercy of any who courted his affection, intoxicated his imagination, and then led him into vice. His Memoir shows how he lost his fellowship at Oriel College, Oxford, at the end of his probationary year. He had been warned by the authorities against his sin of intemperance; and he bent his whole soul to get through that probationary year. For eleven months, and many days of the twelfth, he lived soberly and studied well. Then the old tempters agreed in London to go down to Oxford and get hold of Hartley. They went down on the top of the coach, got access to his room, made him drunk, and carried him with them to

London; and he was not to be found when he should have passed. The story of his death is but too like this.

His fellowship lost, he came, ruinously humbled, to live in this District, at first under compulsion to take pupils, whom, of course, he could not manage. On the death of his mother, an annuity was purchased for him, and paid quarterly, to keep him out of debt, if possible. He could not take care of money, and he was often hungry, and often begged the loan of a sixpence; and when the publicans made him welcome to what he pleased to have, in consideration of the company he brought together, to hear his wonderful talk, his wit, and his dreams, he was helpless in the snare. We must remember that he was a fine scholar, as well as a dreamer and a humorist; and there was no order of intellect, from the sage to the peasant, which could resist the charm of his discourse. He had taken his degree with high distinction at Oxford; and yet the old Westmoreland "statesman," who, offered whisky and water, accepts the one and says the other can be had anywhere, would sit long to hear what Hartley had to tell of what he had seen or dreamed. At gentlemen's tables, it was a chance how he might talk,—sublimely, sweetly, or with a want of tact which made sad confusion. In the midst of the great black-frost at the close of 1848, he was at a small dinner-party at the house of a widow lady, about four miles from his lodgings. During dinner, some scandal was talked about some friends of his to whom he was warmly attached. He became excited on their behalf,—took Champagne before he had eaten enough, and, before the ladies left the table, was no longer master of himself. His host, a very young man, permitted some practical joking: brandy was ordered, and given to the unconscious Hartley; and by eleven o'clock he was clearly unfit to walk home alone. His hostess sent her footman with him, to see him home. The man took him through Ambleside, and then left him to find his way for the other two miles. The cold was as severe as any ever known in this climate; and it was six in the morning when his landlady heard some noise in the porch, and found Hartley stumbling in. She put him to bed, put hot bricks to his feet, and tried all the proper means; and in the middle of the day he insisted on getting up and going out. He called at the house of a friend, Dr. S——, near Ambleside. The kind physician scolded him for coming out, sent for a carriage, took him home, and put him to bed. He never rose again, but died on the 6th of January, 1849. The young host and the old hostess have followed him, after deeply deploring that unhappy day.

It was sweet, as well as sorrowful, to see how he was mourned. Everybody, from his old landlady, who cared for him like a mother, to the infant-school children, missed Hartley Coleridge. I went to his funeral at Grasmere. The rapid Rotha rippled and dashed over the stones beside the churchyard; the yews rose dark from the faded grass of the graves; and in mighty contrast to both, Helvellyn stood, in wintry silence, and sheeted with spotless snow. Among the mourners Wordsworth was conspicuous, with his white hair and patriarchal aspect. He had no cause for painful emotions on his own account; for he had been a faithful friend to the doomed victim who was now beyond the reach of his tempters. While there was any hope that stern remonstrance might rouse the feeble will and strengthen the suffering conscience to relive itself, such remonstrance was pressed; and when the case was past hope, Wordsworth's door was ever open to his old friend's son. Wordsworth could stand by that open grave without a misgiving about his own share in the scene which was here closing; and calm and simply grave he looked. He might mourn over the life; but he could scarcely grieve at the death. The grave was close behind the family group of the Wordsworth tombs. It shows, above the name and dates, a sculptured crown of thorns and Greek cross, with the legend, "By the Cross and Passion, Good Lord, deliver me!"

One had come and gone meantime who was as express a contrast to Hartley Coleridge as could be imagined,—a man of energy, activity, stern self-discipline, and singular strength of will. Such a cast of character was an inexplicable puzzle to poor Hartley. He showed this by giving his impression of another person of the same general mode of life,—that A. B. was "a monomaniac about everything." It was to rest a hard-worked mind and body, and to satisfy a genuine need of his nature, that Dr. Arnold[150] came here from Rugby with his family,—first, to lodgings for an occasional holiday, and afterwards to a house of his own, at Christmas and Midsummer, and with the intention of living permanently at Fox How, when he should give up his work at Rugby.

He was first at a house at the foot of Rydal Mount, at

Christmas, 1831, "with the road on one side of the garden, and the Rotha on the other, which goes brawling away under our windows with its perpetual music. The higher mountains that bound our view are all snow-capped; but it is all snug, and warm, and green in the valley. Nowhere on earth have I ever seen a spot of more perfect and enjoyable beauty, with not a single object out of tune with it, look which way I will." He built Fox How, two or three years later, and at once began his course of hospitality by having lads of the sixth form as his guests,—not for purposes of study, but of recreation, and, yet more, to give them that element of education which consists in familiarity with the noblest natural scenery. The hue and cry which arose when he showed himself a reformer, in Church matters as in politics, followed him here, as we see by his letters; and it was not till his "Life and Correspondence"[151] appeared that his neighbors here understood him. It has always been difficult, perhaps, for them to understand anything modern, or at all vivacious. Everybody respected Dr. Arnold for his energy and industry, his services to education, and his devotedness to human welfare; but they were afraid of his supposed opinions. Not the less heartily did he honor everything that was admirable in them; and when he was gone, they remembered his ways, and cherished every trace of him, in a manner which showed how they would have made much of him, if their own timid prejudices had not stood in the way. They point out to this day the spot where they saw him stand, without his hat, on Rotha bridge, watching the gush of the river under the wooded bank, or gazing into the basin of vapors within the *cul-de-sac* of Fairfield,—the same view which he looked on from his study, as he sat on his sofa, surrounded by books. The neighbors show the little pier at Waterhead whence he watched the morning or the evening light on the lake, the place where he bathed, and the tracks in the mountains which led to his favorite ridges. Everybody has read his "Life and Correspondence," and therefore knows what his mode of life was here, and how great was his enjoyment of it. We have all read of the mountain-trips in summer, and the skating on Rydal Lake in winter,—and how his train of children enjoyed everything with him, as far as they could. It was but for a few years; and the time never came for him to retire hither from Rugby. In June, 1842, he had completed his fourteenth year at Rugby, and was particularly in need, under some harassing cares, of the solace and repose which a few hours more would have brought him, when he was cut off by an illness of two hours. On the day when he was to have been returning to Fox How, some of his children were travelling thence to his funeral. His biographer tells us how strong was the consternation at Rugby, when the tidings spread on that Sunday morning, "Dr. Arnold is dead." Not slight was the emotion throughout this valley, when the news passed from house to house, the next day. As I write, I see the windows which were closed that day, and the trees round the house,—so grown up since he walked among them!—and the course of the Rotha, which winds and ripples at the foot of his garden. I never saw him, for I did not come here till two years after; but I have seen his widow pass on into her honored old age, and his children part off into their various homes, and their several callings in life,—to meet in the beloved house at Fox How, at Christmas, and at many another time.

This leaves only Southey and the Wordsworths; and their ending was not far off. The old poet had seen almost too much of these endings. One day, when I found a stoppage in the road at the foot of Rydal Mount, from a sale of furniture, such as is common in this neighborhood, every spring and autumn, I met Mr. Wordsworth,—not looking observant and amused, but in his blackest mood of melancholy, and evidently wanting to get out of the way. He said he did not like the sight: he had seen so many of these sales; he had seen Southey's, not long before; and these things reminded him how soon there must be a sale at Rydal Mount. It was remarked by a third person that this was rather a wilful way of being miserable; but I never saw a stronger love of life than there was in them all, even so late in their day as this. Mrs. Wordsworth, then past her three-score years and ten, observed to me that the worst of living here was that it made one so unwilling to go. It seems but lately that she said so; yet she nursed to their graves her daughter and her husband and his sister, and she herself became blind; so that it was not hard "to go," when the time came.

Southey's decline was painful to witness,—even as his beloved wife's had been to himself. He never got over her loss; and his mind was decidedly shaken before he made the second marriage which has been so much talked over.

One most touching scene there was when he had become unconscious of all that was said and done around him. Mrs. Southey had been careless of her own interests about money when she married him, and had sought no protection for her own property. When there was manifestly no hope of her husband's mind ever recovering, his brother assembled the family and other witnesses, and showed them a kind of will which he had drawn up, by which Mrs. Southey's property was returned to herself, intact. He said they were all aware that their relative could not, in his condition, make a will, and that he was even unaware of what they were doing; but that it was right that they should pledge themselves by some overt act to fulfil what would certainly have been his wish. The bowed head could not be raised, but the nerveless hand was guided to sign the instrument; and all present agreed to respect it as if it were a veritable will,—as of course they did. The decline was full of painful circumstances; and it must have been with a heart full of sorrow that Wordsworth walked over the hills to attend the funeral.

The next funeral was that of his own daughter Dora,—Mrs. Quillinan. A story has got about, as untrue as it is disagreeable, that Dora lost her health from her father's opposition to her marriage, and that Wordsworth's excessive grief after her death was owing to remorse. I can myself testify to her health having been very good for a considerable interval between that difficulty and her last illness; and this is enough, of itself, to dispose of the story. Her parents considered the marriage an imprudent one; but after securing sufficient time for consideration, they said that she must judge for herself; and there were fine qualities in Mr. Quillinan which could not but win their affection and substantial regard. His first wife, a friend of Dora Wordsworth's, was carried out of the house in which she had just been confined, from fire in the middle of the night; she died from the shock; and she died recommending her husband and her friend to marry. Such is the understood history of the case. After much delay they did marry, and lived near Rydal Mount, where Dora was, as always, the light of the house, as long as she could go to it. But, after a long and painful decline, she died in 1847. Her husband followed soon after Wordsworth's death. He lies in the family corner of Grasmere churchyard, between his two wives. This appeared to be the place reserved for Mrs. Wordsworth, so that Dora would lie between her parents. There seemed now to be no room left for the solitary survivor, and many wondered what would be done; but all had been thought of. Wordsworth's grave had been made deep enough for two; and there his widow now rests.

There was much vivid life in them, however clearly the end was approaching, when I first knew them in 1845. The day after my arrival at a friend's house, they called on me, excited by two kinds of interest. Wordsworth had been extremely gratified by hearing, through a book of mine, how his works were estimated by certain classes of readers in the United States; and he and Mrs. Wordsworth were eager to learn facts and opinions about mesmerism, by which I had just recovered from a long illness, and which they hoped might avail in the case of a daughter-in-law, then in a dying state abroad.[152] After that day, I met them frequently, and was at their house, when I could go. On occasion of my first visit, I was struck by an incident which explained the ridicule we have all heard thrown on the old poet for a self-esteem which he was merely too simple to hide. Nothing could be easier than to make a quiz of what he said to me; but to me it seemed delightful. As he at once talked of his poems, I thought I might; and I observed that he might be interested in knowing which of his poems had been Dr. Channing's[153] favorite. Seeing him really interested, I told him that I had not been many hours under Dr. Channing's roof before he brought me "The Happy Warrior," which, he said, moved him more than any other in the whole series. Wordsworth remarked,—and repeated the remark very earnestly,—that this was evidently applicable to the piece, "not as a poem, not as fulfilling the conditions of poetry, but as a chain of extremely valuable *thoughts*." Then he repeated emphatically,—"a chain of extremely *valuable* thoughts!" This was so true that it seemed as natural for him to say it as Dr. Channing, or any one else.

It is indisputable that his mind and manners were hurt by the prominence which his life at the Lakes—a life very public, under the name of seclusion—gave, in his own eyes, to his own works and conversation; but he was less absorbed in his own objects, less solemn, less severed from ordinary men than is supposed, and has been given out by strangers, who, to the number of eight hundred in a year, have been received by him with a bow, asked to see the garden-terraces where he had meditated this and that work, and dismissed with another bow, and good wishes for their health and pleasure,—the host having, for the most part, not heard, or not attended to, the name of his visitor. I have seen him receive in that way a friend, a Commissioner of Education, whom I ventured to take with me, (a thing I very rarely did,) and in the evening have had a message asking if I knew how Mr. Wordsworth could obtain an interview with this very gentleman, who was said to be in the neighborhood. All this must be very bad for anybody; and so was the distinction of having early chosen this District for a home. When I first came, I told my friends here that I was alarmed for myself, when I saw the spirit of insolence which seemed to possess the cultivated residents, who really did virtually assume that the mountains and vales were somehow their property, or at least a privilege appropriate to superior people like themselves. Wordsworth's sonnets about the railway[154] were a mild expression of his feelings in this direction; and Mrs. Wordsworth, in spite of her excellent sense, took up his song, and declared with unusual warmth that green fields, with daisies and buttercups, were as good for Lancashire operatives as our lakes and valleys. I proposed that the people should judge of this for themselves; but there was no end to ridicule of "the people from Birthwaite" (the end of the railway, five miles off). Some had been seen getting their dinner in the churchyard, and others inquiring how best to get up Loughrigg,—"evidently, quite puzzled, and not knowing where to go." My reply, "that they would know next time," was not at all sympathized in. The effect of this exclusive temper was pernicious in the neighborhood. A petition to Parliament against the railway was not brought to me, as it was well known that I would not sign it; but some little girls undertook my case; and the effect of their parroting of Mr. Wordsworth, about "ourselves" and "the common people" who intrude upon us, was as sad as it was absurd. The whole matter ended rather remarkably. When all were gone but Mrs. Wordsworth, and she was blind, a friend who was as a daughter to her remarked, one summer day, that there were some boys on the Mount in the garden. "Ah!" said Mrs. Wordsworth, "there is no end to those people;—boys from Birthwaite!—boys from Birthwaite!" It was the Prince of Wales, with a companion or two.

The notion of Wordsworth's solemnity and sublimity, as something unremitting, was a total mistake. It probably arose from the want of proportion in his mind, as in his sister's, before referred to. But he relished the common business of life, and not only could take in, but originate a joke. I remember his quizzing a common friend of ours,—one much esteemed by us all,—who had a wonderful ability of falling asleep in an instant, when not talking. Mr. Wordsworth told me of the extreme eagerness of this gentleman, Mrs. Wordsworth, and himself, to see the view over Switzerland from the ridge of the Jura. Mrs. Wordsworth could not walk so fast as the gentlemen, and her husband let the friend go on by himself. When they arrived, a minute or two after him, they found him sitting on a stone in face of all Switzerland, fast asleep. When Mr. Wordworth mimicked the sleep, with his head on one side, anybody could have told whom he was quizzing.—He and Mrs. Wordsworth, but too naturally impressed with the mischief of overwalking in the case of women, took up a wholly mistaken notion that I walked too much. One day I was returning from a circuit of ten miles with a guest, when we met the Wordsworths. They asked where we had been. "By Red Bank to Grasmere." Whereupon Mr. Wordsworth laid his hand on my guest's arm, saying, "There, there! take care what you are about! don't let her lead you about! I can tell you, she has killed off half the gentlemen in the county!"—Mrs. Hemans tells us, that, before she had known him many hours, she was saying to him, "Dear me, Mr. Wordsworth! how can you be so giddy?"

His interest in common things never failed. It has been observed that he and Mrs. Wordsworth did incalculable good by the example they unconsciously set the neighborhood of respectable thrift. There are no really poor people at Rydal, because the great lady at the Hall, Lady Le Fleming, takes care that there shall be none,—at the expense of great moral mischief. But there is a prevalent recklessness, grossness, and mingled extravagance and discomfort in the family management, which, I am told, was far worse when the Wordsworths came than it is now. Going freely among the neighbors, and welcoming and helping them familiarly, the Wordsworths laid their own lives open to observation; and the mingled carefulness and comfort—the good thrift, in short—wrought as a powerful lesson all around. As for what I myself saw,—they took a practical interest in my small purchase of land for my abode; and Mr. Wordsworth often came to consult upon the plan and progress of the house. He used to lie on the grass, beside the young oaks, before the foundations were dug; and he referred me to Mrs. Wordsworth as the best possible authority about the placing of windows and beds. He climbed to the upper rooms before there was a staircase; and we had to set Mrs. Wordsworth as a watch over him, when there was a staircase, but no balustrade. When the garden was laid out, he planted a stone-pine (which is flourishing) under the terrace-wall, washed his hands in the watering-pot, and gave the place and me at once his blessing and some thrifty counsel. When I began farming, he told me an immense deal about his cow; and both of them came to see my first calf, and ascertain whether she had the proper marks of the handsome short-horn of the region. The distinctive impression which the family made on the minds of the people about them was that of practical ability; and it was thoroughly well conveyed by the remark of a man at Rydal, on hearing some talk of Mrs. Wordsworth, a few days after the poet's death:—"She's a gay [rare][155] clever body, who will carry on the business as well as any of 'em."

Nothing could be more affecting than to watch the silent changes in Mrs. Wordsworth's spirits during the ten years which followed the death of her daughter. For many months her husband's gloom was terrible, in the evenings, or in dull weather. Neither of them could see to read much; and the poet was not one who ever pretended to restrain his emotions, or assume a cheerfulness which he did not feel. We all knew that the mother's heart was the bereaved one, however impressed the father's imagination might be by the picture of his own desolation; and we saw her mute about her own trial, and growing whiter in the face and smaller from month to month, while he put no restraint upon his tears and lamentations. The winter evenings were dreary; and in hot summer days the aged wife had to follow him, when he was missed for any time, lest he should be sitting in the sun without his hat. Often she found him asleep on the heated rock. His final illness was wearing and dreary to her; but there her part was clear, and she was adequate to it. "You are going to Dora," she whispered to him, when the issue was no longer doubtful. She thought he did not hear or heed; but some hours after, when some one opened the curtain, he said, "Are you Dora?" Composed and cheerful in the prospect of his approaching rest, and absolutely without solicitude for herself, the wife was everything to him till the last moment; and when he was gone, the anxieties of the self-forgetting woman were over. She attended his funeral, and afterwards chose to fill her accustomed place among the guests who filled the house. She made tea that evening as usual; and the lightening of her spirits from that time forward was evident. It was a lovely April day, the 23d, (Shakespeare's birth- and death-day,) when her task of nursing closed. The news spread fast that the old poet was gone; and we all naturally turned our eyes up to the roof under which he lay. There, above and amidst the young green of the woods, the modest dwelling shone in the sunlight. The smoke went up thin and straight into the air; but the closed windows gave the place a look of death. There he was lying whom we should see no more.

The poor sister remained for five years longer. Travellers, American and others, must remember having found the garden-gate locked at Rydal Mount, and perceiving the reason why, in seeing a little garden-chair, with an emaciated old lady in it, drawn by a nurse round and round the graveled space before the house. That was Miss Wordsworth, taking her daily exercise. It was a great trouble at times, that she could not be placed in some safe privacy; and Wordsworth's feudal loyalty was put to a severe test in the matter. It had been settled that a cottage should be built for his sister, in a field of his, beyond the garden. The plan was made, and the turf marked out, and the digging about to begin, when the great lady at the Hall, Lady Le Fleming, interfered with a prohibition. She assumed the feudal prerogative of determining what should or should not be built on all the lands over which the Le Flemings have borne sway; and her extraordinary determination was, that no dwelling should be built, except on the site of a former one! We could scarcely believe we had not been carried back into the Middle Ages, when we heard it; but the old poet, whom any sovereign in Europe would have been delighted to gratify, submitted with a good grace, and thenceforth rubbed his sister's feet, and coaxed and humored her at home,—trusting his guests to put up with the inconveniences of her state, as he could not remove them from sight and hearing. After she was gone also, Mrs. Wordsworth, entirely blind, and above eighty years of age, seemed to have no cares, except when the errors and troubles of others touched her judgement or sympathy. She was well cared for by nieces and friends. Her plain common sense and cheerfulness appeared in one of the last things she said, a few hours before her death. She remarked on the character of the old hymns, practical and familiar, which people liked when she was young, and which answered some purposes better than the sublimer modern sort. She repeated part of a child's hymn,—very homely, about going straight to school, and taking care of the books, and learning the lesson well,—and broke off, saying, "There! if you want to hear the rest, ask the Bishop o' London. *He* knows it."

Then, all were gone; and there remained only the melancholy breaking up of the old home which had been interesting to the world for forty-six years. Mrs. Wordsworth died in January, 1859. In the May following, the sale took place which Wordsworth had gloomily foreseen so many years before. Everything of value was reserved, and the few articles desired by strangers were bought by commission; and thus the throng at the sale was composed of the ordinary elements. The spectacle was sufficiently painful to make it natural for old friends to stay away. Doors and windows stood wide. The sofa and tea-table where the wisest and best from all parts of the world had held converse were turned out to be examined and bid for. Anybody who chose passed the sacred threshold; the auctioneer's hammer was heard on the terrace; and the hospitable parlor and kitchen were crowded with people swallowing tea in the intervals of their business. One farmer rode six-and-thirty miles that morning to carry home something that had belonged to Wordsworth; and, in default of anything better, he took a patched old table-cover. There was a bed of anemones under the windows, at one end of the house; and a bed of anemones is a treasure in our climate. It was in full bloom in the morning; and before sunset, every blossom was gone, and the bed was trampled into ruin. It was dreary work! The two sons live at a distance; and the house is let to tenants of another name.

I perceive that I have not noticed the poet's laureateship. The truth is, the office never seemed to belong to him; and we forgot it, when not specially reminded of it. We did not like to think of him in court-dress, going through the ceremonies of levee or ball, in his old age. His white hair and dim eyes were better at home among the mountains.

There stand the mountains, from age to age; and there run the rivers, with their full and never-pausing tide, while those who came to live and grow wise beside them are all gone! One after another, they have lain down to their everlasting rest in the valleys where their step and their voices were as familiar as the points of the scenery. The region has changed much since they came as to a retreat. It was they who caused the change, for the most part; and it was not for them to complain of it; but the consequence is, that with them has passed away a peculiar phase of life in England. It is one which can neither be continued nor repeated. The Lake District is no longer a retreat; and any other retreat must have different characteristics, and be illumined by some different order of lights. The case being so, I have felt no scruple in asking the attention of my readers to a long story, and to full details of some of the latest Lights of the Lake District.

Chapter Nine

The World and the Terrace
Two Views from the Knoll[156]

It is with singular alacrity that, in winter evenings, I light the lamp, and unroll my wool-work, and meditate or dream till the arrival of the newspaper tells me that the tea has stood long enough. . . . After tea, if there was news from the seat of war, I called in my maids, who brought down the great atlas, and studied the chances of the campaign with me.[157] Then there was an hour or two for Montaigne, or Bacon, or Shakspere, or Tennyson, or some dear old biography, or last new book from London,—historical, moral or political. Then, when the house and neighbourhood were asleep, there was the half-hour on the terrace, or, if the weather was too bad for that, in the porch,—whence I seldom or never came in without a clear purpose for my next morning's work. I believe that, but for my country life, much of the benefit and enjoyment of my travels, and also of my studies, would have been lost to me.

Fig. 22. Harriet Martineau, 1850 (from Martineau's *Autobiography*)

On my terrace, there were two worlds extended bright before me, even when the midnight darkness hid from my bodily eyes all but the outlines of the solemn mountains that surround our valley on three sides, and the clear opening to the lake on the south. In the one of those worlds, I saw now the magnificent coast of Massachusetts in autumn, or the flowery swamps of Louisiana, or the forests of Georgia in spring, or the Illinois prairie in summer; or the blue Nile, or the brown Sinai, or the gorgeous Petra, or the view of Damascus from the Salahiey; or the Grand Canal under a Venetian sunset, or the Black Forest in twilight, or Malta in the glare of noon, or the broad desert stretching away under the stars, or the Red Sea tossing its superb shells on shore, in the pale dawn.[158] That is one world, all comprehended within my terrace wall, and coming up into the light at my call.

The other and finer scenery is of that world, only beginning to be explored, of Science. The long study of Comte had deeply impressed on me the imagery of the glorious hierarchy of the sciences which he has exhibited.[159] The time was gone by when I could look at objects as mere surface, or separate existences; and since that late labour of love, I had more than ever seen the alliance and concert of the heavenly bodies, and the mutual action and interior composition of the substances which I used to regard as one in themselves, and unconnected in respect to each other. It is truly an exquisite pleasure to dream, after the toil of study, on the sublime abstractions of mathematics; the transcendent scenery unrolled by astronomy; the mysterious, invisible forces dimly hinted to us by Physics; the new conception of the constitution of Matter originated by Chemistry; and then, the inestimable glimpses opened to us, in regard to the nature and destiny of Man . . . .

Wondrous beyond the comprehension of any one mind is the mass of glorious facts, and the series of mighty conceptions laid open; but the shadow of the surrounding darkness rests upon it all. The unknown always engrosses the greater part of the field of vision; and the awe of infinity sanctifies both the study and the dream. Between these worlds, and other interests, literary and political, were my evenings passed, a short year ago. Perhaps no one has had a much more vivid enjoyment than myself of London society of a very high order; and few, I believe, are of a more radically social nature than myself: yet, I may say that there has never been, since I had a home of my own, an evening spent in the most charming intercourse that I would not have exchanged (as far as the mere pleasure was concerned) for one of my ordinary evenings under the lamp within, and the lights of heaven without.

ENDNOTES

1. Excerpted from *Harriet Martineau's Autobiography*, ed. Maria Weston Chapman (Boston: James R. Osgood, 1877), 1:495–97.

2. Martineau moved to the Lake District in 1845.

3. This year saw the publication of Henry George Atkinson and Harriet Martineau's *Letters on the Laws of Man's Nature and Development* (London: John Chapman, 1851). The *Letters*, in which Martineau espoused an atheistic perspective, was acerbically critiqued by the clergy (including her noted Unitarian brother, James Martineau).

4. Martineau wrote her autobiography in 1855, when she believed herself—incorrectly—near life's end.

5. *Sartain's Union Magazine of Literature and Art* 6 (January–June 1850): 38–41, 139–42, 291–98, 355–58, 381–84; 7 (July–December 1850): 28–32, 88–91, 150–53, 227–30, 268–71, 344–47.

6. See, for further details, Martineau's *Life in the Sickroom* (London: E. Moxon, 1845) and *Harriet Martineau's Autobiography* (1877).

7. See, for didactic elaboration, Martineau's tale "Highest House in Wathendale," this volume.

8. John Wilson (1785–1854), Scottish writer who adopted "Christopher North" as his pseudonym; see also Harriet Martineau, "Professor Wilson ('Christopher North')," *Biographical Sketches* (New York: Leypoldt & Holt, 1869), pp. 21–27.

9. See, for further details, Harriet Martineau, "The Bobbin Mill at Ambleside," *Health, Husbandry and Handicraft* (Bradbury and Evans, 1861), pp. 437–47.

10. By the end of the century, according to H. D. Rawnsley in *Life and Nature at the English Lakes* (Glasgow: James MacLehose, 1902), pp. 1–3, the old Market Cross, as well as several other Ambleside landmarks, including the little post office, "wherein one met all the wit and talent of the neighbourhood in olden time," had passed out of existence.

11. See "The Cost of Cottages," this volume.

12. See "Our Farm of Two Acres," this volume.

13. Hannah Nicholson; see, for an interview with Hannah at age eighty-five, regarding Ambleside traditions, Rawnsley's *Life and Nature at the English Lakes* (1902), pp. 3–13. Mrs. Nicholson's son, Cornelius, became an archaeologist whose life is recounted "in a book entitled *A Well-spent Life*, and lately published by Wilson of Kendal."

14. Margaret Nicholson. Neither Hannah nor Margaret ever married. Rawnsley reports in *Life and Nature at the English Lakes* (1902), page 4, that they retired in Ambleside "after the forty-seven years they laboured for the public good and in the service of the Royal Mail."

15. Fredrika Meyer; see, for details of an evening with Ms. Meyer, Martineau's essay for the month of June, this volume.

16. *Riddle,* a coarse-meshed sieve.

17. Mary Wordsworth; see Harriet Martineau, "Mrs. Wordsworth," *Biographical Sketches* (New York: Leypoldt & Holt, 1869), pp. 86–92.

18. The year was 1846. Martineau's *Autobiography* (1:503) reports: "The winter of 1845–6 was . . . the rainiest in the experience of our generation; but the new house was not injured by it; and was ready for occupation when April arrived."

19. The claim to "highest house" has since been supplanted, but the pub house remains open to thirsty passersby.

20. "To Joanna," *The Poetical Works of William Wordsworth*, ed. William Knight (Edinburgh: William Paterson, 1882), 2:156–61.

21. The ritual drama of estate auctions has changed little since Martineau's time. See, for analysis of the tension between "fun" and sadness at such sales, Mary Jo Deegan's participant-observer study of auctions in the United States in *American Ritual Dramas* (Westport, CT: Greenwood Press, 1989), pp. 51–75.

22. H. D. Rawnsley in *Literary Associations of the English Lakes* (Glasgow: James MacLehose and Sons, 1901), 2:193, notes that "In the seventh book of the Excursion his [Robert Walker's] character is admirably sketched"; see "The Excursion: Book Seventh," *The Poetical Works of William Wordsworth* (1882), 5:291–334.

23. "The River Duddon: A Series of Sonnets," *The Poetical Works of William Wordsworth* (1882), 6:302–53.

24. "The Excursion: Book Fourth," *The Poetical Works of William Wordsworth* (1882), 5:148.

25. Fredrika Meyer.

26. Felicia Dorthea Hermans (1793–1835); see *The Poetical Works of Mrs. Hemans* (New York: Thomas Y. Crowell, n.d.).

27. Alexander von Humboldt (1769–1859); see, for example, *Cosmos*, translated from the German by E. C. Otté (London: H. G. Bohn, 1849–1858); see also Harriet Martineau, "Alexander von Humboldt," *Biographical Sketches*, pp. 146–57.

28. The last Saturday in July. The ritual started traditionally at 6:00 PM. In 1854, the site of the ceremony shifted to the then new Church of St. Mary's. See, for further description of the annual event, H. D. Rawnsley, *Life and Nature at the English Lakes* (Glasgow: James MacLehose, 1902), pp. 1–16, which includes the "Rushbearing Hymn," written by Owen Lloyd and sung at Ambleside.

29. Henry Cousins, a joiner by trade.

30. A Puseyite is a follower of Edward Bouverie Pusey (1800–1882), leader of the Oxford Movement (later called the Catholic Revival) in the Church of England.

31. Martineau made good on her promise; see "Our Farm of Two Acres," this volume.

32. Martineau conjoins the "solemn" character of "the unanswered bleat"; see "The Excursion: Book Fourth," *The Poetical Works of William Wordsworth* (1882), 5:160–61.

33. Fredrika Meyer.

34. Tobias Smollett (1721–1771), *The Adventures of Sir Launcelot Greaves* (1762).

35. From the Roman breviary, a prayer for vespers on the sixth Sunday after Pentecost: "Let thy grace, we beseech thee, O Lord, ever go before us and follow us, and may it make us to be continually zealous in doing good works."

36. Ellipsis in the original.

37. A possible reference to William Makepeace Thackeray (1811–1863), *The Irish Sketch-Book* (London: Chapman and Hall, 1845), which recounts: "Two little children were paddling

down the street, one saying to the other, 'Once I had a half-penny, and bought apples with it,'" but the setting is Ireland, not London. Martineau records in her *Autobiography*, however, having read the work during her illness in Tynemouth.

38. "The Excursion: Book Second," *The Poetical Works of William Wordsworth* (1882), 5:80.

39. Obsolete form of "blae-berry"; the common name in Scotland and the North of England of the bilberry or whortle-berry (*Vaccinium myrtillus*), a dwarf hardy shrub abundant on heaths and in mountain woods—the berry is a deep blue-black, about one-quarter inch in diameter.

40. "The Excursion: Book Second," *The Poetical Works of William Wordsworth* (1882), 5:79.

41. *Sloes,* the sharply sour fruit of the blackthorn (*Prunus spinosa*).

42. *Damsons,* small domesticated plums of black or dark purple color.

43. See "The Cost of Cottages," this volume.

44. Shakespeare, *The Merry Wives of Windsor,* 3.3.

45. Martineau wrote a leader on "lynch law" for the *Daily News* (London) 31 July 1856, "About half a century ago. . . ."

46. Ecclesiastes 9:10: "Whatsoever thy hand findest to do, do *it* with thy might; for *there* is no work, nor device, nor knowledge, nor wisdom, in the grave, whither thou goest." See *The Interpreter's Bible* (New York: Abingdon Press, 1956), 5:75.

47. Thomas Gray (1716–1771) toured the lakes during 1–10 October 1769; see *The Correspondence of Thomas Gray,* ed. Paget Toynbee and Leonard Whibley (Oxford: Oxford University Press, 1935), 3:1078–1102. Gray found the tourist facilities wanting: "Came to Ambleside, 18 m: from Keswick meaning to lie there, but on looking into the best bed-chamber dark &

damp as a cellar grew delicate, gave up Winandermere in despair & resolved I would go on to Kendal directly, 15 m: farther."

48. *Wether,* a male sheep.

49. See, for the sad end of Hartley Coleridge, "Lights of the Lake District," this volume.

50. Derwent Coleridge (1800–1883), Hartley's brother.

51. "Lake and Mountain Holidays: I, The Hutchinsons in Grasmere," *People's Journal* 2 (1846): 1–3. The essay is here given the more descriptive title suggested elsewhere by Martineau; see "Lights of the Lake District," this volume.

52. Margaret Gillies, "The Hutchinson Family" (pen and ink drawing), *People's Journal* 1 (1846): 225.

53. Mary Howitt, "The Hutchinson Family," *People's Journal* 1 (1846): 226–29.

54. The White Lion Hotel, in Ambleside, advised in the mid-1800s that "Visitors will find every comfort, good rooms, cleanliness, attention, and moderate charges. There is attached to the Hotel a good Billiard Room [and there is] An omnibuss daily to meet the steamers at Windermere Water head" (from an advertisement appended to the editor's copy of Harriet Martineau, *Complete Guide to the English Lakes* [Windermere: John Garnett, n.d., circa 1855]).

55. Adelaide Kemble (1815–1879), a mezzo soprano and the sister of Fanny Kemble; see, for example, "Hark, Hark the Lark at Heav'n's Gate Sings," a song by Franz Schubert based on a text from Shakespeare and adapted by Adelaide Kemble (London: L. Williams & Son, n.d.).

56. Herbert Hartman, *Harley Coleridge* (Oxford: Oxford University Press, 1931), p. 154, notes the concert was held in "Benson Harrison's garden, Green Bank, Ambleside."

57. Tennyson's the *May Queen* was published in 1832, and the first stanza reads:

You must wake and call me early, call me early, mother dear;
Tomorrow 'ill be the happiest time of all the glad New-year;
Of all the glad New-year, mother, the maddest merriest day;
For I'm to be Queen o' the May, mother, I'm to be Queen o' the May.

The above lines are quoted from *The Poems of Tennyson*, ed. Christopher Ricks (Berkeley: University of California Press, 1987), 1:456.

58. Originally published in *Once a Week* 1 (9 July 1859): 37–40; 1 (16 July 1859): 44–47; and 1 (30 July 1859): 96–100; reprinted in Martineau, *Health, Husbandry, and Handicraft* (London: Bradbury and Evans, 1861), pp. 269–98.

59. William Cobbett (1763–1835); see Cobbett, *Cottage Economy* (London: C. Clement, 1822).

60. A "rood" was a cursory measure of land, of 40 square poles, where a "pole" varied in local usage from six to eight yards.

61. John Sillett, author of *A Practical System of Fork and Spade Industry* (London, 1847); see also *The Evidence of John Sillett, on His Examination before a Committee of the House of Commons* (London: J. Watson, 1848).

62. The Freehold Land Society movement began in Birmingham in 1847 as a political scheme to increase the number of persons qualified, by virtue of being landowners, to vote.

63. See Miss Coulton, *Our Farm of Four Acres and the Money We Made by It* (London: Chapman and Hall, 1859).

64. *Mangold* (or *mangeld-wurzel*) was a variety of beet cultivated primarily as fodder for cattle.

65. Martineau reported on her visits to these locales in:

Society in America (1837), *Retrospect of Western Travel* (1838), and *Eastern Life, Present and Past* (1848).

66. *Parterres* are ornamental flower beds, sometimes designed with gravel or turf walkways.

67. "We find Dr Smith's Disinfectant of such value that my farm man says he would on no account be without it for a day. We get it from Mr. McDoughall, Manchester, and find it preferable even to powdered charcoal." (Note in the original.—Ed.)

68. *Haulm* is the collective term for the stems and stalks of beans, peas, potatoes, and similar cultivated plants.

69. The abbey of Furness was established in 1127 BCE. See Martineau's account of the subsequent fortunes and decline of the abbey in "The English Lake District," this volume.

70. Rotten Row, a promenade in Hyde Park, London, frequented by the fashionable during the Victorian era.

71. Charles Edward Mudie (1818–1890). In 1842, Mudie launched a rental library system with branches in many English towns.

72. William Howitt (1792–1879), British author and a frequent contributor, as was Martineau, to the *People's Journal.*

73. *Once a Week* 2 (14 January 1860): 61–65; reprinted in Martineau, *Health, Husbandry, and Handicraft* (London: Bradbury and Evans, 1861), pp. 72–82.

74. "Home or Hospital," *Once a Week* 1 (19 November 1859): 419–23; reprinted in *Health, Husbandry, and Handicraft* (1861), pp. 60–72.

75. The Fulchers, from Norfolk.

76. Arthur Jackson, who resided at Rose cottage, Ambleside, was a mason and lodging house keeper.

77. John Newton; see the month of November in "A Year at Ambleside," this volume.

78. To the reprinted version of "The Cost of Cottages," in *Health, Husbandry, and Handicraft* (1861), pp. 81–82, Martineau appended a floor plan and the cost details of building a £60 cottage in Westmoreland, as submitted by Jackson.

79. The full citation is: *Report to Her Majesty's Principal Secretary of State for the Home Department, from the Poor Law Commissioners, On an Inquiry into the Sanitary Condition of the Labouring Population of Great Britain; with Appendices* (London: W. Clowes and Sons, 1842).

80. "Cottage Habitations," *English Woman's Journal* 4 (October 1859): 73–82. Copies of this otherwise scarce journal are readily found on microfiche in the massive *Gerritsen Collection of Woman's History*.

81. *English Woman's Journal* 4 (December 1859).

82. From Charles Knight, *The Land We Live In: A Pictorial and Literary Sketch-Book of the British Empire* (London: Charles Knight, circa 1847–50), 2:217–25.

83. Ecclesiastes 9:10 (*The Interpreter's Bible*).

84. See, for examples of Roman remnants still visible today, James Southworth, *Walking the Roman Roads of Cumbria* (London: Robert Hale, 1985).

85. King Stephen, British sovereign from 1135 to 1154.

86. "The wolf is spoken of as a public enemy in edicts of Edward I. and John. Sir Ewen Cameron laid low the last Scotch wolf in 1680. The last presentment for killing wolves in Ireland was made, in the county of Cork, in 1710." (Note in the original.—Ed.)

87. That is, from 1066 to the first decade of the 1700s.

88. The Act of Union, 1706, declared that Scotland and England should have a united parliament as of 1 May 1707.

89. Gretna Green, just over the border in Scotland, pro-

vided legal marriages for runaway couples that wished to marry quickly, without the lengthy formalities required in England.

90. William Wordsworth (1770–1850), the noted romantic poet who lived at Rydal.

91. "The River Duddon: A Series of Sonnets."

92. "*Works*, (edition of 1841, vol. ii. p. 189, note)." (Note in the original.—Ed.)

93. "*History and Antiquities of Westmoreland and Cumberland,* 1777, vol. ii, p. 13." (Note in the original.—Ed.)

94. "The Stepping Stones," numbers IX and X in "The Duddon Sonnets," *The Poetical Works of William Wordsworth* (1882), 6:312–13.

95. Ranulph de Meschines, Earl of Chester (1100–1153).

96. "*A Complete Guide to the Lakes* (1843), p. 59." (Note in the original.—Ed.)

97. The story is recounted in "The Horn of Egremont Castle," *The Poetical Works of William Wordsworth* (1882), 4:6–11.

98. "This term describes the guest as putting in his whittle (his knife) among the provisions of the family." (Note in the original.—Ed.)

99. See William Wordsworth, *Guide to the Lakes*, 5th ed., edited and introduced by Ernest De Sélincourt (Oxford: Oxford University Press,1906; repr. 1970), pp. 113–16.

100. "*History and Antiquities of Westmoreland and Cumberland,* ii. p. 69. Nicolson and Burn." (Note in the original.—Ed.)

101. "The Excursion: Book Fourth," *The Poetical Works of William Wordsworth* (1882), 5:161.

102. "Joined in one solemn and capricious grove"—a line from "Yew Trees," *The Poetical Works of William Wordsworth* (1882), 2:321–24.

103. Robert Southey (1774–1843).

104. "*The Tourist's New Guide*, by Wm. Green. 1819.Vol. ii., p. 469." (Note in the original.—Ed.)

105. "Mr. Smith, quoted in Green's *Tourist's New Guide*. ii., 473." (Note in the original.—Ed.)

106. Flintoft's model is preserved in the Keswick Museum and Art Gallery, Fitz Park, Station Road, Keswick.

107. The saga of Cuthbert and Herbert was early recounted by The Venerable Bede in his *Ecclesiastical History of England*.

108. See Wordsworth, *Guide to the Lakes*, 5th ed. (Oxford University Press, 1977), p. 38.

109. Carbureted hydrogen, or coal gas; azote, or nitrogen.

110. "The Somnambulist," *The Poetical Works of William Wordsworth* (1882), 7:382–88. In a prefatory note to the poem, Wordsworth recounts an alternative origin for the story: "While we were making an excursion together in the part of the lake District we heard that Mr. Glover, the artist, while lodging at Lyulph's Tower, had been disturbed by a loud shriek, and upon rising he had learnt that it had come from a young woman in the house who was in the habit of walking in her sleep. In that state she had gone down stairs, and, while attempting to open the outer door, either from some difficulty or the effect of the cold stone upon her feet, had uttered the cry which alarmed him. It seemed to us all that this might serve as a hint for a poem, and the story here told was constructed and soon after put into verse by me as it now stands."

111. Bernard Gilpin (1517–1558), a leader in the Reformation; see *The Life of Bernard Gilpin* (London: W. I. and T. P., 1636).

112. At this point, Martineau noted that her treatment "of the fourth section of the lake scenery is much shortened by a

full account having been given in No. V of this work of Windemere, Ambleside, and Rydal." Her reference is to the unsigned essay, presumably by Charles Knight, on "Windermere" in *The Land We Live In* (London: Charles Knight, circa 1847–1850), 1:66–80.

113. "The Excursion: Book Second—The Solitary," *The Poetical Works of William Wordsworth* (1882), 5:64–104.

114. Autolicus (*or* Autolycus), a rogue in Shakespeare's *A Winter's Tale.*

115. Elizabeth Smith; see "Lights of the Lake District," this volume.

116. *Household Words* 3 (19 July 1851): 389–96. Evidence for Martineau's authorship of this unsigned tale is provided by Anne Lohrli, *Household Words* (University of Toronto Press, 1973), p. 360.

117. The Border wars, between England and Scotland, spanned four hundred years from the time of Edward I to the parliamentary union in 1707.

118. Napoleon Bonaparte was born Napoleon Buonaparte. The family later adopted the French spelling of their originally Corsican name.

119. "Bedlam" refers to a specific London lunatic asylum and derives from a contraction of "Bethlehem"(the name of a religious house subsequently reorganized as a foundation for lunatics).

120. From the *Atlantic Monthly* 7 (May 1861): 541–58.

121. Thomas Gray (1716–1771).

122. William Wordsworth (1770–1850).

123. Robert Southey (1774–1843).

124. William Wilberforce (1759–1833), influential British politician and vigorous abolitionist.

125. Elizabeth Smith (1776–1806); her major works were published posthumously.

126. *The Book of Job*, translated from the Hebrew by Elizabeth Smith (Bath: Richard Crutwell, 1810).

127. Friedrich Gottlieb Klopstock (1724–1803), German lyric poet. See *Memoirs of Frederick and Margaret Klopstock*, comp. and trans. Elizabeth Smith (Bath: R. Crutwell, 1809).

128. Elizabeth Hamilton (1748–1816) and Thomas Bowdler (1754–1825); Bowdler's expurgated edition of Shakespeare gave rise to the term *to bowdlerize.*

129. Alfred Tennyson (1809–1892) married Emily Sarah Sellwood in 1850. See, on their postnuptial stay in the Lake District, *Alfred Lord Tennyson: A Memoir*, by his son (London: Macmillan, 1898), 2:133–35.

130. *Memoirs of William Wordsworth*, by Christopher Wordsworth (London: E. Moxon, 1851).

131. Samuel Taylor Coleridge (1772–1834).

132. Dorothy Wordsworth (1771–1855).

133. Sir George Howland Beaumont (1753–1827); see *Memoirs of William Wordsworth* (1851), 1:258–80.

134. St. Thomas's Day, the twenty-first of December.

135. "The Excursion: Book Fifth," *The Poetical Works of William Wordsworth* (1882), 5:199–240.

136. Mary Fricker married Robert Lovell, Sarah Fricker married S. T. Coleridge, and Edith Fricker married Robert Southey.

137. Thomas De Quincey (1785–1859); see, for his personal perspective, his *Recollections of the Lake Poets*, edited from the 1834 and 1840 journals by Edward Sackville-West (London: Purnell and Sons, 1948); see also Harriet Martineau, "Thomas De Quincey," *Biographical Sketches*, pp. 93–101.

138. John Wilson (1785–1854), Scottish writer who adopted the pseudonym "Christopher North."

139. Sir Walter Scott (1771–1832).

140. George Canning (1770–1827), statesman and prime minister of England.

141. John Bolton, of Storrs Hall, Bowness, organized the Regatta in 1825.

142. Thomas Campbell (1777–1844).

143. Richard Watson (1737–1816); see, for his autobiography, *Anecdotes of the Life of Richard Watson* (London: T. Cadell and W. Davies, 1817).

144. Felicia Dorthea Hemans (1793–1835), a noted poet.

145. See *Memorials of Mrs. Hemans, With Illustrations of Her Literary Character from Her Private Correspondence*, ed. Henry F. Chorley (London: Saunders and Otley, 1836).

146. Charles Lamb (1775–1834) and his sister, Mary.

147. John Gibson Lockhart, *Memoirs of the Life of Sir Walter Scott* (Edinburgh: R. Cadell, 1837–38). See also Harriet Martineau, "John Gibson Lockhart," *Biographical Sketches*, pp. 28–36.

148. "To Tennyson, after Hearing Abby Hutchinson Sing 'The May-Queen' at Ambleside." This poem is appended in full to Martineau's "Frolics with the Hutchinsons," this volume.

149. Hartley Coleridge, *Poems*, with a memoir of his life by his brother (London: Edward Moxon, 1851).

150. Dr. Thomas Arnold (1793–1842), father of Matthew Arnold.

151. See Arthur Penrhyn Stanley, *Life and Correspondence of Thomas Arnold* (London: B. Fellowes, 1844).

152. Martineau was a staunch advocate of mesmerism; see, for example, her *Letters on Mesmerism* (London: E. Moxon, 1845).

153. William Ellery Channing (1780–1842); Martineau provides a sketch of her visit with Channing in her *Retrospect of Western Travel* (New York: Harper & Brothers, 1838), 2:117–28.

154. "Steam-boats, Viaducts, and Railways," *Poetical Works of William Wordsworth* (1882), 7:378–79; "On the Projected Kendal and Windermere Railway," ibid., 8:147–48.

155. Brackets in the original.

156. Excerpted from *Harriet Martineau's Autobiography*, ed. Maria Weston Chapman (Boston: James R. Osgood, 1877), 2:89–91.

157. These are Martineau's recollections from the year 1854 (ibid., 2:88).

158. See, for Martineau's major travel writings, her *Society in America* (1837), *Retrospect of Western Travel* (1838), and *Eastern Life, Present and Past* (1848); on how to be an astute traveler, consult *How to Observe Morals and Manners* (1838); and, finally, additional details on her travels are found throughout her *Autobiography.*

159. See especially, the preface to *The Positive Philosophy of Auguste Comte*, freely translated and condensed by Harriet Martineau (London: John Chapman 1853). See, for more specifics, *Harriet Martineau's Autobiography* (James R. Osgood 1877), 2:57–59; Susan Hoecker-Drysdale, "Harriet Martineau and the Positivism of Auguste Comte," in *Harriet Martineau: Theoretical & Methodological Perspectives*, ed. Michael R. Hill and Susan Hoecker-Drysdale (Routledge 2001), pp. 169–89; and Harriet Martineau, "On Edward Lombe, Translating Auguste Comte, and the Liberal English Press: A Previously Unpublished Letter," edited and with an introduction by Michael R. Hill, *Sociological Origins* 3, no. 2 (forthcoming).

INDEX

Note: page references for graphic illustrations appear in **boldface**.